W9-DIW-727

DOWN
THE
RIVER

BOOKS BY EDWARD ABBEY

Fiction
Good News
The Monkey Wrench Gang
Black Sun
Fire on the Mountain
The Brave Cowboy
Jonathan Troy

Personal History
Abbey's Road
The Journey Home
Desert Solitaire

Natural History
Desert Images (with David Muench)
The Hidden Canyon (with John Blaustein)
Cactus Country (with Ernst Haas)
Slickrock (with Philip Hyde)
Appalachian Wilderness (with Eliot Porter)

Down
the
River

Edward Abbey

With drawings by the author

E. P. Dutton ～ New York

"Down the River With Henry Thoreau" © 1981 by Edward Abbey first appeared in *Down the River with Henry Thoreau/Walden* and is reprinted by courtesy of Peregrine Smith, Inc. Portions of *Down the River* have been published, in somewhat different form and sometimes under different titles, in *Backpacker Magazine, GEO, Harper's Magazine, The New York Times, Outside, Rocky Mountain Magazine, Rolling Stone, Running, Sierra Club Wilderness Calendar.* Copyright © 1978, 1979, 1980, 1981, 1982 by Edward Abbey.

Grateful acknowledgment is made for permission to excerpt from "The Eagle and the Mole," by Elinor Wylie, published in *Collected Poems* (New York: Alfred A. Knopf, Inc., 1932); and from "The Days of Forty-Nine," new words and new music adaptation by Frank Warner; collected, adapted, and arranged by John A. Lomax; TRO—© copyright 1947, renewed 1975 by Ludlow Music, Inc., New York, New York.

Copyright © 1982 by Edward Abbey

All rights reserved. Printed in the U.S.A.

No part of this publication may be reproduced or transmitted in any form or by any means, electronic or mechanical, including photocopy, recording or any information storage and retrieval system now known or to be invented, without permission in writing from the publisher, except by a reviewer who wishes to quote brief passages in connection with a review written for inclusion in a magazine, newspaper or broadcast.

Published in the United States by E. P. Dutton, Inc., 2 Park Avenue, New York, N.Y. 10016

Library of Congress Cataloging in Publication Data
Abbey, Edward,
    Down the river.
    I. Title.
PS3551.B2D68 1982   814'.54   81-19429
                                    AACR2

ISBN: 0-525-09524-1 (cloth)
       0-525-47676-8 (paper)
Published simultaneously in Canada by Clarke, Irwin & Company Limited, Toronto and Vancouver

Book Design by Nicola Mazzella

10 9 8 7 6 5 4 3 2 1

First Edition

To Don Congdon,
friend and counselor for twenty-one years,
and also to my fellow river rats

Shall we gather at the river
Where bright angel feet have trod;
With its crystal tide forever
Flowing by the throne of God?
  —Robert Lowry, 1864

Every man has to go down the river some time.
  —Paul Revere Abbey, 1959

Contents

DOWN
THE
RIVER

Preliminary Notes

For twenty-three years now I've been floating rivers. Always downstream, the easy and natural way. The way Huck Finn and Jim did it, La Salle and Marquette, the mountain men, Major Powell, a few hundred others.

For me this floating began near home on Crooked Crick in the Allegheny Mountains of western Pennsylvania. (The wrong side of the mountains.) My brother Hoots and I built a boat. He was nine years old, I was ten. To be honest, we didn't build it, we stole it. From my father. Nor was it exactly a boat. Actually it was a rectangular wooden box, about four foot by three and one foot deep, used for mixing cement in. In the words of singer Katie Lee, another river rat, our boat "had no stern and had no bow/ It looked just like a garbage scow." The bottom was flat, the insides well caulked with dried concrete. To my brother and me it resembled a boat. With immense effort we dragged, pushed, and weaseled this thing down through the woods to the creek, a labor of several hours. It was very heavy. We slid it down a muskrat slide and shoved it into the water, climbing aboard. There was room for us both; we were small. We clung to the gunwales as our scow sank peacefully and immediately to the bottom of the creek, leaving us sitting in water up to our necks.

That was very long ago.

My next river trip took place twenty-five years later when my friend Ralph Newcomb and I launched two inflatable dinghies on the Rio Colorado and floated through twelve days and 150 miles of Utah's Glen Canyon. Before the dam. I have described that journey elsewhere.

Many river trips followed, mostly in the American Southwest. Some of those, too, I have written about in other books—hallucinations on the Green River, floating down the Rio Grande through the canyons of Big Bend, a dory expedition through the Grand Canyon. There have been many others on many rivers. I have had more than my share, since the rivers began getting crowded, and don't intend to do any more. Or hardly any. (Would still like to see the Bío-Bío. The Owyhee. The Congo. The Kolyma. The Mississippi and the Amazon.) But in general, no more. It's time for some of us to stay home for a while and leave room on the rivers for you other folks.

This book is about some recent boat trips and about related things now going, going—sold!—down the river. "Dreams! [for example] adorations! illuminations! religions!" as Allen Ginsberg has noted, in his wry and quiet manner; "the whole boatload of sensitive bullshit! . . . gone down the flood!"

"The rivers are our brothers," said Chief Seattle. "They quench our thirst. The rivers carry our canoes and feed our children. . . . You must give to the rivers the kindness you would give your brothers."

Chief Seattle did not understand what was coming. How could he have imagined, for instance, that a time might arrive when the rivers would not even be fit to drink from? But certain consolations remain. Thoreau said, "Who hears the rippling of rivers will not utterly despair of anything." That makes sense.

"I love any discourse of rivers . . ." said Izaak Walton. Pascal said, in *Thought # 17,* "Rivers are roads that move, and carry us where we wish to go." "I wish all roads were rivers," said Céline in *Guignol's Band.* "Oh, Shenandoah, I long to hear you." The voices come. "Oh, the moonlight's fair tonight upon the Wabash . . ." The riverine voices come flooding in. "Way down upon de Swanee ribber, far far away . . ." "Oh, it's a monstrous big river," said Huck. "Away, I'm bound away, 'cross the wide Missouri." "I love all things that flow," said Joyce. "I like rivers better than oceans," wrote E. A. Robinson, "for we see both sides." "A thousand years hence the river will run as it did," wrote Thomas Fuller in his *Gnomologia* in 1732, anticipating the damnation of the Vale of Rhonda, of Hetch Hetchy, of Glen Canyon—to name but a few. The rivers will run, and the mountain streams that feed them: "By shallow waters to whose falls," sang Marlowe, "melodious birds sing madrigals." Tugboats croak on the Hackensack, young lovers in the Charles. "A mountain and a river are good neighbors," wrote George Herbert in 1639. "The river glideth at his own sweet will," wrote the gentle Wordsworth in 1802; ah yes, William, like for instance the Conemaugh at Johnstown, Pennsylvania, in 1936.

Rivers, rivers, we can never—well, hardly ever—have enough of them. The rivers go by and down and on, while transient ghosts place ephemeral toes in the solid, sullied, substantial waters: "Dat ol' man river," Heraclitus said, "he jus' keeps rollin' along. . . ."

A wind is rising. And the rivers flow.

Fasten your life jackets.

None of the essays in this book requires elucidation, other than to say, as in everything I write, they are meant to serve as antidotes to despair. Despair leads to boredom, electronic games, computer hacking, poetry, and other bad habits.

A friend of mine in New York who also writes books for a living, and good ones, cheerful, buoyant, tough-minded, sends me a most untypical cry from the heart:

". . . I'm worrying more about the purposefulness of my work, and its value too. . . . I think, like Isaac Singer, that you and I are writing in a dying language of a dying world, and that none of us has been able to face the scorching heat of this truth, and decide what to do or even think in response. . . ."

I replied by return postcard in words to this effect, "Be of good cheer, the military-industrial state will soon collapse. Meanwhile we must do all in our power to oppose, resist, and subvert its desperate aggrandizements. As a matter of course. As a matter of honor."

A naïve optimism predicated on wistful hope. Not good enough. For better comfort I turned to an old letter from my father:

> Ed,
>   . . . I tell time by the sun and the time of year by the squirrels. I watched one today taking butternuts from the top of the tree next to the tool shed. He was really in a hurry. So I reckon that means an early winter. And the wooly worms have heavy coats and the woodbine twineth. That means I'm just as happy as if I had good sense. . . .
>   I am not worrying about you. I am not worrying about anybody. Peace is pretty good. As for me I'm really enjoying my decrepit old age. I am busy, interestedly busy building my rock shop, and as I do everything (ahem) I'm doing a neat job. The fireplace and rock chimney has had me stumped but by trial and error and varied advice I am getting it up. I hope that squirrel is just busy and not working against time or I might not finish before the snow flies.
>   You better make that river trip. Every man has to go down the river some time. I have some money I wont need till I need it. You can dig it up when you get here or I'll send you a can full. . . .

My old man. He became eighty years old last February. In April we went for a walk down the Kaibab Trail, seven miles to the bottom of the Grand Canyon. We watched what's left of the Colorado River roll by for an hour, then walked back to the rim by way of the Bright Angel Trail, nine miles long and five thousand feet up. Rain fell on us most of the way. The old man complained some but not as much as I did. He got angry only when I offered to carry his pack.

My daughter Susie is close to thirteen now and rows a little plastic skiff through dangerous rapids on the Green and San Juan rivers.

I'm beginning to think that my father and my daughter and I are indestructible. We brag a lot. This won't do.

Still thinking of my friend's aberrant gloom, I searched through my notebooks and sent him this translation of a Zuñi Indian ceremonial song (*with flutes & drums*):

> Everybody wake up! (*flutes*)
> Open your eyes! Stand up! (*drums*)
> Be children of the light—strong, swift,
>   sure of foot!
> Hurry, Clouds, from the four quarters
>   of the world!
> Come, Ice, cover the fields
>   that seeds may grow!
> Come, Big Snows, that the rivers will flow
>   this summer!
> All hearts be glad!

That too makes sense, I think. Keep those rivers moving. Keep that Hudson slithering—in its massive sluggish oily viscid fashion—past the piers and under the orange peels of Manhattan. Let it flow.

I had no better answer for my friend back east in his vertiginous city. A postcard and a song were all that I could offer. Bread on the river. I trust it is enough.

Think like a mountain, urged Aldo Leopold. Quite so. And feel like a river, says I. Shakespeare understood the process:

> The current that with gentle murmur glides
> Thou knowest, being stopped, impatiently doth rage;
> But when his fair course is not hindered
> He makes sweet music with th' enamelled stones,
> Giving a gentle kiss to every sedge
> He overtaketh in his pilgrimage.

A few essays in this book deal with unpleasant and ungrateful subjects—the damnation of another river, the militarization of the open range, the manufacture of nuclear weapons, the industrialization of agriculture. They were written from a sense of duty, as well as for the easy money; I much prefer sweeter, funnier, happier themes.

Environmental journalism is not a cheerful field of work. The opposition is severe, well-funded, and becoming more brutal each year. After years of indifference, the managers of the corporate sector and their hired scribes (*Commentary, National Review, Time, Newsweek, Fortune, Wall Street Journal,* et al.) have finally awakened to the fact that environmentalism, if taken seriously, is a greater threat to the Perpetual Power & Growth Machine than labor unions or Communism. Labor unions can be broken or bought off, and in our nation they mostly have been, while international Communism, though a competitor for planetary power, does not threaten the basic system: Communists like capitalists believe above all in technology, the ever-expanding economy (nice self-contradiction!), industrialism, militarism, centralized control—the complete domination of nature and human beings. The more intense the rivalry the more alike the two sides become; the differences between the men at the top are merely ideological, like the different colors of opposing football teams. As Orwell pointed out in the conclusion of *Animal Farm,* when the ruling administrators from the two sides convened for a conference, they all looked—to the animals outside looking in—much the same. Which was which? The animals could not tell.

When I published magazine articles objecting to the pollution of our Western skies, or the strip-mining of our rangelands, the editors and I would receive, by automated feedback, dozens of letters like these:

> . . . *If Mr. Abbey is so in love with wilderness, he should take his beer cans and his warped head and go far back in the hills and stay there. The world would be glad to see the last of him and it is obvious he has no place in civilized society.*
>
> Daryl S. Allen
> Scottsdale, Arizona

How wonderful it must be to live in the journalistic world, free of concern for honest reporting—and selling verbiage as profitably as the Lexington Avenue hookers sell their wares. . . .

> Frederick L. Conroy
> W. Redding, Connecticut
> *[Home of Charles Ives!]*

. . . Please consider that many of us are totally unenthused by the sheer effrontery of these self-centered godlike creatures who, in the fullness of their pitiful little egos and monstrous conceits, appoint themselves as the sole arbiters of conservation. . . .

> J. Thomas Pulliam
> Palm Springs, California

. . . I suggest that Abbey purchase ten six-packs of Schlitz, enclose himself in his garage inside his pickup truck, start the motor and see if he can drink all of the beer. . . .

> J. R. Skousen
> Lake Forest, Illinois

And so forth. I have dozens of such communications in my treasured file of nasty letters, some on heavyweight corporation stationery, many unprintable in a decent book meant for family reading, most of them from men connected with the mining ("Mining Is Everybody's Future"), lumbering, land development, or construction industries. The Empire strikes back.

But I've been lucky. So far nobody has attempted to bomb my house, kidnap my daughter, or torture my friends—routine events, as we know, both in the Communist world and in such stern components of the Free World as Argentina, Brazil, Chile, Uruguay, Paraguay, Guatemala, El Salvador, Honduras, Peru, Colombia, South Korea, South Africa, the Philippines, etc. Ill-wishers cannot get at me through economic means because, despite thirty years of earnest effort, I remain one of the few veterans of World War II who has not yet been able to find a steady job.

Nevertheless—I welcome more letters. I want to hear from my readers, whoever you are. I want to know what's going on out there in the great American boiling pot. My mailing address is P.O. Box 628, Oracle, Arizona. And if you want to talk, give me a ring on this here new telephone machine we've got on the kitchen wall. My number is three shorts, three longs, three shorts. ($\cdots$ — — — $\cdots$) Crank real hard.

I have a friend named Marilyn McElhenny. She lives in Jackson, Wyoming. She is a wildlife biologist by profession but makes her living these days as a florist. She is a sweet, rosy, generous, thoroughly delightful young woman, pretty as a marigold. She owns a dog, a shaggy yellow mutt named Toley, ingenuous and friendly, though he lost a leg a few years back while rock climbing near Moab, Utah. Long ago I promised Miss McElhenny that I would put her and her dog in a book.

Here they are.

Some people send poems.

Far Away

My head is upon
A far away hill
And my soul is lying
Beneath its tree.
The sun's and wind's
Enchanted touch does fill
Memory of days
Spent with you and me.

H. Boney
Greencastle, Pennsylvania

Reviewers may note that I include two book reviews of my own in this assemblage. The reasons are two: (1) to indulge a weakness for malicious mischief at the expense of a pair of overinflated reputations, always a healthy exercise for the amateur critic, and (2) to prepare the way for a salute to those among contemporary American novelists whom I truly admire, such as William Gaddis, Thomas Pynchon, Don Delillo, Robert Coover, Kurt Vonnegut, E. L. Doctorow, Gilbert Sorrentino, William Kotzwinkle, Thomas Berger, Joseph Heller, Wallace Stegner, Robert Stone, Joseph McElroy, and others I have mentioned before. Missing from my little list are a number of well-known names. I am aware of the omission and can only explain it in this wise: although the others among current writers are gifted, much esteemed, earnest, and industrious fellows, they uniformly lack (it seems to me) those powers of imaginative technique, intensity of vision, and high moral purpose—concern for right and wrong, justice and injustice, truth and falsehood, beauty and ugliness—that form and inform the work of those I most respect.

I might also say, regarding reviews and reviewers, that I have yet to read a review of any of my own books which I could not have written much better myself.

Meanwhile, back to the river. On with the river, day by day, down to the ultimate sea. Shall we gather at the river? Why not? One more river one more time. And then no more. And then that ancient river must flow right on down without me.

E. A.

Independence Day, 1981

PART I

Thoreau and
Other Friends

1

Down the River
with Henry Thoreau

November 4, 1980

Our river is the Green River in southeast Utah. We load our boats at a place called Mineral Bottom, where prospectors once searched for gold, later for copper, still later for uranium. With little luck. With me are five friends plus the ghost of a sixth: in my ammo can—the river runner's handbag—I carry a worn and greasy paperback copy of a book called *Walden, or Life in the Woods*. Not for thirty years have I looked inside this book; now for the first time since my school days I shall. Thoreau's mind has been haunting mine for most of my life. It seems proper now to reread him. What better place than on this golden river called the Green? In the clear tranquillity of November? Through the red rock canyons known as Labyrinth, Stillwater, and Cataract in one of the sweetest, brightest, grandest, and loneliest of primitive regions still remaining in our America?

Questions. Every statement raises more and newer questions. We shall never be done with questioning, so long as men and women remain human. QUESTION AUTHORITY reads a bumper sticker I saw the other day in Moab, Utah. Thoreau would doubtless have amended that to read "Always Question Authority." I would add only the word "All" before the word "Authority." Including, of course, the authority of Henry David himself.

Here we are, slipping away in the early morning of another Election Day. A couple of us did vote this morning but we are not, really, good citizens. Voting for the lesser evil on the grounds that otherwise we'd be stuck with the greater evil. Poor grounds for choice, certainly. Losing grounds.

We will not see other humans or learn of the election results for ten days to come. And so we prefer it. We like it that way. What could be older than the news? We shall treasure the bliss of our ignorance for as long as we can. "The man who goes each day to the village to hear the latest news has not heard from himself in a long time." Who said that? Henry, naturally. The arrogant, insolent village crank.

I think of another bumper sticker, one I've seen several times in several places this year: NOBODY FOR PRESIDENT. Amen. The word is getting around. Henry would have approved. Heartily. For he also said, "That government is best which governs not at all."

Year by year the institutions that dominate our lives grow ever bigger, more complicated, massive, impersonal, and powerful. Whether governmental, corporate, military, or technological—and how can any one of these be disentangled from the others?—they weigh on society as the pyramids of Egypt weighed on the backs of those who were conscripted to build them. The pyramids of power. Five thousand years later the people of Egypt still have not recovered. They remain a passive and powerless mass of subjects. Mere fellahin, expendable and interchangeable units in a social megamachine. As if the pride and spirit had been crushed from them forever.

In many a clear conclusion we find ourselves anticipated by the hoer of beans on the shores of Walden Pond. "As for the Pyramids," wrote Henry, "there is nothing to wonder at in them so much as the fact that so many men could be found degraded enough to spend their lives constructing a tomb for some ambitious booby, whom it would have been wiser and manlier to have drowned in the Nile. . . ."

Some critic has endeavored to answer this observation by claiming that the pyramid projects provided winter employment for swarms of peasants who might otherwise have been forced to endure long seasons of idleness and hunger. But where did the funds come from, the surplus grain, to support and feed these hundreds of thousands of two-legged pismires? Why, from the taxes levied on the produce of their *useful* work in the rice fields of the Nile Delta. The slaves were twice exploited. Every year. Just as the moon rides, concrete monuments, and industrial war machines of contemporary empire-states, whether capitalist or Communist, are funded by compulsory taxation, erected and maintained by what is in effect compulsory labor.

The river flows. The river will not wait. Let's get these boats on the current. Loaded with food, bedrolls, cooking gear—four gourmet cooks in a party of six (plus ghost)—they ride on the water, tethered to shore. Two boats, one an eighteen-foot rubber raft, the other an aluminum dory. Oar-powered. We scramble on board, the swampers untie the lines, the oarsmen heave at their oars. Rennie Russell (author of *On the Loose*) operates the raft; a long-connected, lean fellow named Dusty Teale rows the dory.

We glide down the golden waters of Labyrinth Canyon. The water here is smooth as oil, the current slow. The sandstone walls rise fifteen hundred feet above us, radiant with sunlight, manganese and iron oxides, stained with old tapestries of organic residues left on the rock faces by occasional waterfalls. On shore, wheeling away from us, the stands of willow glow in autumn copper; beyond the willow are the green-gold cottonwoods. Two ravens fly along the rim, talking about us. Henry would like it here.

November 5, 1980

We did not go far yesterday. We rowed and drifted two miles down the river and then made camp for the night on a silt bank at the water's edge. There had been nobody but ourselves at Mineral Bottom but the purpose, nonetheless, was to "get away from the crowd," as Rennie Russell explained. We understood. We cooked our supper by firelight and flashlight, ate beneath the stars. Somebody uncorked a bottle of wine. Rennie played his guitar, his friend Ted Seeley played the fiddle, and Dusty Teale played the mandolin. We all sang. Our music ascended to the sky, echoing softly from the cliffs. The river poured quietly seaward, making no sound but here and there, now and then, a gurgle of bubbles, a trilling of ripples off the hulls of our half-beached boats.

Sometime during the night a deer stalks nervously past our camp. I hear the noise and, when I get up before daybreak, I see the dainty heart-shaped tracks. I kindle the fire and build the morning's first pot of black, rich, cowboy coffee, and drink in solitude the first cupful, warming my hands around the hot cup. The last stars fade, the sky becomes brighter, passing through the green glow of dawn into the fiery splendor of sunrise.

The others straggle up, one by one, and join me around the fire. We stare at the shining sky, the shining river, the high canyon walls, mostly in silence, until one among us volunteers to begin breakfast. Yes, indeed, we are a lucky little group. Privileged, no doubt. At ease out here on the edge of nowhere, loafing into the day, enjoying the very best of the luckiest of nations, while around the world billions of other humans are sweating, fighting, striving, procreating, starving. As always, I try hard to feel guilty. Once again I fail.

"If I knew for a certainty that some man was coming to my house with the conscious intention of doing me good," writes our Henry, "I would run for my life."

We Americans cannot save the world. Even Christ failed at that. We Americans have our hands full in trying to save ourselves. And we've barely tried. The Peace Corps was a lovely idea—for idle and idealistic young Americans. Gave them a chance to see a bit of the world, learn something. But as an effort to "improve" the lives of other peoples, the inhabitants of the so-called underdeveloped nations (our nation is overdeveloped), it was an act of cultural arrogance. A piece of insolence. The one thing we could do for a country like Mexico, for example, is to stop every illegal immigrant at the border, give him a good rifle and a case of ammunition, and send him home. Let the Mexicans solve their customary problems in their customary manner.

If this seems a cruel and sneering suggestion, consider the current working alternative: leaving our borders open to unlimited immigration until—and it won't take long—the social, political, economic life of the United States is reduced to the level of life in Juarez. Guadalajara. Mexico City. San Salvador. Haiti. India. To a common peneplain of overcrowding, squalor, misery, oppression, torture, and hate.

What could Henry have said to this supposition? He lived in a relatively spacious America of only 24 million people, of whom one-sixth were slaves. A mere 140 years later we have grown to a population ten times larger, and we are nearly all slaves. We are slaves in the sense that we depend for our daily survival upon an expand-or-expire agro-industrial empire—a crackpot machine—that the specialists cannot comprehend and the managers cannot manage. Which is, furthermore, devouring world resources at an exponential rate. We are, most of us, dependent employees.

What would Henry have said? He said, "In wildness is the preservation of the world." He said, somewhere deep in his thirty-nine-volume *Journal*, "I go to my solitary woodland walks as the homesick return to their homes." He said, "It would be better if there were but one inhabitant to a square mile, as where I live." Perhaps he did sense what was coming. His last words, whispered from the deathbed, are reported to us as being "moose . . . Indians . . ."

Looking upriver toward Tidwell Bottom, a half mile away, I see a lone horse grazing on the bunch grass, the Indian rice grass, the saltbush, and sand sage of the river's old floodplain. One horse, unhobbled and untended, thirty miles from the nearest ranch or human habitation, it forages on its own. That horse, I'm thinking, may be the one that got away from me years ago, in another desert place, far from here. Leave it alone. That particular horse has found at least a temporary solution to the question of survival. Survival with honor, I mean, for what other form of survival is worth the trouble? That horse has chosen, or stumbled into, solitude and independence. Let it be. Thoreau defined happiness as "simplicity, independence, magnanimity and trust."

But solitude? Horses are gregarious beasts, like us. This lone horse on Tidwell Bottom may be paying a high price for its freedom, perhaps in some form of equine madness. A desolation of the soul corresponding to the grand desolation of the landscape that lies beyond these canyon walls.

"I never found the companion that was so companionable as solitude," writes Henry. "To be in company, even with the best, is soon wearisome and dissipating."

Perhaps his ghost will forgive us if we suspect an element of *extra-vagance* in the above statement. Thoreau had a merry time in the writing of *Walden;* it is an exuberant book, crackling with humor, good humor, gaiety, with joy in the power of words and phrases, in ideas and emotions so powerful they tend constantly toward the outermost limit of communicable thought.

"The sun is but a morning star." Ah yes, but what exactly does that mean? Maybe the sun is also an evening star. Maybe the phrase had no exact meaning even in Thoreau's mind. He was, at times, what we today might call a put-on artist. He loved to shock and exasperate; Emerson complains of Henry's "contrariness." The power of Thoreau's assertion lies not in its meaning but in its exhilarating suggestiveness. Like poetry and music, the words imply more than words can make explicit.

Henry was no hermit. Hardly even a recluse. His celebrated cabin at Walden Pond—some of his neighbors called it a "shanty"—was two miles from Concord Common. A half-hour walk from pond to post office. Henry lived in it for only two years and two months. He had frequent human visitors, sometimes too many, he complained, and admitted that his daily rambles took him almost every day into Concord. When he tired of his own cooking and his own companionship he was always welcome at the Emersons' for a free dinner. Although it seems that he earned his keep there. He worked on and off for years as Emerson's household handyman, repairing and maintaining things that the great Ralph Waldo was too busy or too incompetent to attend to himself. "Emerson," noted Thoreau in a letter, "is too much the gentleman to push a wheelbarrow." When Mrs. Emerson complained that the chickens were scratching up her flower beds, Henry attached little cloth booties to the chickens' feet. A witty fellow. Better and easier than keeping them fenced in. When Emerson was off on his European lecture tours, Thoreau would look after not only Emerson's house but also Emerson's children and wife.

We shall now discuss the sexual life of Henry David Thoreau.

November 6, 1980

Awaking as usual sometime before the dawn, frost on my beard and sleeping bag, I see four powerful lights standing in a vertical row on the eastern sky. They are Saturn, Jupiter, Mars, and, pale crescent on a darkened disc, the old moon. The three great planets seem to be rising from the cusps of the moon. I stare for a long time at this strange, startling apparition, a spectacle I have never before seen in all my years on planet Earth. What does it mean? If ever I've seen a portent in the sky this must be it. Spirit both forms and informs the universe, thought the New England transcendentalists, of whom Thoreau was one; all Nature, they believed, is but symbolic of a greater spiritual reality beyond. And within.

Watching the planets, I stumble about last night's campfire, breaking twigs, filling the coffeepot. I dip waterbuckets in the river; the water chills my hands. I stare long at the beautiful, dimming lights in the sky but can find there no meaning other than the lights' intrinsic beauty. As far as I can perceive, the planets signify nothing but themselves. "Such suchness," as my Zen friends say. And that is all. And that is enough. And that is more than we can make head or tail of.

"Reality is fabulous," said Henry; "be it life or death, we crave nothing but reality." And goes on to describe in precise, accurate, glittering detail the most subtle and minute aspects of life in and about his Walden Pond; the "pulse" of water skaters, for instance, advancing from shore across the surface of the lake. Appearance *is* reality, Thoreau implies; or so it appears to me. I begin to think he outgrew transcendentalism rather early in his career, at about the same time that he was overcoming the influence of his onetime mentor Emerson; Thoreau and the transcendentalists had little in common—in the long run—but their long noses, as a friend of mine has pointed out.

Scrambled eggs, bacon, green chiles for breakfast, with hot *salsa,* toasted tortillas, and leftover baked potatoes sliced and fried. A gallon or two of coffee, tea and—for me—the usual breakfast beer. Henry would not have approved of this gourmandising. To hell with him. I do not approve of his fastidious puritanism. For one who claims to crave nothing but reality, he frets too much about *purity.* Purity, purity, he preaches, in the most unctuous of his many sermons, a chapter of *Walden* called "Higher Laws."

"The wonder is how they, how you and I," he writes, "can live this slimy, beastly life, eating and drinking. . . ." Like Dick Gregory, Thoreau recommends a diet of raw fruits and vegetables; like a Pythagorean, he finds even beans impure, since the flatulence that beans induce disturbs his more ethereal meditations. (He would not agree with most men that "farting is such sweet sorrow.") But confesses at one point to a sudden violent lust for wild woodchuck, devoured raw. No wonder; Henry was probably anemic.

He raised beans not to eat but to sell—his only cash crop. During his lifetime his beans sold better than his books. When a publisher shipped back to Thoreau 706 unsellable copies of his *A Week on the Concord and Merrimack Rivers* (the author had himself paid for the printing of the book), Henry noted in his *Journal,* "I now have a library of 900 volumes, over 700 of which I wrote myself."

Although professing disdain for do-gooders, Thoreau once lectured a poor Irish immigrant, a neighbor, on the advisability of changing his ways. "I tried to help him with my experience . . ." but the Irishman, John Field, was only bewildered by Thoreau's earnest preaching. "Poor John Field!" Thoreau concludes; "I trust he does not read this, unless he will improve by it. . . ."

Nathaniel Hawthorne, who lived in Concord for a time and knew Thoreau, called him "an intolerable bore."

On the subject of sex, as we would expect, Henry betrays a considerable nervous agitation. "The generative energy, which, when we are loose, dissipates and makes us unclean, when we are continent invigorates and inspires us. Chastity is the flowering of man. . . ." (But not of flowers?) "We are conscious of an animal in us, which awakens in proportion as our higher nature slumbers. It is reptile and sensual. . . ." "He is blessed who is assured that the animal is dying out in him day by day. . . ." In a letter to his friend Harrison Blake, Henry writes: "What the essential difference between man and woman is, that they should be thus attracted to one another, no one has satisfactorily answered."

Poor Henry. We are reminded of that line in Whitman (another great American oddball), in which our good gray poet said of women, "They attract with a fierce, undeniable attraction," while the context of the poem makes it clear that Whitman himself found young men and boys much more undeniable.

Poor Thoreau. But he could also write, in the late essay "Walking," "The wildness of the savage is but a faint symbol of the awful ferity with which good men and lovers meet." Ferity—now there's a word. What could it have meant to Thoreau? Our greatest nature lover did not have a loving nature. A woman acquaintance of Henry's said she'd sooner take the arm of an elm tree than that of Thoreau.

Poor Henry David Thoreau. His short (forty-five years), quiet, passionate life apparently held little passion for the opposite sex. His relationship with Emerson's wife Lidian was no more than a long brother-sisterly friendship. Thoreau never married. There is no evidence that he ever enjoyed a mutual love affair with any human, female or otherwise. He once fell in love with and proposed marriage to a young woman by the name of Ellen Sewall; she rejected him, bluntly and coldly. He tried once more with a girl named Mary Russell; she turned him down. For a young man of Thoreau's hypersensitive character, these must have been cruel, perhaps disabling blows to what little male ego and confidence he possessed to begin with. It left him shattered, we may assume, on that side of life; he never again approached a woman with romantic intentions on his mind. He became a professional bachelor, scornful of wives and marriage. He lived and probably died a virgin, pure as shriven snow. Except for those sensual reptiles coiling and uncoiling down in the root cellar of his being. Ah, purity!

But we make too much of this kind of thing nowadays. Modern men and women are obsessed with the sexual; it is the only realm of primordial adventure still left to most of us. Like apes in a zoo, we spend our energies on the one field of play remaining; human lives otherwise are pretty well caged in by the walls, bars, chains, and locked gates of our industrial culture. In the relatively wild, free America of Henry's time there was plenty of opportunity for every kind of adventure, although Henry himself did not, it seems to me, take advantage of those opportunities. (He could have toured the Western plains with George Catlin!) He led an unnecessarily constrained existence, and not only in the "generative" region.

Thoreau the spinster-poet. In the year 1850, when Henry reached the age of thirty-three, Emily Dickinson in nearby Amherst became twenty. Somebody should have brought the two together. They might have hit it off. I imagine this scene, however, immediately following the honeymoon:

EMILY (raising her pen)
    Henry, you haven't taken out the garbage.
HENRY (raising his flute)
    Take it out yourself.

What tunes did Thoreau play on that flute of his? He never tells us; we would like to know. And what difference would a marriage—with a woman—have made in Henry's life? In his work? In that message to the world by which he challenges us, as do all the greatest writers, to change our lives? He taunts, he sermonizes, he condemns, he propounds conundrums, he orates and exhorts us:

"Wherever a man goes, men will pursue and paw him with their dirty institutions. . . ."

"I found that by working six weeks a year I could meet all the expenses of living."

"Tell those who worry about their health that they may be already dead."

"When thousands are thrown out of employment, it suggests they were not well-employed."

"If you stand right fronting and face to face with a fact, you will see the sun glimmer on both its surfaces, as if it were a scimitar, and feel its sweet edge dividing you through the heart and marrow, and so you will happily conclude your mortal career."

". . . The hero is commonly the simplest and obscurest of men."

". . . Little is to be expected of a nation when the vegetable mould is exhausted, and it is compelled to make manure of the bones of its fathers."

"Genius is a light which makes the darkness visible, like the lightning's flash, which perchance shatters the temple of knowledge itself. . . ."

"When, in the course of ages, American liberty has become a fiction of the past—as it is to some extent a fiction of the present—the poets of the world will be inspired by American mythology."

"We should go forth on the shortest walk . . . in the spirit of undying adventure, never to return."

". . . If I repent of anything, it is very likely to be my good behavior. What demon possessed me that I behaved so well?"

"No man is so poor that he need sit on a pumpkin; that is shiftless-ness."

"I would rather sit on a pumpkin and have it all to myself than be crowded on a velvet cushion."

"A man is rich in proportion to the number of things which he can afford to let alone."

"We live meanly, like ants, though the fable tells us that we were long ago changed into men. . . ."

"A living dog is better than a dead lion. Shall a man go and hang himself because he belongs to the race of pygmies, and not be the big-gest pygmy that he can?"

"I will endeavor to speak a good word for the truth."

"Rather than love, than money, than fame, give me truth."

"Any truth is better than make-believe."

And so forth.

November 7, 1980

On down this here Greenish river. We cast off, row south past Woodruff, Point, and Saddlehorse bottoms, past Upheaval Bottom and Hardscrabble Bottom. Wherever the river makes a bend—and this river comes near, in places, to bowknots—there is another flat area, a bottom, covered with silt, sand, gravel, grown up with grass and brush and cactus and, near shore, trees: willow, cottonwood, box elder, and jungles of tamarisk.

The tamarisk does not belong here, has become a pest, a water-loving exotic engaged in the process of driving out the cot-tonwoods and willows. A native of arid North Africa, the tamarisk was imported to the American Southwest fifty years ago by con-servation *experts*—dirt management specialists—in hopes that it

would help prevent streambank erosion. The cause of the erosion
was flooding, and the primary cause of the flooding, then as now,
was livestock grazing.

Oars at rest, we drift for a while. The Riverine String Band
take up their instruments and play. The antique, rowdy, vibrant
music from England and Ireland by way of Appalachia and the
Rocky Mountains floats on the air, rises like smoke toward the
high rimrock of the canyon walls, fades by infinitesimal gradations
into the stillness of eternity. Where else could it go?

Ted Seeley prolongs the pause, then fills the silence with a solo
on the fiddle, a Canadian invention called "Screechin' Old
Woman and Growlin' Old Man." This dialogue continues for
some time, concluding with a triumphant outburst from the Old
Woman.

We miss the landing off the inside channel at Wild Horse
Bench and have to fight our way through thickets of tamarisk and
cane to the open ground of Fort Bottom. We make lunch on crack-
ers, canned tuna, and chopped black olives in the shade of a cottonwood by the side of a long-abandoned log cabin. A trapper,
prospector, or cow thief might have lived here—or all three of
them—a century ago. Names and initials adorn the lintel of the
doorway. The roof is open to the sky.

We climb a hill of clay and shale and limestone ledges to inspect at close hand an ancient ruin of stone on the summit. An
Anasazi structure, probably seven or eight hundred years old, it
commands a broad view of river and canyon for many miles both
up and downstream, and offers a glimpse of the higher lands beyond. We can see the great Buttes of the Cross, Candlestick Tower,
Junction Butte (where the Green River meets the Colorado River),
Ekker Butte, Grandview Point, North Point, and parts of the
White Rim. Nobody human lives at those places, or in the leagues
of monolithic stone between them. We find pleasure in that knowledge. From this vantage point everything looks about the same
as it did when Major John Wesley Powell and his mates first saw
it in 1869. Photographs made by members of his party dem-
onstrate that nothing much has changed except the vegetation

types along the river, as in the case of tamarisk replacing willow.

We return to our river. A magisterial magpie sails before us across the barren fields. Two ravens and a hawk watch our lazy procession downstream past the long straightaway of Potato Bottom. We make camp before sundown on an island of white sand in the middle of the river. A driftwood fire under an iron pot cooks our vegetable stew. Russell mixes a batch of heavy-duty cornbread in the Dutch oven, sets the oven on the hot coals, and piles more coals on the rimmed lid. The cornbread bakes. We drink our beer, sip our rum, and listen to a pack of coyotes yammering like idiots away off in the twilight.

"I wonder who won the election," says one member of our party—our boatwoman Lorna Corson.

"The coyotes can explain everything," says Rennie Russell.

It's going to be a cold and frosty night. We add wood to the fire and put on sweaters and coats. The nights are long in November; darkness by six. The challenge is to keep the fire going and conversation and music alive until a decent bedtime arrives. Ten hours is too long to spend curled in a sleeping bag. The body knows this if the brain does not. That must be why I wake up every morning long before the sun appears. And why I remain sitting here, alone on my log, after the others have crept away, one by one, to their scattered beds.

Henry gazes at me through the flames of the campfire. From beyond the veil. Edward, he says, what are you doing here? Henry, I reply, what are you doing out there?

How easy for Thoreau to preach simplicity, asceticism and voluntary poverty when, as some think, he had none but himself to care for during his forty-five years. How easy to work part-time for a living when you have neither wife nor children to support. (When you have no payments to meet on house, car, pickup truck, cabin cruiser, life insurance, medical insurance, summer place, college educations, dinette set, color TVs, athletic club, real estate investments, holidays in Europe and the Caribbean. . . .)

Why Henry never took a wife has probably more to do with his own eccentric personality than with his doctrine of independence-through-simplicity. But if he had *wanted* a partner, and had been able to find one willing to share his doctrine, then it seems reasonable to suppose that the two of them—with their little Thoreaus—could have managed to live a family life on Thoreauvian principles. Henry might have been compelled to make pencils, survey woodlots, and give public lectures for twenty-four weeks, rather than only six, each year, but his integrity as a free man would still have been preserved. There is no reason—other than the comic incongruity of imagining Henry Thoreau as husband and father—to suppose that his bachelorhood invalidates his arguments. If there was tragedy in the life of Thoreau, that tragedy lies not in any theoretical contradiction between what Henry advocated and how he lived but in his basic loneliness. He was a psychic loner all his life.

But a family man nevertheless. Except for his two years and two months at Walden Pond, his student years at Harvard, and occasional excursions to Canada, Cape Cod, and Maine, Thoreau lived most of his life in and upon the bosom of family—Emerson's family, part of the time, and the Thoreau family—mother, sister, uncles, and aunts—during the remainder.

When his father died Henry took over the management of the family's pencil-making business, a cottage industry carried on in the family home. Always a clever fellow with his hands, Henry developed a better way of manufacturing pencils, and a better product. Some think that the onset of his tuberculosis, which eventually killed him, was hastened by the atmosphere of fine powdered graphite in which he earned a part of his keep.

A part of it: Thoreau had no wish to become a businessman—"Trade curses everything it handles"—and never gave to pencils more than a small part of his time.

He was considered an excellent surveyor by his townsmen and his services were much in demand. His work still serves as the basis of many property lines in and around the city of Concord. There is a document in the Morgan Library in New York, a map of Walden Pond, signed "H. D. Thoreau, Civil Engineer."

But as with pencil-making, so with surveying—Thoreau

would not allow it to become a full-time career. Whatever he did, he did well; he was an expert craftsman in everything to which he put his hand. But to no wage-earning occupation would he give his life. He had, he said, "other business." And this other business awaited him out in the woods, where, as he wrote, "I was better known."

What was this other business? It is the subject of *Walden*, of his further books and essays, and of the thirty-nine volumes of his *Journal*, from which, to a considerable extent, the books were quarried. Thoreau's subject is the greatest available to any writer, thinker and human being, one which I cannot summarize in any but the most banal of phrases: "meaning," or "the meaning of life" (meaning *all* life, of course, not human life only), or in the technical usage preferred by professional philosophers, "the significance of existence."

It is this attempt to encircle with words the essence of being itself—with or without a capital *B*—which gives to Henry's prose-poetry the disturbing, haunting, heart-opening quality that some call mysticism. Like the most ambitious poets and artists, he was trying to get it all into his work, whatever "it" may signify, whatever "all" may include. Living a life full of wonder—wonderful—Henry tries to impart that wonder to his readers.

"There is nothing inorganic. . . . The earth is not a mere fragment of dead history, stratum upon stratum, like the leaves of a book, to be studied by geologists and antiquaries chiefly, but living poetry like the leaves of a tree, which precede flowers and fruit; not a fossil earth but a living earth. . . ."

That the earth, considered whole, is a kind of living being, might well seem like nonsense to the hardheaded among us. Worse than nonsense—mystical nonsense. But let us remember that a hard head, like any dense-hulled and thick-shelled nut, can enclose, out of necessity, only a tiny kernel of meat. Thinking meat, in this case. The hard head reveals, therefore, while attempting to conceal and shelter, its tiny, soft, delicate, and suspicious mind.

The statement about earth is clear enough. And probably true. To some, self-evident, though not empirically verifiable within the present limitations of scientific method. Such verification requires a more sophisticated science than we possess at present. It requires a science with room for more than data and information, a science that includes sympathy for the object under study, and more than sympathy, love. A love based on prolonged contact and interaction. Intercourse, if possible. Observation informed by sympathy, love, intuition. Numbers, charts, diagrams, and formulas are not in themselves sufficient. The face of science as currently construed is a face that only a mathematician could love. The root meaning of "science" is "knowledge"; to see and to see truly, a qualitative, not merely quantitative, understanding.

For an example of science in the whole and wholesome sense read Thoreau's description of an owl's behavior in "Winter Visitors." Thoreau observes the living animal in its native habitat, and watches it for weeks. For an example of science in its debased sense take this: According to the L.A. *Times,* a psychologist in Los Angeles defends laboratory experimentation on captive dogs with the assertion that "little is known about the psychology of dogs." Anyone who has ever kept a dog knows more about dogs than that psychologist—who doubtless considers himself a legitimate scientist—will learn in a year of Sundays.

Or this: Researchers in San Francisco have confined chimpanzees in airtight glass cubicles (gas chambers) in order to study the effect of various dosages of chemically polluted air on these "manlike organisms." As if there were not already available five million human inhabitants of the Los Angeles basin, and a hundred other places, ready, willing, and eager to supply personally informed testimony on the subject under scrutiny. Leaving aside any consideration of ethics, morality, and justice, there are more intelligent ways to study living creatures. Or nonliving creations: rocks have rights too.

That which today calls itself science gives us more and more information, an indigestible glut of information, and less and less understanding. Thoreau was well aware of this tendency and foresaw its fatal consequences. He could see the tendency in himself, even as he partially succumbed to it. Many of the later *Journals* are filled with little but the enumeration of statistical data concerning such local Concord phenomena as the rise and fall of lake levels, or the thickness of the ice on Flint's Pond on a January morning. Tedious reading—pages and pages of "factoids," as Norman Mailer would call them—attached to no coherent theory, illuminated by neither insight nor outlook nor speculation.

Henry may have had a long-range purpose in mind but he did not live long enough to fulfill it. Kneeling in the snow on a winter's day to count the tree rings in a stump, he caught the cold that led to his death on May 6, 1862. He succumbed not partially but finally to facticity.

Why'd you do it, Henry? I ask him through the flames.

The bearded face with the large, soft, dark eyes, mournful and thoughtful as the face of Lincoln, smiles back at me but offers no answer. He evades the question by suggesting other questions in his better-known, "mystical" vein:

"There was a dead horse in the hollow by the path to my house, which compelled me sometimes to go out of my way, especially in the night when the air was heavy, but the assurance it gave me of the strong appetite and inviolable health of Nature was my compensation for this. I love to see that Nature is so rife with life that myriads can be afforded to be sacrificed and suffered to prey on one another. . . . The impression made on a wise man is that of universal innocence. Compassion is a very untenable ground. It must be expeditious. Its pleadings will not bear to be stereotyped."

Henry, I say, what the devil do you mean?

He smiles again and says, "I observed a very small and graceful hawk, like a nighthawk, alternately soaring like a ripple and tumbling a rod or two over and over, showing the underside of its wings, which gleamed like a satin ribbon in the sun. . . . The merlin it seemed to me it might be called; but I care not for its name. It was the most ethereal flight I have ever witnessed. It did not simply flutter like a butterfly, nor soar like the larger hawks, but it sported with proud reliance in the fields of the air. . . . It appeared to have no companion in the universe . . . and to need none but the morning and the ether with which it played. It was not lonely, but made all the earth lonely beneath it."

Very pretty, Henry. Are you speaking for yourself? I watch his lined, gentle face, the face of his middle age (though he had no later) as recorded in photographs, and cannot help but read there the expression, engraved, of a patient, melancholy resignation. All babies look identical; boys and adolescents resemble one another, in their bewildered hopefulness, more than they differ. But eventually the inner nature of the man appears on his outer surface. Character begins to shine through. Year by year a man reveals himself, while those with nothing to show, show it. Differentiation becomes individuation. By the age of forty, if not before, a man is responsible for his face. The same is true of women too, certainly, although women, obeying the biological imperative, strive harder than men to preserve an appearance of youthfulness—the reproductive look—and lose it sooner. Appearance *is* reality.

Henry replies not to my question but, as befits a ghostly seer, to my thought: "Nothing can rightly compel a simple and brave man to a vulgar sadness."

We'll go along with that, Henry; you've been accused of many things but no one, to my knowledge, has yet accused you of vulgarity. Though Emerson, reacting to your night in jail for refusing to pay the poll tax, called the gesture "mean and skulking and in bad taste." In bad taste! How typically Emersonian. Robert Louis Stevenson too called you a "skulker" on the grounds that you preached more strongly than you practiced, later recanting when he learned of your activity in the antislavery movement. The contemporary author Alan Harrington, in his book *The Immortalist,* accuses you of writing, at times, like "an accountant of the spirit." That charge he bases on your vague remarks concerning immorality, and on such lines as "Goodness is the only investment that never fails."

Still other current critics, taking their cue from those whom Nabokov specified as "the Viennese quacks," would deflect the force of your attacks on custom, organized religion, and the state by suggesting that you suffered from a complex of complexes, naturally including the castration complex and the Oedipus complex. Your defiance of authority, they maintain, was in reality no more than the rebelliousness of an adolescent rejecting his father—in this case the meek and mousy John Thoreau.

Whatever grain of truth may be in this diagnosis, such criticism betrays the paternalistic condescension of these critics toward human beings in general. The good citizen, they seem to be saying, is like the obedient child; the rebellious man is a bad boy. "The people are like children," said our own beloved, gone but not forgotten, Richard Nixon. The psychiatric approach to dissidence has been most logically applied in the Soviet Union, where opposition to the state is regarded and treated as a form of mental illness.

In any case, Henry cannot be compelled to confess to a vulgar sadness. The vulgarity resides in the tactics of literary Freudianism. Of the opposition. Psychoanalysis is the neurosis of the psychoanalyst—and of the psychoanalytic critic. Why should we bother any more with this garbage? I thought we stopped talking about Freud back in 1952. Sometime near the end of the Studebaker era.

Fading beyond the last flames of the fire, Henry lulls me to sleep with one of his more soporific homilies:

"The light which puts out our eyes is darkness to us. Only that day dawns to which we are awake. There is more day to dawn. The sun . . ."

Yes, yes, Henry, we know. How true. Whatever it means. How late it is. Whatever the hour.

I rise from my log, heap the coals of the fire together, and by their glimmering light and the cold light of the stars fumble my way back and into the luxury of my goosedown nest. Staring up at mighty Orion, trying to count six of the seven Pleiades, a solemn thought comes to me: We Are Not Alone.

I nuzzle my companion's cold nose, the only part of her not burrowed deep in her sleeping bag. She stirs but does not wake. We're not alone, I whisper in her ear. I know, she says; shut up and go to sleep. Smiling, I face the black sky and the sapphire stars.

Mark Twain was right. Better the savage wasteland with Eve than Paradise without her. Where she is, there is Paradise.

Poor Henry.

And then I hear that voice again, far off but clear: "All Nature is my bride."

November 8, 1980

Who won the election? What election? Mere vapors on the gelid air, like the breath from my lungs. I rebuild the fire on the embers of last night's fire. I construct the coffee, adding fresh grounds to yesterday's. One by one, five human forms reassemble themselves about me, repeating themselves, with minor variations, for another golden day. The two vegetarians in our group—Rennie and Lorna—prepare their breakfast oatmeal, a viscous gray slime. I dump two pounds of Buck-sliced bacon into the expedition's wok, to the horror of the vegetarians, and stir it roughly about with a fork. Stir-cooking. The four carnivores look on with hungry eyes. The vegetarians smile in pity. "Pig meat," says Lorna, "for the four fat pork faces." "Eat your pussy food," says Dusty Teale, "and be quiet."

The melody of morning. Black-throated desert sparrows chatter in the willows: *chirr . . . chirr . . . chit chit chit.* The sun comes up, a glaring cymbal, over yonder canyon rim. Quickly the temperature rises five, ten, twenty degrees, at the rate of a degree a minute, from freezing to fifty-two. Or so it feels. We peel off parkas, sweaters, shirts, thermal underwear. Ravens croak, a rock falls, the river flows.

The fluvial life. The alluvial shore. "A river is superior to a lake," writes Henry in his *Journal*, "in its liberating influence. It has motion and indefinite length. . . . With its rapid current it is a slightly fluttering wing. River towns are winged towns."

Down the river. Lorna rows the dory, I row the raft. We are edified by water music from our string trio, a rich enchanting tune out of Peru called "Urubamba." The song goes on and on and never long enough. The Indians must have composed it for a journey down the Amazon.

Fresh slides appear on the mud banks; a beaver plops into the water ahead of us, disappears. The beavers are making a comeback on the Green. Time for D. Julien, Jim Bridger, Joe Meek, Jed Smith, and Jim Beckwourth to reappear. Eternal recurrence, announced Nietzsche. Time for the mountain men to return. The American West has not given us, so far, sufficient men to match our mountains. Or not since the death of Crazy Horse, Sitting Bull, Dull Knife, Red Cloud, Chief Joseph, Little Wolf, Red Shirt, Gall, Geronimo, Cochise, Tenaya (to name but a few), and their comrades. With their defeat died a bold, brave, heroic way of life, one as fine as anything recorded history has to show us. Speaking for myself, I'd sooner have been a liver-eating, savage horseman, riding with Red Cloud, than a slave-owning sophist sipping tempered wine in Periclean Athens. For example. Even Attila the Hun, known locally as the Scourge of God, brought more fresh air and freedom into Europe than the crowd who gave us the syllogism and geometry, Aristotle and his *Categories*, Plato and his *Laws*.

Instead of mountain men we are cursed with a plague of diggers, drillers, borers, grubbers; of asphalt-spreaders, dam-builders, overgrazers, clear-cutters, and strip-miners whose object seems to be to make our mountains match our men—making molehills out of mountains for a race of rodents—for the rat race.

Oh well . . . revenge is on the way. We see it in those high thin clouds far on the northern sky. We feel it in those rumbles of discontent deep in the cupboards of the earth: tectonic crockery trembling on the continental shelves. We hear it down the slipface of the dunes, a blue wind moaning out of nowhere. We smell it on the air: the smell of danger. Death before dishonor? That's right. What else? Liberty or death? Naturally.

When no one else would do it, it was Thoreau, Henry Thoreau the intolerable bore, the mean skulker, the "quaint stump figure of a man," as William Dean Howells saw him, who rang the

Concord firebell to summon the villagers to a speech by Emerson attacking slavery. And when John Brown stood on trial for his life, when all America, even the most ardent abolitionists, was denouncing him, it was himself—Henry—who delivered a public address first in Concord, then in Boston, not only defending but praising, even eulogizing, the "madman" of Harpers Ferry.

We go on. Sheer rock—the White Rim—rises from the river's left shore. We pause at noon to fill our water jugs from a series of potholes half filled with last week's rainwater. We drink, and sitting in the sunlight on the pale sandstone, make our lunch—slabs of dark bread, quite authentic, from a bohemian bakery in Moab; a serious hard-core hippie peanut butter, heavy as wet concrete, from some beatnik food coop in Durango, Colorado (where Teale and Corson live); raspberry jam; and wild honey, thick as axle grease, for esophageal lubrication.

"What is your favorite dish?" another guest asked Thoreau as they sat down to a sumptuous Emersonian dinner.

"The nearest," Henry replied.

"At Harvard they teach all branches of learning," said Ralph Waldo.

"But none of the roots," said Henry.

Refusing to pay a dollar for his Harvard diploma, he said, "Let every sheep keep its own skin." When objections were raised to his habit of exaggeration, Henry said, "You must speak loud to those who are hard of hearing." Asked to write for the *Ladies' Companion,* he declined on the grounds that he "could not write anything companionable." He defines a pearl as "the hardened tear of a diseased clam, murdered in its old age." On the art of writing he said to a correspondent, "You must work very long to write short sentences." And added that "the one great rule of composition . . . is to speak the truth." Describing the flavor of a certain wild apple, he wrote that it was "sour enough to set a squirrel's teeth on edge, or make a jay scream."

And so on. The man seemingly composed wisecracks and epigrams in his sleep. Even on his deathbed. "Henry, have you made your peace with God?" asked a relative. "I am not aware that we had ever quarreled, Aunt," said Henry. To another visitor, attempting to arouse in him a decent Christian concern with the next world, Henry said, "One world at a time."

One could make a book of Henry's sayings. And call it *Essais. Areopagitica. Walden.*

Many of his friends, neighbors, relatives, and relative friends must have sighed in relief when Henry finally croaked his last, mumbling "moose . . . Indians . . . " and was safely buried under Concord sod. Peace, they thought, at long last. But, to paraphrase the corpse, they had *somewhat hastily* concluded that he was dead.

His passing did not go unnoticed outside of Concord. Thoreau had achieved regional notoriety by 1862. But at the time when the giants of New England literature were thought to be Emerson, Hawthorne, Alcott, Channing, Irving, Longfellow, Dr. Lowell, and Dr. Holmes, Thoreau was but a minor writer. Not even a major minor writer.

Today we see it differently. In the ultimate democracy of time, Henry has outlived his contemporaries. Hawthorne and Emerson are still read, at least in university English departments, and it may be that in a few elementary schools up in Maine and Minnesota children are being compelled to read Longfellow's *Hiawatha* (I doubt it; doubt that they can, even under compulsion), but as for the others they are forgotten by everyone but specialists in American literature. Thoreau, however, becomes more significant with each passing decade. The deeper our United States sinks into industrialism, urbanism, militarism—with the rest of the world doing its best to emulate America—the more poignant, strong, and appealing becomes Thoreau's demand for the right of every man, every woman, every child, every dog, every tree, every snail darter, every lousewort, every living thing, to live its own life in its own way at its own pace in its own square mile of home. Or in its own stretch of river.

Looking at my water-soaked, beer-stained, grease-spotted cheap paperback copy of *Walden,* I see that mine was from the thirty-third printing. And this is only one of at least a dozen current American editions of the book. *Walden* has been published abroad in every country where English can be read, as in India—

God knows they need it there—or can be translated, as in Russia, where they need it even more. The Kremlin's commissars of literature have classified Thoreau as a nineteenth-century social reformer, proving once again that censors can read but seldom understand.

The village crank becomes a world figure. As his own Johnny Appleseed, he sows the seeds of liberty around the planet, even on what looks like the most unpromising soil. Out of Concord, apples of discord. Truth threatens power, now and always.

We walk up a small side canyon toward an area called Soda Springs Basin; the canyon branches and branches again, forming more canyons. The floor of each is flood-leveled sand, the walls perpendicular sandstone. Each canyon resembles a winding corridor in a labyrinth. We listen for the breathing of the Minotaur but find only cottonwoods glowing green and gold against the red rock, rabbitbrush with its mustard-yellow bloom, mule-ear sunflowers facing the sunlight, their coarse petals the color of butter, and the skull and curled horns of a desert bighorn ram, half buried in the auburn sand.

The canyons go on and on, twisting for miles into the plateau beyond. We turn back without reaching Soda Springs. On our return Dusty Teale takes up the bighorn trophy, carries it back to the dory and mounts it on the bow, giving his boat dignity, class, an unearned but warlike glamour.

We camp today at Anderson Bottom, across the river from Unknown Bottom. We find pictographs and petroglyphs here, pictures of deer, bighorns, warriors, and spectral figures representing—who knows—gods, spirits, demons. They do not trouble us. We cook our dinner and sing our songs and go to sleep.

November 9, 1980

Early in the morning I hear coyotes singing again, calling up the sun. There's something about the coyotes that reminds me of Henry. What is it? After a moment the answer comes.

Down near Tucson, Arizona, where I sometimes live—a grim and grimy little-big town, swarming with nervous policemen, dope dealers, resolute rapists, and geriatric bank robbers, but let this pass for the moment—the suburban parts of the city are infested with pet dogs. Every home owner in these precincts believes that he needs whatever burglar protection he can get; and he is correct. Most evenings at twilight the wild coyotes come stealing in from the desert to penetrate the suburbs, raid garbage cans, catch and eat a few cats, dogs, and other domesticated beasts. When this occurs the dogs raise a grim clamor, roaring like maniacs, and launch themselves in hot but tentative pursuit of the coyotes. The coyotes retreat into the brush and cactus, where they stop, facing the town, to wait and sit and laugh at the dogs. They yip, yap, yelp, howl, and holler, teasing the dogs, taunting them, enticing them with the old-time call of the wild. And the dogs stand and tremble, shaking with indecision, furious, hating themselves, tempted to join the coyotes, run off with them into the hills, but— afraid. Afraid to give up the comfort, security, and safety of their housebound existence. Afraid of the unknown and dangerous.

Thoreau was our suburban coyote. Town dwellers have always found him exasperating.

"I have traveled a good deal in Concord; and everywhere, in shops and offices and fields, the inhabitants have appeared to me to be doing penance in a thousand remarkable ways. . . . By a seeming fate, commonly called necessity, they are employed, as it says in an old book, laying up treasures which moth and rust will corrupt and thieves break through and steal. It is a fool's life, as they will find when they get to the end of it, if not before. . . . I sometimes wonder that we can be so frivolous. . . . As if you could kill time without injuring eternity."

Oh, come now, Henry, stop yapping at us. Go make love to a pine tree (all Nature being your bride). Lay off. Leave us alone. But he will not stop.

"The mass of men lead lives of quiet desperation. What is called resignation is confirmed desperation. . . . A stereotyped but unconscious despair is concealed even under what are called the games and amusements of mankind. There is no play in them."

But is it *true* that the mass of men lead lives of quiet desperation? And if so, did Henry escape such desperation himself? And
who, if anyone, can answer these questions?

As many have noted, the mass of men—and women—lead
lives today of *un*quiet desperation. A frantic busyness ("business")
pervades our society wherever we look—in city and country,
among young and old and middle-aged, married and unmarried,
all races, classes, sexes, in work and play, in religion, the arts, the
sciences, and perhaps most conspicuously in the self-conscious cult
of meditation, retreat, withdrawal. The symptoms of universal un-
ease and dis-ease are apparent on every side. We hear the demand
by conventional economists for increased "productivity," for example. Productivity of what? for whose benefit? to what end? by
what means and at what cost? Those questions are not considered.
We are belabored by the insistence on the part of our politicians,
businessmen and military leaders, and the claque of scriveners who
serve them, that "growth" and "power" are intrinsic goods, of
which we can never have enough, or even too much. As if gigan-
tism were an end in itself. As if a commendable rat were a rat
twelve hands high at the shoulders—and still growing. As if we
could never have peace on this planet until one state dominates all
others.

The secondary symptoms show up in the lives of individuals,
the banalities of everyday soap opera: crime, divorce, runaway
children, loneliness, alcoholism, mental breakdown. We live in a
society where suicide (in its many forms) appears to more and
more as a sensible solution; as a viable alternative; as a workable
option.

Yes, there are many who seem to be happy in their lives and
work. But strange lives, queer work. Space technicians, for example, busily refining a new type of inertial guidance system for an
intercontinental ballistic missile bearing hydrogen bombs. Laboratory biologists testing the ability of mice, dogs, and chimpanzees to
cultivate cancer on a diet of cigarettes and Holsum bread, to pro-
pel a treadmill under electric stimuli, to survive zero gravity in a

centrifuge. And the indefatigable R. Buckminster Fuller hurtling around the globe by supersonic jet with six wristwatches strapped to each forearm, each watch set to a different time zone. "The world is big," says Fuller, "but it is comprehensible."

And also, to be fair, young dancers in a classroom; an old sculptor hacking in fury at a block of apple wood; a pinto bean farmer in Cortez, Colorado, surveying his fields with satisfaction on a rainy day in July (those rare farmers, whom Thoreau dismissed with such contempt, we now regard with envy); a solitary fly fisherman unzipping his fly on the banks of the Madison River; wet childen playing on a shining, sun-dazzled beach.

Compared with ours, Thoreau's was an open, quiet, agrarian society, relatively clean and uncluttered. The factory system was only getting under way in his time, though he took note of it when he remarked that "the shop girls have no privacy, even in their thoughts." In his day England, not America, was "the workhouse of the world." (America now in the process of being succeeded by Japan.) What would Henry think of New England, of the United States, of the Western world, in the year 1980? 1984? 2001? Would he not assert, confidently as before, that the mass of humans continue to lead lives of quiet desperation?

Quiet desperation. The bite of the phrase comes from the unexpected, incongruous juxtaposition of ordinarily antithetical words. The power of it comes from our sense of its illuminating force— "a light which makes the darkness visible." Henry's shocking pronouncement continues to resonate in our minds, with deeper vibrations, 130 years after he made it. He allows for exceptions, indicating the "mass of men," not all men, but as for the truth of his observation no Gallup Poll can tell us; each must look into his own heart and mind and then deny it if he can.

And what about Henry himself? When one of his friends, William Ellery Channing, declared morosely that no man could be happy "under present conditions," Thoreau replied without hesitation, "But I am." He spent nearly a year at his dying and near the end, too weak to write any more, he dictated the following, in answer to a letter from his friend Blake:

"You ask particularly after my health. I *suppose* that I have not many months to live; but of course I know nothing about it. I may add that I am enjoying existence as much as ever, and regret nothing."

When the town jailer, Sam Staples, the same who had locked Thoreau up for a night many years before, and had also become a friend, paid a visit to the dying man, he reported to Emerson: "Never spent an hour with more satisfaction. Never saw a man dying with so much pleasure and peace." A trifle lugubrious, but revealing. Henry's sister Sophia wrote, near his end, "It is not possible to be sad in his presence. No shadow attaches to anything connected with my precious brother. His whole life impresses me as a grand miracle. . . . "

A cheerful stoic all the way, Thoreau refused any drugs to ease the pain or let him sleep; he rejected opiates, according to Channing, "on the ground that he preferred to endure the worst sufferings with a clear mind rather than sink into a narcotic dream." As he would never admit to a vulgar sadness, so he would not allow himself to surrender to mere physical pain.

It must have seemed to Henry during his last year that his life as an author had been a failure. Only two of his books were published during his lifetime and neither received much recognition. His contemporaries, without exception—Emerson included—had consigned him to oblivion, and Henry could not have been unaware of the general opinion. But even in this he refused to acknowledge defeat. Noting the dismal sales of his books, he wrote in his *Journal:* "I believe that the result is more inspiring and better for me than if thousands had bought my wares. It affects my privacy less and leaves me freer."

Emerson declared that Thoreau was a coldly unemotional man, stoical but never cheerful; Emerson had so convinced himself of this that when, in editing some of Thoreau's letters for publication, he came across passages that indicated otherwise, he deleted them. But Ralph Waldo's son Edward, in his book *Henry Thoreau as Remembered by a Young Friend,* wrote that Henry loved to sing and dance, and was always popular with the children of Concord.

In her *Memories of Hawthorne,* Hawthorne's daughter Rose gives us this picture of Thoreau ice skating, with Emerson and Hawthorne, on the frozen Concord River: "Hawthorne," she writes, "moved like a self-impelled Greek statue, stately and grave" (the marble faun); Emerson "closed the line, evidently too weary to hold himself erect, pitching headforemost ..."; while Thoreau, circling around them, "performed dithyrambic dances and Bacchic leaps."

But what of the photographs of Henry referred to earlier, the daguerreotype in his thirty-ninth year by B. W. Maxham, made in 1856, and the ambrotype by E. S. Dunshee, made in 1861? Trying to get some sense of the man himself, in himself, which I do not get from his words alone, or from the accounts of Thoreau by others, I find myself looking again and again at these old pictures. Yes, the eyes are unusually large, very sensitive and thoughtful, as is the expression of the whole face. The nose is too long, the chin too small, neither an ornament; the face deeply lined, the brow high, the hair and beard luxuriant. A passable face, if not a handsome one. And it still seems to me that I read in his eyes, in his look, an elemental melancholy. A resigned sadness. But the man was ailing with tuberculosis when the former picture was made, within a year of his death when the second was made. These facts should explain the thoughtful look, justify a certain weariness. In neither picture can we see what might be considered a trace of self-pity—the *vulgar* sadness. And in neither can we perceive the faintest hint of any kind of desperation. Henry may have been lonely; he was never a desperate man.

What does it matter? For us it is Henry's words and ideas that count, or more exactly, the symbiotic and synergistic mutually reinforcing logic of word and idea, and his successful efforts to embody both in symbolic acts. If it were true that he never had a happy moment (I doubt this) in his entire life, he surely had an intense empathy with the sensations of happiness:

"... I have penetrated to those meadows on the morning of many a first spring day, jumping from hummock to hummock, from willow root to willow root, when the wild river valley and the woods were bathed in so pure and bright a light as would have waked the dead, if they had been slumbering in their graves, as some suppose. There needs no stronger proof of immortality."

The paragraph is from the springtime of Henry's life. *Walden* is a young man's book, most of it written before his thirtieth year. But the infatuation with the sun and sunlight carries on into the premature autumn of his years as well; he never gave them up, never surrendered. Near the end of his life he wrote:

"We walked [jumping has become walking, but the spirit remains the same] in so pure and bright a light, gilding the withered grass and leaves, so softly and serenely bright, I thought I had never bathed in such a golden flood, without a ripple or a murmur to it. The west side of every wood and rising ground gleamed like the boundary of Elysium, and the sun on our backs seemed like a gentle herdsman driving us home at evening."

And concluding: "So we saunter toward the Holy Land, till one day the sun shall shine more brightly than ever he has done, shall perchance shine into our minds and hearts, and light up our whole lives with a great awakening light, as warm and serene and golden as on a bankside in autumn."

November 10, 1980

Onward, into Stillwater Canyon. We have left Labyrinth behind, though how Major Powell distinguished the two is hard to determine. The current is slow, but no slower than before, the canyons as serpentine as ever. In the few straight stretches of water we gain a view of Candlestick Tower, now behind us, and off to the southwest, ahead, the great sandstone monadnock three hundred feet high known as Cleopatra's Chair, "bathed," as Henry would say, "in a golden flood of sunlight."

We row around an anvil-shaped butte called Turk's Head. Hard to see any reason for the name. Is there any reason, out here, for any name? These huge walls and giant towers and vast mazy avenues of stone resist attempts at verbal reduction. The historical view, the geological view, the esthetical view, the rock climber's view, give us only aspects of a massive *presence* that remains fundamentally unknowable. The world is big and it is incomprehensible.

A hot, still morning in Stillwater Canyon. We row and rest and glide, at two miles per hour, between riparian jungles of rusty willow, coppery tamarisk, brown cane, and gold-leaf cottonwoods. On the shaded side the crickets sing their dirgelike monotone. They know, if we don't, that winter is coming.

But today is very warm for mid-November. An Indian-summer day. Looking at the rich brown river, jungle on both banks, I think how splendid it would be, and apposite, to see the rugose snout of an alligator come sliding through the water toward us. We need alligators here. Crocodiles, also. A few brontosauri, pteranodons, and rocs with twenty-five-foot wingspan would not be amiss. How tragic that we humans arrived too late, to the best of our conscious recollection, to have witnessed the fun and frolic of the giant thunder lizards in their time of glory. Why was that great chapter ripped too soon from the Book of Life? I would give ten years off the beginning of my life to see, only once, *Tyrannosaurus rex* come rearing up from the elms of Central Park, a Morgan police horse screaming in its jaws. We can never have enough of nature.

We explore a couple of unnamed side canyons on the right, searching for a natural stone arch I found ten years ago, on a previous river journey. Hallucination Arch, we named it then, a lovely span of two-tone rosy sandstone—not shown on any map—somewhere high in the northern fringes of the Maze. We do not find it this time. We pass without investigating a third unknown canyon; that must have been the right one.

We camp for two nights at the mouth of Jasper Canyon, spend the day between the nights exploring Jasper's higher ramifications, toward the heart of the Maze. If the Maze has a heart. We go on the following day, down the river, and come sailing out one fine afternoon into the confluence of the two great desert streams. The Green meets the Colorado. They do not immediately merge, however, but flow along side by side like traffic lanes on a freeway, the greenish Colorado, the brownish Green, with a thin line of flotsam serving as median.

Henry never was a joiner either.

"Know all men by these presents that I, Henry Thoreau, do not wish to be considered a member of any incorporated body which I have not joined."

A crusty character, Thoreau. An unpeeled man. A man with the bark on him.

We camp today at Spanish Bottom, near the first rapids of Cataract Canyon. Sitting around our fire at sundown, four of us gnawing on spareribs, the other two picking at their pussy food— tofu and spinach leaves and stewed kelp (it looks like the testicles of a sick octopus)—we hear the roar of tons of silty water plunging among the limestone molars of Brown Betty Rapid: teeth set on edge. The thunderous vibrations rise and fall, come and go, with the shifting evening winds.

We spend the next day wandering about the top of the Maze, under the shadows of Lizard Rock, Standing Rock, the Chimney, looking down into five-hundred-foot-deep canyons, into the stems, branches, and limbs of an arboreal system of part-time drainages. It took a liberal allowance of time, indeed, for the rare storms of the canyon country to carve out of solid rock these intricate canyons, each with its unscalable walls, boxlike heads, stomach-turning dropoffs. A man could spend the better part of a life exploring this one area, getting to know, so far as possible, its broad outline and its intimate details. You could make your summer camp on Pete's Mesa, your winter camp down in Ernie's Country, and use Candlestick Spire all year round for a personalized private sundial. And die, when you're ready, with the secret center of the Maze clutched to your bosom. Or, more likely, never found.

Henry spent his life—or earned his life—exploring little more than the area surrounding his hometown of Concord. His jaunts beyond his own territory do not amount to much. He traveled once to Minnesota, seeking health, but that was a failure. He never came west, although, as he says, he preferred walking in a westerly direction. He never saw our Rocky Mountains, or the Grand Canyon, or the Maze. He never reached the Amazon, Alaska, Antarctica, the Upper Nile, or the Mountains of the Moon. He journeyed once to Staten Island but was not impressed.

Instead, he made a world out of Walden Pond, Concord, and their environs. He walked, he explored, every day and many nights, he learned to know his world as few ever know any world. Once, as he walked in the woods with a friend (Thoreau had many friends, we come to realize, if not one in his lifetime with whom he could truly, deeply share his life; it is we, his readers, over a century later, who must be and are his true companions), the friend expressed his long-felt wish to find an Indian arrowhead. At once Henry stopped, bent down, and picked one up.

November 14, 1980

Today will be our last day on the river. We plan to run the rapids of Cataract Canyon this morning, camp on Lake Powell this afternoon, go on to Hite Marina and back to civilization, such as it is, tomorrow.

I rise early, as usual, and before breakfast go for a walk into the fields of Spanish Bottom. I see two sharp-shinned hawks roosting in a cottonwood. A tree of trembling leaves, pale gold and acid green. The hawks rise at my approach, circle, return to the tree as I go on. Out in the field, one hundred yards away, I see an erect neck, a rodentian head, a pair of muley ears displayed in sharp silhouette against the redrock cliffs. I stop, we stare at each other— the transient human, the ephemeral desert mule deer. Then I notice other deer scattered beyond the first: one, two, three, four, five—nine all told. Two with antlers.

My first thought is *meat*. Unworthy thought—but there they are, waiting, half of them standing broadside to me, their dear beating hearts on level with the top of the sand sage, saltbush, rice grass. Two of them within a hundred yards—easy range for a thirty-thirty. Meat means survival. Survival, by Christ, with honor. With *honor!* When the cities lie at the monster's feet, we shall come here, my friends, my very few friends and I, my sons and my daughter, and we will survive. We shall live.

My second thought is more fitting, for the moment. Leave them in peace. Let them be. Efface yourself, for a change, and let the wild things be.

What would Henry say? Henry said, "There is a period in the history of the individual, as of the race, when the hunters are the 'best men,' as the Algonquins called them. We cannot but pity the boy who has never fired a gun; he is no more humane, while his education has been sadly neglected." But then he goes on to say: "No humane being, past the thoughtless age of boyhood, will wantonly murder any creature which holds its life by the same tenure that he does. The hare in its extremity cries like a child. I warn you, mothers, that my sympathies do not make the usual *philanthropic* distinctions." Is that his last word on the subject? Hardly. Henry had many words for every subject, and no last word for any. He also writes, "But I see that if I were to live in a wilderness, I should become . . . a fisher and hunter in earnest."

So let them be for now. I turn back to camp, making one step. The deer take alarm, finally, and move off at a walk. I watch. Their fear becomes contagious. One begins to run, they all run, bounding away toward the talus slopes of the canyon wall. I watch them leap upward into the rocks, expending energy with optimum ease, going farther and rising higher until they disappear, one by one, somewhere among the boulders and junipers at the foot of the vertical wall.

Back to camp and breakfast. We load the boats, secure the hatches, lash down all baggage, strap on life jackets, face the river and the sun, the growing roar of the rapids. First Brown Betty, then Ben Hur and Capsize Rapids, then the Big Drop and Satan's Gut. Delightful names, and fitting. We feel the familiar rush of adrenaline as it courses through our blood. We've been here before, however, and know that we'll get through. Most likely. The odds are good. Our brave boatman and boatwoman, Dusty and Lorna, ply the oars and steer our fragile craft into the glassy tongue of the first rapid. The brawling waters roar below, rainbows of broken sunlight dance in the spray. We descend.

Henry thou should be with us now.

I look for his name in the water, his face in the airy foam. He must be here. Wherever there are deer and hawks, wherever there is liberty and danger, wherever there is wilderness, wherever there is a living river, Henry Thoreau will find his eternal home.

2

Watching the Birds: The Windhover

We used to live, my wife and I, in a glassy cabin on a mountain peak, surrounded by a national forest. Our job was to watch. Watch what? Well, watch just about everything. To us it seemed like the center of the world. When clouds gathered, we watched for lightning, where it struck. After the lightning we'd watch for smoke in the trees and when and if it appeared, a few hours later or a couple of days later, we'd locate the smoke with our precision fire-finder and radio the news to forest headquarters. The report generally went like this: "Phoenix, this is Aztec Peak, ten-seventy-three." (10-73 is forest radio code for fire.)

"Go ahead, Aztec."

"We've got a little smoke for you at zero-four-two degrees and thirty minutes, southwest side of Two Bar Ridge. It's a single snag, blue-gray smoke, small volume, intermittent puffs. Light wind from the west. Heavy fuel but not spreading."

"Ten-four, Aztec. Let us know if it grows."

While fire crews were dispatched to find and put out the fire, my wife and I returned to our job of watching. We watched the clouds again and the weather, and approaching and departing storms. We watched the sun go down behind Four Peaks and the Superstition Mountains, that sundown legend retold and recurring every evening, day after day after day. We saw the planet Venus bright as radium floating close to the shoulder of the new moon. We watched the stars, and meteor showers, and the snaky ripple of cloud-to-cloud lightning coursing across the sky at night.

We watched the birds. One day a little nuthatch flew into our cabin through an open window, banged its silly head against the closed window opposite, and dropped to the floor. I picked up the tiny bird, holding it in my palm. I could feel the beating of its furious heart. I set it down on the catwalk outside, in the sunlight. After a while the nuthatch came to, shook its head, lofted its wings, and fluttered off. What can you think of a bird that crashes into glass and creeps headfirst down the trunk of a pine?

The forest spread below us in summer in seventeen different shades of green. There were yellow pine and piñon pine, blue spruce and Engelmann spruce, white fir and Douglas fir, quaking aspen, New Mexican locust, alligator juniper, and four kinds of oak. Along the rimrock of the escarpment, where warm air rose from the canyons beneath, grew manzanita, agave, sotol, and several species of cactus—prickly pear, pincushion, fishhook. Far down in the canyons, where water flowed, though not always on the surface, we could see sycamore, alder, cottonwood, walnut, hackberry, wild cherry, and wild grape. And a hundred other kinds of tree, shrub, and vine that I would probably never learn to identify by name.

The naming of things is a useful mnemonic device, enabling us to distinguish and utilize and remember what otherwise might remain an undifferentiated sensory blur, but I don't think names tell us much of character, essence, meaning. Einstein thought that the most mysterious aspect of the universe (if it is, indeed, a *uni*-verse, not a pluri-verse) is what he called its "comprehensibility."

Being primarily a mathematician and only secondarily a violinist, Einstein saw the world as comprehensible because so many of its properties and so much of its behavior can be described through mathematical formulas. The atomic bomb and Hiroshima made a convincing argument for his point of view. As does the ignition of juniper twigs, by the agency of friction, into heat, smoke, and flame. Mass is transformed into energy, emitting light. Employing fire lookouts.

Even so, I find something narrow and too specialized in Einstein's summary of the situation. The specialist's viewpoint may go deep but it cannot go all the way through. How could it if the world, though finite, is unbounded? Nor does its practical utility—atomic bombs—make up for its lack of breadth. All special theories suffer from this defect. The lizard sunning itself on a stone would no doubt tell us that time, space, sun, and earth exist to serve the lizard's interests; the lizard, too, must see the world as perfectly comprehensible, reducible to a rational formula. Relative to the context, the lizard's metaphysical system seems as complete as Einstein's.

But to me the most mysterious thing about the universe is not its comprehensibility but the fact that it exists. And the same mystery attaches to everything within it. The world is permeated through and through by mystery. By the incomprehensible. By creatures like you and me and Einstein and the lizards.

Modern science and technology have given us the engineering techniques to measure, analyze, and take apart the immediate neighborhood, including the neighbors. But this knowledge adds not much to our understanding of things. "Knowledge is power," said Francis Bacon, great-great-grandfather of the nuclear age. Power, exactly—that's been the point of the game all along. But power does not lead to wisdom, even less to understanding. Sympathy, love, physical contact—touching—are better means to so fine an end.

Vague talk, I agree. This blather about mystery is probably no more than a confession of intellectual laziness. Let's have no more metaphysical apologetics. Throw metaphysic to the dogs, I say, and watch the birds. I'd rather contemplate the noble turkey vulture soaring on the air, contemplating me, than speculate further on Einstein's theories, astrophysics, or the significance of the latest computer printouts from Kitt Peak Observatory and NASA. The computer tapers (tapirs?) have a word for it: GIGO. Garbage In, Garbage Out. Output equals Input. Numbers in, numbers out—nothing more. NINO, a double negation. Anything reduced to numbers and algebra is not very interesting. Useful, of course, for the processing of data, physical relations, human beings—but not interesting.

The vultures are interesting. In the morning they would rise, one by one, from their communal roost a quarter-mile below our lookout, and disperse themselves to the four quarters of the firmament. Each patrols its chosen—or allocated—territory, rising so high and sailing so far it soon becomes invisible to human eyes, even when our human eyes are aided by Bausch & Lomb 7×50 binoculars. But although we cannot always see them, the buzzards keep an eye on one another as well as on the panorama of life and death below, and when one bird descends for an actual or potential lunch its mates notice and come from miles away to join the feast. This is the principle of evolutionary success: mutual aid.

At evening, near sundown, the vultures would return. Friendly, tolerant, gregarious birds, they liked to roost each night on the same dead pine below. One by one they spiraled downward, weaving transparent figures in the air while others maintained a holding pattern, sinking slowly, gradually—as if reluctant to leave the heights—toward the lime-spattered branches of the snag. They might even have had nests down in there somewhere, although I could never see one, with little buzzard chicks waiting for supper. Try to imagine a baby vulture.

Gathered on their favorite dead tree, heads nodding together, the vultures resembled from our vantage point a convocation of bald, politic funeral directors discussing business prospects—always good. Dependable. The mature birds have red, wrinkled, featherless heads; the heads of the young are a bluish color and also naked. The heads are bald because it's neater, safer, more sanitary, given the line of work. If you made your living by thrusting your beak and eyes and ears and neck deep into the rotting entrails, say, of a dead cow, you too would prefer to be bald as a buzzard. Feathers on the head would impede a hasty withdrawal, when necessary, and might provide lodging for maggots, beetles, worms, and bacteria. Best for the trade to keep sleek and tidy.

I respect vultures myself, even like them, I guess, in a way, and fully expect someday to join them, internally at least. One should plan one's reincarnation with care. I like especially the idea of floating among the clouds all day, seldom stirring a feather, meditating on whatever it is that vultures meditate about. It looks like a good life, from down here.

We had some golden eagles in the area too, but seldom got a look at them. Uncommon and elitist birds, aloof as warlords, they generally hang out as far as possible from human habitat. Who could blame them? Sheepmen and many others shoot them on sight, on general principles. Our hero Ernest Hemingway could not resist the temptation to bag an eagle now and then, though he hated himself afterward. Not an easy job to be, or to have been, Ernest Hemingway. Elinor Wylie advised emulation:

> Avoid the reeking herd,
> Shun the polluted flock,
> Live like that stoic bird
> The eagle of the rock.

But she spent most of her time in New York City. Can't blame her either. Every bird in its proper place.

The redtail hawk is a handsome character. I enjoyed watching the local hunter come planing through the pass between our mountaintop and the adjoining peak, there to catch the wind and hover in place for a while, head twitching back and forth as it scans the forest below. When he—or she—spots something live and edible, down she goes at an angle of forty-five degrees, feet first, talons extended, wings uplifted, feathers all aflutter, looking like a Victorian lady in skirts and ruffled pantaloons jumping off a bridge.

The hawk disappears into the woods. I watch, binoculars ready. She rises seconds later from the trees with something wriggling, alive, in her right foot. A field mouse. The hawk sails high in the air. The mouse is fighting, bites the hawk on the shank (I can see these details without difficulty), and the startled redtail drops her prey. The mouse falls down and away, also at an angle of forty-five degrees, carried eastward by the wind. The hawk stoops, swoops, and recaptures the mouse a hundred feet above the treetops, carries it to the broken-off top of a pine, perches there, still holding the struggling mouse in her claws, and makes one quick stab of beak to the mouse's head. I see a spurt of red. The mouse is still. The hawk gulps down her lunch raw and whole, in one piece, as an owl does. *Hors rodentine.* Later, after craw and gizzard have done their work, the hawk will regurgitate a tiny ball of fur and toenails.

We watched the storms of late afternoon. Sun descending in a welter of brawling purple clouds. Spokes of gold wheel across the sky, jags and jets of lightning flicker from cloud to cloud and from cloud to earth. Mighty kettledrums thunder in the distance. My wind gauge reads thirty-five knots. The trees sway, the wind booms through the forest.

Watching the vultures gather below, I noticed a disturbance. A small gray-backed falcon was diving among the vultures, harrying the laggards. It was a peregrine falcon—rare but not extinct. Watching through the glasses, I saw one vulture actually flapping its wings to escape the falcon—an unusual exertion for a vulture. The falcon strikes, their bodies collide in what appears to me as a glancing blow. A few vulture feathers float off on the wind. The vulture flaps into the shelter of the trees, swearing quietly, apparently unharmed. Tiring of this sport, the falcon skims upward in a sweeping arc, shooting through the circling vultures, winging higher and higher into the sky, and stops at the apex of its parabola to hover there, still as a star, facing the wind, the lightning, the advancing storm.

The falcon hangs in space for second after second, motionless, as if suspended on a thread, its wings, body, and spirit in perfect equilibrium with the streaming torrents of the air. Give your heart to the hawks, urged Robinson Jeffers. Okay, I thought, I'll do that. For this one splendid moment. Until the falcon sheers off on the wind and vanishes in storm and light.

Appealing as I find the idea of reincarnation, I must confess that it has a flaw: to wit, there is not a shred of evidence suggesting it might be true. The idea has nothing going for it but desire, the restless aspiration of the human mind. But when was aspiration ever intimidated by fact? Given a choice, I plan to be a long-winged fantailed bird next time around.

Which one? Vulture, eagle, hawk, falcon, crane, heron, wood ibis? Well, I believe I was a wood ibis once, back in the good old days of the Pleistocene epoch. And from what I already know of passion, violence, the intensity of the blood, I think I'll pass on eagle, hawk, or falcon this time. For a lifetime or two, or maybe three, I think I'll settle for the sedate career, serene and soaring, of the humble turkey buzzard. And if any falcon comes around making trouble I'll spit in his eye. Or hers. And contemplate this world we love from a silent and considerable height.

3

Meeting the Bear

In the evening I descend from my tower and go for a walk in the woods.

What tower? What woods? Hard, ·brutal questions, which I decline to answer. The specificity demanded I regard as an invasion of privacy. But I shall offer a few clues (out of homage to Nabokov) for the entertainment of any readers who may still be with me. Think of Montaigne. Yeats. Rapunzel. Childe Roland. Of Stephen Dedalus and "stately, plump Buck Mulligan." Of a warm, secret place for the gestation of ideas—not so much an ivory as an ovary tower. It matters little if the ideas fail to emerge.

Like the American Legion and the American Medical Association, I am pleased to report that my mind has not been violated by an original thought since the end of World War II. If it ever ended. Though a sucker for philosophy all of my life I am not a thinker but—a toucher. A *feeler,* groping his way with the white cane of the senses through the hairy jungle of life. I believe in nothing that I cannot touch, kiss, embrace—whether a woman, a child, a rock, a tree, a bear, a shaggy dog. The rest is hearsay. If God is not present in this young prickly pear jabbing its spines into my shin, then God will have to get by without my help. I'm sorry but that's the way I feel. The message in the bottle is not for me.

As for the woods, let us say that they lie in a slovenly manner across a disorderly range of middle-aged mountains somewhere between Sombrero Butte on the east, Noisy Mountain to the south, Malicious Gap on the west, and several small rivers—a bit farther off—to the north and northwest, namely, those the Spanish called Fool Creek, Little Red, the River of Souls, and the River of Dolors. (Not dollars.) These are honest hints, fairly offered. Anyone familiar with the geography of the American West can work it out.

What do I do up in that tower all day? Nothing. Or nearly nothing. Or to phrase it positively, I participate in the nothingness of Being, as Heidegger would say. Somebody has to do it. No easy task, which is why they pay me $4.25 an hour. And who are They? Another riddle. They live in the castle, that's all I know. The paychecks come in the mail, regularly but always two weeks late. The signature is illegible, the code numbers indecipherable. A strange business and for a long time, when I thought about it, it troubled me. Then I stopped thinking about it and it troubled me no more. A form of grace, I suppose, this money—like manna—from Heaven. But it works, it's legal tender, it pays for the bacon, the beans, the beer, the turnips and onions.

I've been mostly alone in this place since the year I was born, and there are times when I think the solitude may have affected my mental stability in a possibly unhealthy way. That's why I descend each evening, rain or shine, for a walk in the woods. My dog Ellie barks with delight as I come, clanging like a jailer, down the fifty-two steel steps of the tower. I open a gate in the fence. We plunge off the brow of the mountain, down the trail into the twilight forest. The Dark Forest. Perhaps I'm a Ranger of some kind. Was I not a student of Dark Forestry, long ago, in that medieval school? Was it Heidelberg? Wittenberg? Edinburgh? In some former life? Pale phantom memories float like clouds across the eroded topography of a sick and disordered mind.

Bear scat lies steaming on the trail. Reality. Fresh reality, warm to the touch, full of berry seeds. The mess resembles red caviar. Almost whimpering in the ecstasy of her excitement, Ellie dives into the brush. I call her back. Reluctantly, or maybe not so reluctantly, she returns. Part Labrador, part German shepherd, two years old, she whines, growls, shivers all over as she strives for speech, trying to tell me something of urgent importance. I pause to stroke and quiet her. I know, I tell her, I know, I know. . .

We go on, downward into the gloom. The setting sun flickers through the treetops, through the oak and fir and yellow pine. We pass beneath the vultures' roost, where they gather each evening, and I am startled as always when the stillness is shattered by the sudden violent beating of ponderous wings. Once aloft they circle in silence until we've passed on. They never learn. But neither do I.

From a certain distance, from just beyond the zone of cautious silence that always surrounds a human walking through nature, comes the call of the hermit thrush. A silvery music, a flute song, simple and sweet and piercing to the heart. A twilight music, painful in its beauty. If there is a Heaven, an ideal realm beyond space and time, it must contain the hermit thrush. Otherwise, what good is it? And there must be trees too, of course. And mountains. And a sun that sets each evening and rises each morning. And winding through the woods, a trail with pine needles, stones, oak leaves, fresh bear shit. Naturally.

A mirror image of the earth we know, is that the best that I can imagine? This little planetary world, with its torture, cruelty, insult, degradation, greed, stupidity, spiraling without significance other than itself toward some black hole in the singularity of Einstein's universe? The mind strains toward an understanding, toward some idea of ultimate, absolute perfection—or of absolute horror. Either will do. But can no more grasp it, can no more define and communicate this thing than can Ellie my dog make explicit her emotions to me.

Forget it. We diverge onto an older, dimmer path, one that leads slightly uphill toward a small brown stagnant pond I know. When we get there I sit down on a log, keeping Ellie at my feet, and wait, watch, listen.

A cloud of gnats, like the molecules of a gas confined within an invisible retort, dances in place at one side of the pond. A few dragonflies, some red, some blue—four-winged, ornate, glittering, Victorian creatures—skim above the water. Water striders walk upon it, making the most delicate of ripples. My dog loves to slosh into the water, pursue those insouciant insects, snap them up and gulp them down. But this time I restrain her, waiting for something more interesting. For what? I don't know, yet.

The sun goes down. The song of the hermit thrush becomes distant, hesitant, fading into evening.

The twilight condenses. But the new moon will light our way out of here. Or I can always feel my way. It's straight uphill back to the lookout tower. Cannot get lost. Far off, an owl hoots, once, twice, echoed by another at an equally vague location. Then all becomes quiet. We wait.

The dog stiffens with tension beneath my hand. I can feel even before I hear it the soft snarl beginning deep in her throat. I press down, hushing her alarm.

Out of the silence, surprisingly close, upwind, comes the noise of a heavy, shambling body forcing its way with arrogant or perhaps only carefree indifference through the scrub oak, thorny locust, jumbled and decaying logs. I hear sniffing and snorting sounds, the unmistakable, unintelligible mutter of another oafish hermit talking to himself. But I can see nothing, nobody. The sounds come closer, stop. Still as a bump on the log, I hold Ellie down (though she makes no effort to rise) and stare into the dark beyond the pond.

The bear is staring at me. It is a mature male, a huge and powerful black bear, golden-brown despite its breed, and it stands—*looms*—above the oak brush on the other side of the water. The bear peers directly at where I sit but cannot really see me, cannot quite perceive and identify what I am. The close-set red eyes squint with effort, the ears twitch, the nostrils flex in the up-turned black muzzle, trying to smell me out. We are so close to one another that if I wanted to I could count the flies circling around the bear's massive head. I can smell him. I can smell that odor, rich rank tangy as skunk, of wild and living beast.

I can't speak for the bear, but for myself I can say that I feel no trace of fear. It never occurs to me to feel fear. Instead I am overcome by the usual naïve presumption that this bear, like any other stranger, will like me, be pleased to meet me, want to know me better. This same enchanted innocence has borne me in and out of a hundred Saturday night cowboy bars without a scuffle and once carried me for a season safely through the streets of Bedford-Stuyvesant in Brooklyn during a previous incarnation as a public-welfare caseworker. As with a day of rock climbing, the fear comes afterward during sleep, in those hectic dreams that wake you at four o'clock in the morning.

And, so, I begin to rise, extending my hand in greeting. Now at last the bear perceives me, giving a start as he catches the scent of man the enemy. The bear shakes his head, somersaults backward and crashes away through the tangle, disappearing into our history.

That's all that happens. Nothing more. Ellie stops trembling. I let her chase the water striders for a while (back home on the farm we called them water skippers). The new moon floats like a slice of lemon on the wine-dark sky. Its light comes down in columns through the dark trees.

After a time I get up, grope along the path to the main trail, Ellie cruising in wide circles around me, and trudge uphill toward my tower on the mountain's summit. The vultures, well settled in their roost, let us pass this time without reaction.

What does it mean? Where will it all end? The questions now seem trivial, meaningless. For the present, why should we care? We have seen the bear and are content.

4

Planting a Tree

My wife and I and my daughter live (for the moment) in a little house near the bright, doomed city of Tucson, Arizona. We like it here. Most of the time. Our backyard includes a portion of the Sonoran Desert, extending from here to the California border and down into Mexico. Mesquite trees grow nearby, enough to supply fuel for the Franklin stove when the nights are cold, enough to cook the occasional pork chop, or toast the tortilla, on the grill under the decaying Chinese elm.

Out back is the dry creekbed, full of sand, called a "wash" in this country, winding through the trees and cactus toward the Tucson Mountains five miles away. We'll climb those hills yet, maybe. Rattlesnakes live in the rocky grottoes along the wash. Sometimes they come to the house for a social call. We found one coiled on the *Welcome* mat by the front door Sunday evening. Our cat has disappeared.

There are still a few bands of javelina—wild semi-pigs—out there. They come by at night, driving the dogs into hysterics of outrage, which the javelinas ignore. Coyotes howl at us when they feel like it, usually in the mornings and again around sundown, when I rile them some with my flute—they seem partial to "Greensleeves," played on the upper register. We have an elf owl living in a hole in the big saguaro cactus by the driveway, and three pygmy owls, bobbing and weaving like boxers, up in the palm at evening. There are packrats in the woodpile and scorpions under the bark of the logs; I usually find one when I'm splitting firewood.

So it's pretty nice here. We'd like to stay for a while, a lifetime or two, before trying something else. But we probably won't. We came down here from Utah four years ago, for practical reasons, now satisfied. We are free to leave whenever we wish.

The city remains at a comfortable distance. We hear the murmur of it by day, when the wind is from the east, and see its campfires glow by night—those dying embers. The police helicopters circle like fireflies above Tucson, Arizona, all night long, maintaining order. The homicide rate hangs steady at 3.2 per diem per 1,000,000, including lowriders, dope peddlers, and defenseless winos. All is well. Eighteen Titan missile bases ring the city, guarding us from their enemies. The life expectancy of the average Tucsonan, therefore, is thirty minutes—or whatever it takes for an ICBM to shuttle from there to here. Everything is A-OK. We sleep good.

Still, the city creeps closer, day by day. While the two great contemporary empires are dying—one in Afghanistan and Poland, the other in Vietnam, Iran, Nicaragua, El Salvador. And though I welcome their defeat, their pain and fear make them more dangerous than ever. Like mortally wounded tyrannosaurs, they thrash about in frenzy, seeking enemies, destroying thousands of innocent lives with each blind spasm of reaction. And still the city creeps closer. I find a correlation in these movements. I foresee the day when we shall be obliged to strike camp, once again.

Where to this time? Home to Utah? Back to Appalachia? On

to Australia? Down the river of eternal recurrence? It doesn't matter too much. There is no final escape, merely a series of tactical retreats, until we find the stone wall at our backs, bedrock beneath our feet.

Ah well, enough of this skulking rhetoric. Before we go we will plant a tree. I cleared away some ragweed yesterday, dug a thigh-deep hole this morning, and planted a young budding cottonwood this afternoon. We soaked the hole with well water, mixed in the peat moss and the carefully set-aside topsoil, and lowered the root ball of the sapling into its new home. The tree shivered as I packed the earth around its base. A shiver of pleasure. A good omen. A few weeks of warm weather and the little green leaves will be trembling in the sunlight. A few good years and the tree will be shading the front porch and then the roof of the house. If the house is still here. If someone, or something, as I hope, is still enjoying this house, this place, this garden of rock and sand and paloverde, of sunshine and delight.

We ourselves may never see this cottonwood reach maturity, probably will never take pleasure in its shade or birds or witness the pale gold of its autumn leaves. But somebody will. Something will. In fifty years Tucson will have shrunk back to what it once was, a town of adobe huts by the trickling Santa Cruz, a happier place than it is now, and our tree will be here, with or without us. In that anticipation I find satisfaction enough.

PART II

Politicks and Rivers

5

Notes from a Cold River

First Day

We put on the Tatshenshini at a place called Dalton Post in the Canadian Yukon. Nobody here but a few locals, fishing for salmon. Subdued excitement among the boatmen: Two of them had seen a big grizzly nearby, only a couple of hours before. They call the bear a GRIZ up here; GRIZZ in the plural form. Always capitalized, of course, spoken, written, or in the mind. GRIZZ—the one hairy element in an otherwise manageable scene, adding the tang of genuine danger to a jaunt through the woods. Lord Grizzly, or Old Ephraim, as the mountain men called him.

The five boats—property of Sobek, Inc., an international river-running outfit—are rigged, loaded, coffeepot stowed away, shotguns lashed on top of the duffel. The boatmen are ready, the river is rushing past, there is nothing to do but go. We look at one another: this is it, the moment of maximum anticipation, the moment of silence when the conductor lifts his baton—the pause before the charge. We launch off, onto the green-gray and swirling water, into the 140 miles of mountain wilderness between here and Dry Bay—our takeout point—on the Gulf of Alaska. Down the Tatshenshini: one more river. May there always be one more.

Snow-dappled peaks rise in the distance, seven or eight thousand feet high. Most of them are unnamed, very few of them ever climbed. Hills in the middle distance are covered with what looks like green plush—alder jungles, almost impenetrable to a man. (But not to a bear.) On the banks of the river is a dark forest of birch, spruce, hemlock, poplar, and as everywhere, the alders. The country has a tropical look, lush and green, but the first splash of the river into the boat dispels that fancy. This is a river of icy water—of *gletscher milch,* as the Swiss would call it. Forty-nine degrees Fahrenheit.

We run some lively rapids, continuous for a mile. More icy water in my face, down my neck, inside my pants. Most refreshing. Bald eagles go winging by, as common here as buzzards in the desert. When we stop for lunch I see moose sign on the path, clusters of them here and there, each dropping the size and shape of a dove's egg. And the same color—brown. I keep looking for Lord GRIZ, keep expecting that humped figure to come crashing out of the jungle, looking for me. But when I go probing into the gloom of the alder thickets I see only flies, and hear only mosquitoes, and smell only rotting leaves. Very quiet in there. A sense of—deception. I can hear a voice saying, *Nobody here but us shadows, boss. . . .*

We make camp that first afternoon on a broad, beautiful, pebble shore. There are no sand beaches on this river. I forget why not. For supper we eat scalloped potatoes and good, tough, mastfed pork chops. Splendid. The sun keeps dribbling along the northwest horizon, unwilling to go down. The endless sub-Arctic evening. We linger around the fire, waiting for night to come so we can go to bed. "What time is it?" somebody asks. And a fellow with a watch looks at it and says, "Eleven-thirty." We go to bed in the twilight; so far as I know it never did get dark that night.

Second Day

Awake in silvery light under a clouded sky. Sunshine plays on the snowy Alsek Range to the west, the Noisy Mountains beyond, both a part of the greater St. Elias Range. We're still in the Yukon; Alaska is another day or two downriver. Not that it makes any difference out here.

Before breakfast a couple of the boatmen and a few of the passengers wade icy Silver Creek and slog through a stinking, mosquito-infested swamp to see the moose in a nearby moose pond. But the moose are gone when we get there. On the way back I see claw marks on the trunk of a white spruce, higher than I can reach. Somebody's been sharpening his fingernails here. The boatmen caress their double-barreled, twelve-gauge shotguns, loaded with double-ought buckshot. It's all psychological, of course; none of us would actually shoot a bear. Except in self-defense.

Pancakes and eggs for breakfast. Well-built coffee. The "dwarf hummingbirds" (Tatshenshini mosquitoes) are hungry too; we feed together. In fact this is the hungriest country I have ever seen in my life; not only the bugs but the humans, we do not eat to live but live to eat. Too much fresh air, maybe. Or that river water, which looks like dishwater but tastes delicious. Though much too silty, this time of year, for fishing.

Down the river again, a river becoming colder, wider, siltier all the time. A broad stream with braided channels, some navigable and some not; it keeps the boatmen alert. The country looks more and more like Idaho, less and less, as I had thought in Juneau and Haines, like West Virginia.

I ride in Mark Jensen's boat today. A big, rowdy, jolly fellow, about thirty I'd guess, with a demonic gleam in his blue eyes—Jensen is the cook. Cooks are always dangerous, but this one seems friendly. He looks like a Viking and sings like Jimmy Buffett, only better. He comes from Vernal, Utah, of old Mormon stock. But I'm no bigot; I can overlook something like that. Especially when he drinks good whiskey and is willing to share it.

And then there's this other passenger in the boat, I forget his name, who says he used to coauthor scripts for "Star Trek" and "Mission Impossible." That's all right too; everybody has to make a living somehow. Always polite, I ask him what he thinks of my hero, Thomas Pynchon. "Pynchon," he says with a sneer, "could never get his junk published in any real sci-fi magazine." Dear me, I think, that's probably true. And what kind of work is this passenger doing now? He's a space-science engineer by trade, he tells me, working on a new satellite program for the Pentagon. Tell me about it, I say. Sorry, he says, classified stuff—but you'd be astounded if I told you. No, I say, I'd only be depressed and disgusted. Thus nipping in the bud a fruitless and tedious conversation.

At evening we put in at a side stream called Sediment Creek. Here we shall camp for two long twilight nights. The plan is to hike up Goat Ridge tomorrow to see those hairy Asiatic antelope that tourists call "mountain goats."

Booze with the boatmen while fixing supper. Raw jokes, coarse laughter, tall tales—some of these lads, working for this Sobek outfit, have been all over the world. Down the Omo River in Abyssinia, fighting off crocodiles with a paddle. Living on nothing but fish for six days on the Rio Brio in Argentina. Shot at by young *bandidos* in southern Mexico. Playing tennis with John Lindsay in Sagaponack, Long Island. Trading beans for beer with headhunters in New Guinea. . . . The stories get wilder, taller, falling over into farce.

Third Day

Revenge: I dip my cupped hands in a mountain pool, drink a swarm of wriggling mosquito larvae with my water. The little fetuses go gliding down my gullet, bound for an entertaining trip through the entrenched meanders of my intestines. I feel no guilt, they've got a fighting chance.

Up Goat Ridge today. But first I creep off deep into the woods for a solitary crap. Has to be done. Squatting there with my pants down, feeding the mosquitoes, I think, naturally, of GRIZZ. Each falling pine cone, each snapping twig, makes me think my time has come. What a way to die. Nothing like the possible presence of a GRIZ to add zest to an otherwise routine chore. But Old Ephraim fails to show.

We go up the mountain in a long file like P.O.W.'s, escorted by our shotgun-bearing boatmen. We traverse an open, wind-swept, grassy ridge, bright with flowers: the miniature and exquisite blue forget-me-nots (Alaska's state flower); bluebells o' Scotland; wild rose; yarrow; hemlock; purple lupine; the red (or western) columbine; and acres of buttercups.

Above timberline very soon, in this northerly latitude, we pass snowfields with trickling seeps, rock slides where pikas whistle at us, and the dens, all over the place, of little hairy marmots.

Fresh bear scat on the trail. And great rough gouges torn from the sod, where some bear has been digging into the marmot tunnels.

We see the mountain goats, far off and across a valley, several flocks of them grazing on the grass. We climb higher and find one old he-goat alone, perched near a crag. The photographers spread out in a wide skirmish line and advance carefully upon him. He watches, not stirring a hair, until they get almost within shooting distance, then ambles easily over the edge and vanishes.

Far above us stand the snow-covered peaks, dozens of them marching in solemn, sawtoothed file toward the horizon. Between the mountains, like blue tongues, hang the glaciers. We descend the ridge and see, at a distance, our first bear, a black bear with a honey-colored stripe down its back. Unaware of us, it shambles loosely along, fur coat rippling, across a slope of scree. With ease, with nonchalance, never missing a step. And disappears into the alder jungle.

We go on. Down through the dark woods, with trip leader

Bartley Royal Henderson IV (also from Vernal, Utah) calling out as he leads the way, "Ho, bear, hey, GRIZ, it's only us. . . ."

Back to camp, where the cook has long preceded us. "Grits on!" he announces. The famished hikers scramble for the cook tent, banging spoons and cups and plates. *"Chilook-a-nuck,"* says boatman Jim Slade. A Sherpa phrase, he explains, which means "I'm almost dead." Always good for a laugh in Nepal.

These boatmen. These jet-set river guides. With names like those of outlaws from a Western movie. Jensen, Henderson, Slade; and the other two—Stan Boor and Tom Moody. Bright, handsome, talented young men with many skills, equally adept at river running, cooking, rock climbing, glacier trekking, search and rescue, fishing, hunting, skiing, guitar, harmonica, song. True outdoorsmen, who not only know but also love the out-of-doors. And indeed, how could you know it *unless* you loved it? As on any commercial river trip, the boatmen—and often, these days, the boatwomen—are the best part of the trip. The most interesting part. The rest is scenery. Which keeps floating past before you can get the feel of it, or even get a good look at it. But that's the price we pay for keeping on schedule. The life span of modern techno-industrial man must be the shortest in human history. Or does it only seem that way?

Fourth Day

Early start. Down the cold river through a gorge over huge gray "pressure" or "compression" waves, we rollick in our rubber boats. Out of the gorge; the river becomes wider, shallower. Here and there we scrape bottom and have to rock and jiggle our passage over the gravel bars, while the boatman feels about with his long oar.

Great view of the far Elias Range, blowing with clouds and snow. All those many peaks just sitting there, useless, unbagged. My mountain-climbing friends—Roger Grette, Bill Hoy, Susan Sontag, Norman Podhoretz, Leon Edel—would have a nervous fit if they were here.

Odd how the glaciers begin at the very summit of the peaks—as if dumped there from the sky. And then, from the summit, they start oozing toward the river like long blue snouts of frozen snot. Grumbling and crumbling as they advance.

The boatmen seek the deeper channels. The passengers, getting bored and depressed, start baiting one another, as always happens on the fourth day with six to go.

On my boat is a beautiful, silver-haired woman from Madison, Wisconsin, who confesses to being, by profession, an "occupational therapist."

"Maybe you could help my brother-in-law," says a joker.

"What's wrong?" says the therapist.

"He needs a job," the wag says. "Shock treatment."

She smiles patiently. On the adjacent boat are two young women named Jenny and Ginny. "All women are the same," says a grinning oaf, playing the devil, "so they might as well be named the same." "You'll be able to tell the difference," Jenny replies, "when you grow up."

Into the endless evening. More banter. We go ashore.

Suppertime again, thank God. Shotguns are stacked before the cook tent, one with a flower in its muzzle. Shaggy spruce trees beyond, snowy mountains in the distance, and all these rugged characters in Pendleton shirts sitting around the open campfire, eating spaghetti and meatballs and watching the coffeepot boil over. It looks exactly like a scene from the cover of *Field & Stream*. Or *Alaska* magazine. The essence of the American dream.

The wind has been blowing ice water in our faces all day. Now, at evening, the wind stops. Completely. Why? The answer is clear: to give the mosquitoes a chance to come out and feed. To join us for supper.

Fifth Day

In the morning a boatman pours a sleek drowned mouse out of the cold coffeepot. A passenger complains. "It's all right," the boatman says. "The mouse is dead."

Some wise guy has sneaked into the cook tent and placed a

large, gray, hairy, dried-out wolf turd on cook Jensen's best pan-cake griddle. Without a word he serves it back to me on my plate. I could one-up him by eating it, but I throw it away, letting Jensen enjoy his petty victory.

Wolf tracks, bear shit, and moose sign everywhere, but so far we have seen no wildlife but the eagles, one black bear, and a few mountain goats. Which aren't even true goats. "Don't talk to me about it," Henderson says. "See the management."

We do a short run down the river, then stop for lunch and a walk up a glacial moraine. The glaciers are getting closer every day, millions of tons of pale blue ice bulging down through their U-shaped cirques, but this is our first walk up an actual terminal moraine. We come to a dome-shaped pile of rocks about twenty feet high. This, we learn, is a kame, a deposit left here by the re-treating glacier. Some of us climb it—overcoming a kame—and let it go at that.

We lie in the sunshine, on the warm grass, and stare at the mountains, the endless snow-covered mountains, range after range, standing beyond the dark forest. The glaciers wink and glitter, running with streams of melted ice. Now and then, so remote as to be barely audible, comes the rumble of readjustment, the clash and crash of falling ice. Flowers and ice, sunlight and snow—it looks like Switzerland. But shaggier. Like Colorado. But colder. Even now, on this bright afternoon, in a field of flowers, Alaska seems to me a cold and somber land. I can imagine all too easily what it will be like here in two or three months: this meadow buried under ten feet of crusted snow, ice floes grinding in the river, wolves howling under the moon. And some poor, anxious-looking devil in a bearskin coat facing the long Arctic night with nothing but a little campfire and a bottle of Yukon Jack.

(Comparisons are invidious. Granted. But I must confess: After thirty-four years in the American Southwest, after too much time spent dawdling about in places like Grand Canyon, Death Valley, the Maze, the Superstition Mountains, the San Rafael Reef and the Waterpocket Fold, the San Juan Mountains and the Gran Desierto, Baja California, Glen Canyon and the Dirty Devil River, Desolation Canyon and the Pariah River, the Book Cliffs and the Kaiparowits Plateau and Big Bend and White Sands, the Red Desert and Black Rock and Barranca del Cobre, Factory Butte and Monument Valley, Slickhorn Gulch, Buckskin Gulch, Thieves' Mountain, Montezuma's Head, Cabeza de Prieta, Cabezon, Telluride and Lone Pine and the Smoke Creek Desert, Moab and Upheaval Dome, White Rim and Druid Arch—*to name but a few*—and seeing the full moon rise over the 13,000-foot peaks of Sierra La Sal, while the setting sun turns watermelon pink a 2,000-foot vertical wall of sandstone in the foreground, then—and I'll admit I'm spoiled—then by comparison Alaska seems, well, sort of . . . *banal.* But not bad, not bad.)

We camp this evening near the confluence of the Alsek and Tatshenshini rivers. Glorious views in all directions—snow and ice and mountains fifty or sixty miles away. Far up the Alsek Valley is a distant ghostly pyramid of snow that might be, just might be, Mount Logan, 19,850 feet above sea level. We get out the maps and try to determine landmarks, direction, distance. No one is certain. But it is a big mountain. And far away. My friend Grette did bag that one, come to think of it—if it is Logan.

We need a bath. A sauna. We lower the cook tent to half its normal height, dig a shallow pit in the ground under the tent, heat rocks in the fire, shovel the rosy, glowing rocks into the pit, strip, crawl into the tent, and suffer. Jim Slade, sauna boss, tosses water on the rocks and on us, in turn, until all present are satisfactorily steamed. Then we crawl out and plunge into the river. Shocking— but exhilarating, as always. The sensation afterward, prolonged, is one of intense and profound well-being. We linger naked around the fire, enjoying the twilight, the roar of glacial streams around us, the gleam of far-off mountains, and don't go to bed until around "midnight," when the sun finally goes behind the western peaks.

Sixth Day

"Grits on!" cries Jensen, offering to the breakfast crowd his excellent green chile omelets, with bacon, biscuits, jam, coffee, and various other side dishes. "Throw a lip over that, Ed," he says, shoveling a gigantic four-egg omelet onto my plate, "and when it's gone come back for another."

Don't mind if I do. We eat and eat, gorging ourselves like swine, and go back for seconds, thirds. God, but I'm hungry. If everybody else wasn't in the same condition, I'd think my personal old tapeworm was having his relatives in for a family reunion.

On down this greasy river. Mountains like Matterhorns looming ahead, cutting off our exit to the sea. No matter, the river rolls on, augmented now by the Alsek, and looking about half a mile wide. A glacial Mississippi. Silent waterfalls—too distant to be heard—gush from the soft green of the mountainsides; it looks like Venezuela. It looks like the mountains of China; I expect to see panda bear loping out of the green hills of laurel and alder, paddling into the river to swim along. It looks like Siberia; it looks like Alaska. It does not look like West Virginia. Not anymore.

We stop on shore and go for another walk, up the mountain, following a glacial torrent that has carved the only pathway through the alder jungles. On the first snow field our party splits, half going one way, half another. The party I'm in struggles on up the snow, tops out on a ridge, and sprawls on the slabs of rock for a rest. A glacier hangs above us, its face riddled with ice caves. Now and then a small avalanche of snow, ice, and rock comes sliding over the upper rim of the glacier. We move farther out on the ridge.

Now we can see the other party—five people, with one shotgun-carrying boatman—crawling up a snowy couloir. On their right, perhaps five hundred yards away and below, out of their field of vision, is a bear. The bear is angling toward them, going uphill as if it were downhill. We study the bear through field glasses but cannot determine its make—too far away. But Henderson thinks it might be *Ursus horribilis,* the grizzly. He stands and shouts a warning to the others; they don't appear to hear him but keep on going, up the snow, to a ridge like ours but higher, where they disappear. The bear follows, right on their trail.

There is nothing we can do but watch and wait, and make

bets on which will return first: four or five running humans or one fat and strolling bear. Or neither. We listen for the sound of the shotgun but hear nothing.

Eventually the people reappear, all of them, walking back down the hill, unhurried, not pursued. Anticlimax. We rejoin them below, learning that the bear had been only another black bear, which ran down the other side of the ridge when they saw it and it saw them.

We camp today by No Name Glacier, which we will explore tomorrow. Giant tacos for supper; I heap my plate with an awesome pile of refried beans, hamburger, grated cheese, diced tomato, diced onions, diced chile, chopped lettuce, and hot *salsa,* all resting, of course, on a toasted tortilla, and somehow throw a lip over the whole thing. Amazing. Disgusting. I return for seconds.

"What makes you an authority on the Southwest, Abbey," some punk kid says to me over the campfire.

"Why do you ask?"

"I was born there," he says.

"How old are you?"

"Thirty-one."

"Well, I made my home there in '47," I says. "So I've lived there longer than you, sonny."

Afterward the lying begins.

Seventh Day

We go for a walk on the glacier. On top of it, over the knobby, speckled, gritty back of the beast. Its stomach grumbles far below as unimaginable tonnages of compacted ice grind over one another, over the rock toward the river. What color is this thing?

A pale turquoise blue, I'd say. Or chrysocolla blue. Not so, says another, but more like—battery terminal corrosion blue. We peer into what appear to be bottomless crevasses. Pure oblivion down in there. If you fell in you'd disappear forever. Slip down, and down, and down, into the intense blue inane, between walls of freezing glass, under dripping stalactites of ice, until you wedged yourself, finally, into a crack too narrow for further descent. And there you would wait and wait and wait, waiting until the glacier ground you into *gletscher milch*. Turning your bones to silt and your flesh, eventually, into salmon eggs.

Fearful places. We tread carefully as we prowl around these things. One misstep and you're going, gone. Of course the boatmen carry ropes in their packs. But how long are the ropes? How deep are these crevasses?

Here is a kind of millrace in the glacier, a stream of water disappearing down a hole. What glaciologists call a moulin—a mill. I drop a few stones into the mill. They go clunking and clattering out of sight. And over here is something different, a blue grotto full of blue ice water. The color, the bland depths, the quiet menace, remind me of the core of a nuclear reactor. A man could splash about in there for maybe five minutes, I suppose, before dying. No one cares to try it.

We go on for a mile or two, up and across the glacier's wrinkled back, until we come to a kind of badlands in the ice, a mass of crags and pinnacles and caves and crevasses and knife-edge ridges hundreds of feet high, where farther progress is impossible without crampons, ropes, ice axes, nerve—a great deal of nerve—and skill.

Good place to stop and eat lunch.

Afterward we lie about in the sun, listening to the sound of the glacier moving, twitching, creeping. A sound like the rumble of empty oil drums. Three of the boatmen, who have the right equipment and claim they know what they are doing, go around the badlands and on up the glacier. By the time they diminish to the apparent size of flies, they've gone a tenth of the way up it.

Somebody complains about the flies: "These Alaskan flies aren't satisfied with crap—they go for blood."

We return to camp. "How about a light snack before dinner?" someone suggests. We have a little something.

The other boatmen return from the glacier. The five of them hunch together in the cook tent, taking what they call a head sauna. More songs and laughter. What makes these river guides such lively folks, always—as Henry Miller advocated—"always merry and bright"?

I've got my theories. My theory is that a vigorous, free, out-doors life is good for people. It fills them with cheer and high spir-its, leading to health and a long life. Despite the claims of medical technicians such as Lewis Thomas, official spokesman for the cancer industry, it is not more and newer drugs we need, not better living through chemotherapy, but rather clean air. Clean water. Good fresh real food. And plenty of self-directed physical activity.

Medical science has succeeded in reducing infant mortality rates, thus creating the catastrophe of overpopulation, but it has not—despite medical myth—lengthened the normal life span. "Three score years and ten," now as in biblical times, remains the norm. And in fact the longest-lived people on earth, we hear, are the primitive peasants of places like Ecuador, the Caucasus Mountains, Afghanistan. Certainly not the inhabitants of Dr. Thomas's Sloan-Kettering Memorial Hospital in New York City.

Eighth and Ninth Days

I'm getting homesick. I miss my woman. I miss my own mountains. I miss my desert. I miss—my home.

"A man whose emotions are alive," wrote Saul Bellow, "is at home anywhere." Now that may be true for an urbanite like Bel-low, who has lived his life inside walls and under a roof; big cities, it's true, are pretty much the same everywhere. But a countryman feels different, knows better; a countryman has a place on earth that is his own, and much as he may love to wander, as I myself do, he loves the wandering more because he has a place to return to, a place where he belongs. A place to live and when his time comes, a place to die. The earth has fed me for half a century; I owe the earth a body. The debt shall be paid.

Daydreaming.

Where are we? We're floating down this weird river deep in southeast Alaska. We make camp at Alsek Bay, a kind of parking lot for icebergs. The bay is full of them. Marvelous fantasy creations in blue ice, floating on water as still as glass. Blue submarines, aircraft carriers, castles, whales, sharks, tugboats of ice. Each with a mirror image of itself in the cold blue water.

Water temperature here is 40° F. Air temperature is 49°. A day of drizzling rain. Some sulk in their tents. A few of us defy the rain, keep the fire going, drink "magic coffee" all day long. (Magic coffee is one part bourbon to three, maybe two, parts coffee.)

Bart Henderson tells his bear story. It was right here, on Alsek Bay, that he was chased by a GRIZ. He and two passengers were walking on the shore, hoping to see an iceberg heel over, a glacier calve. No shotgun slung on his shoulder that time. A grizzly bear was out in the bay, on a floe; it jumped off and swam toward them. They ran back toward camp. They had gone only a few hundred yards when the bear reached land. They ran harder, with Bart in the lead. (He was trip leader.) For some reason the two passengers veered off in a different direction, not following Bart. The bear chose to follow Bart, staying about fifteen to twenty feet behind him, not closing the gap though it could easily have done so. (There are no trees to climb in this area.) The GRIZ chased Bart for half a mile until camp came in sight and other people, some with weapons.

At that point the bear sprinted off on another line. Bart says he had run so hard he damaged his lungs, was spitting blood for three days afterward. While running he'd turned his head once to look at the bear; what he thought he saw on the bear's face, he says, was curiosity—a "noncommittal" curiosity. The bear haunted his dreams for three years.

Alone in my tent tonight—and I sleep well apart from everyone else, as is my habit—I unsheathe my knife and lay it on the tent floor close at hand. Not to fight off a bear with, but to slash my way quickly out the back of the tent in case Lord Grizzly should come nosing around the entrance.

Tenth Day

First up in the morning, as usual—old men have guilty dreams—I
start the fire and build the coffee. Our culture runs on coffee and
gasoline, the first often tasting like the second. We can survive
without gasoline, as we are doing on this oar-powered river trip,
and we can live without coffee for a time, when some other chemical concoction is available—Mormon tea, for example—but if ever
both gasoline and coffee were taken from us, how could America
endure?

The passengers crawl from their dew-covered tents: the space
engineer, clutching his copy of Tolkien's *The Hobbit*. (And I had
thought only children read Tolkien.) The beautiful silver-haired
woman from Madison, with whom I am secretly in love. After nine
days on this muddy river she looks as fresh, bright, cheery, and trig
as she did on the first. (I asked her once how she did it. Secret midnight baths? A folding tub in her tent? "I have a clean mind," she
told me.) Ginny and Jenny with their thoughtful, genial, watchful
husbands. The fellow from Pennsylvania who looks like a movie
star, and the big friendly, lumpish bearlike man from Chicago who
fell in the river one day, from a boat, while it was still tied up on
shore. A trucking industry executive and his son. Two young
brothers, Dave and Robert Shore, one a Sobek boatman on vaca-
tion and the other a physician, with their father, a game old gent
who goes everywhere, misses nothing, takes part in everything.
And the five regular boatmen—Bart and Mark and Stan and Jim
and Tom. Good men. If we were going into war again I can't think
of any I'd rather have on our side. I mean, all of these good men
and women. And if they were on the other side I'd join the other
side.

Last Day

We shove off, down the River (as outfitters say) of No Financial
Return. Icebergs about the size of Volkswagen buses jostle us for

space in the main channel. The cameras click and snap like a herd of crickets. Somebody plays his harmonica and Mark Jensen sings a song called "Pencil-Thin Mustache." The clouds begin to lift and we get a glimpse, from time to time, of the breathtaking crown of Mount Fairweather, serene and splendid, 15,300 feet above the sea and only a few miles from the coast.

We pause at a fishing camp, where the boatmen buy two big sockeye salmon—caught in the bay—for dinner tonight. Baked salmon is the plan, stuffed with onions and rice and tomatoes and garlic and other good fruits from the earth. As we go on I see a light plane at rest on the camp landing strip: civilization is now only a flight away. Tomorrow morning we fly from Dry Bay back to Haines, Alaska; from there to Juneau and Seattle.

"What's there to do in Haines?" I ask Jensen.

"Well," he says, "there's the Pioneer Club, where you can get clubbed by a pioneer. And there's the Rip Tide Bar, where you can get ripped and tied."

The river is broad, shining, placid as it nears the ocean. I imagine I can smell the sea in the air. And sure enough, gulls begin to appear, screaming for lunch, and a sea lion rises from the current to watch us, for a minute, with its large and wistful eyes.

We set up our last camp beside the airstrip near the fishing village of Dry Bay. We unload, de-rig, and deflate the five rubber boats. Stanley Boor and Mark Jensen prepare the salmon and set them to baking over a smoky fire. The river blends with the bay and the bay with the sea and the sea melts, without dividing line, into a golden sky. The gulls glide over the golden water. The evening goes on forever.

6

MX

Where is Carl Sagan when we need him most? While he indulges his fantasies of life on other worlds in gorgeous color TV, his scientific coworkers here on poor beleaguered planet Earth are making practical preparations for the extermination of life on *this* world. One world at a time, Dr. Sagan. Where are Lewis Thomas, Alvin Toffler, Jeremy Bernstein, Tom Wolfe, Buckminster Fuller, Gerard O'Neill, Timothy P. Leary, and the other apologists for the glossy technocracy rising around us in walls of aluminum and glass? And behind chain-link fences topped with barbed wire? The MX— Missile Experimental—casts a long shadow over the American West, and across most of Western civilization, for that matter. A shadow that extends from Tonopah, Nevada, to Vladivostok, Kamchatka, Siberia.

One lunatic armed with a rusty ax can create a respectable

amount of terror in any decent community. But for real lunacy on the grand scale you need a committee (better yet, an institution), staffed with hundreds and thousands of well-trained technicians, economists, intellectuals, engineers, and administrators. There are two such institutions flourishing at this time: one is known as the Kremlin, the other as the Pentagon. Intricately engaged with one another in a Mutual Admiration Debate (MAD), they have created between them the grand finale of the contemporary nightmare.

I have on my desk before me (as I write this) a handsome brochure promoting the beauty and benefits of the MX Mobile Defense System. The document is unsigned—prepared by a committee—but comes obviously from some Air Force cranny in the Pentagon. Except for the fact that it is printed in the American language, it would serve the Kremlin equally well. I have no doubt that copies of it, with translation attached, are passing at this very hour from desk to desk among the Pentagon's counterparts in Moscow.

This brochure describes MX in admirably tough, laconic language: "The Problem: Growing Soviet military power. . . . The Solution: Mobility. . . . The Challenge: Hiding a missile in the open. . ."

Listen to this:

> Each of the 200 MX missiles is carried in a launcher which in turn is placed inside an enclosed transporter. The transporter travels a dirt road connecting 23 empty shelters located at the ends of spur roads. The launcher with its missile is secretly deposited in one of the shelters, then the transporter continues along the road to the other shelters, at each one simulating the process of depositing the launcher. Thus the Soviets are confronted with 4,600 possible locations for the 200 missiles. . . .

The classic shell game. One imagines the Kremlin generals and admirals scratching at their crew cuts: "What the devil are we going to do about this, *tovarichi?*" And they still have all those American B-52s with their cruise missiles, all those American nuclear submarines with their Tridents and Poseidons to worry about. Not to mention the Armand Hammer salesmen and Mormon missionaries with their nuclear suitcases circulating through the Moscow subway system. The boys at the K. ponder the question for a minute or two before the solution—"multiplicity"—to the problem—"growing American military power"—comes to one of them: "Comrades," says General Ripov, "no problem: we build more missiles."

Of course the Soviets can no longer raise enough grain to feed their ever-growing population. But that is no difficulty either: the Americans, Canadians, and Australians will feed their people, for a fair return in Siberian gold, of course, thereby permitting the Soviet authorities to allocate more of their national resources to the ever-continuing nuclear arms race. In this way everybody wins. Or as the Pentagon brochure explains it:

> MX will present new business opportunities for companies during construction and operation. . . . New business will in turn stimulate new job and career opportunities. Some—such as administration, fire protection, security, clerical, construction and maintenance—will result directly from the construction and base operation. Many other jobs will arise indirectly as a result of construction and permanent area growth. Payroll dollars from the construction workers and the permanent base personnel will be spent on restaurants, cars, new homes, clothing and other consumer goods. This will build up the capital in local banks available for loans, boost collections of state and local taxes, and help to maintain the stability of the communities for the future.

Boom-town building—the economics shell game. Where are Milton Friedman and William Simon and George Gilder when we need them to explain the connections between military spending, inflation, unemployment, poverty, crime, and declining productivity? The Missile Experimental may be a beautiful thing to look at, from an engineering point of view, but it seems clear that no one can eat it, wear it, live in it, or make love to it. The labor, brains, materials, and money required to build the thing must be subtracted from resources that might otherwise be expended upon food, clothing, shelter (human shelter), and, who knows, even love. Frills. Froufrou.

Still, there is love of a sort involved in this project. My Air Force brochure goes on to describe "The Builders: An aerospace team effort" in terms as precise and glittering as tooled metal:

Stage I. This solid-fuel rocket motor generates approximately ½ million pounds of thrust. Design, assembly and testing of the rocket motor and structure will be the responsibility of Thiokol Inc. in Brigham City, Utah. Also, Thiokol will design, assemble and test the explosive charges which enable destruction of a test missile in the event of a serious malfunction.

Stage II. This stage also is propelled by solid fuel and develops 250,000 to 300,000 pounds of thrust. It includes a new feature called an extendable nozzle exit cone (ENEC). The conical thrust chamber which directs the engine thrust is in two nesting sections. Upon separation from Stage I, one segment extends from the end of the other to make the cone longer. . . . Aerojet Solid Rocket Propulsion Co. of Sacramento, California, is responsible for design, assembly and development testing of the rocket motor, the ENEC, and other components of the second stage.

Stage III. This solid fuel stage also uses an extendable nozzle exit cone. Its ENEC is made up of three nested sections which extend on ignition for greater efficiency. Stage III develops about 100,000 to 125,000 pounds of thrust to boost the remaining Stage IV/post-boost vehicle to its highest point. Hercules Inc. at Magna, Utah, is responsible for design, assembly and testing. . . .

Stage IV. The last stage uses storable liquid propellants to carry out the maneuvers required of the post-boost vehicle. . . . The Rocketdyne Division of Rockwell International, Canoga Park, California, is responsible . . .

Guidance and Control. Along with propulsion, Stage IV houses computers, communications equipment, and other electronics which guide and control the missile from launch through release of the re-entry vehicles. The Autonetics Group/Rockwell International in Anaheim, California, is responsible. . .

AIRS. An instrument called an advanced inertial reference sphere (AIRS) provides the flight computer with a steady stream of information on the missile's movements during flight. AIRS is a gyroscope-stabilized, freely rotating sphere about a foot in diameter that provides a reference point in guiding the missile along its pre-set flight path. AIRS will be designed, built and tested by Northrop Corporation at Palos Verdes Peninsula, California.

SFIR. The specific force integrated receiver, or SFIR, is also part of the missile guidance, navigation and control system, supplying the flight computers with information about the missile's speed and acceleration. Honeywell Inc., St. Petersburg, Florida, is responsible. . .

Now we come to the point of it all.

Re-Entry System. This system includes the nose-cone, the mechanisms to eject it after Stage IV leaves the earth's atmosphere, and the structure containing the warheads. The warheads are General Electric Mark 12As [sounds like a new-type dishwasher] which are dropped in ballistic trajectories signaled by the Stage IV guidance computers. Design, assembly and testing of the re-entry system will be the responsibility of AVCO Inc., Wilmington, Massachusetts.

The End.

A marvelous flying machine. But although the MX project is budgeted for a minimum of $33 billion (more likely $100 billion when cost overruns, tips, and bribes are included), the design appears to contain one serious flaw: there is no place in this 71-foot-long, 192,000 pound vehicle for human beings. There is no passenger compartment for the scientists, generals, and corporation executives who should be allowed—should be honored—should be *compelled,* at gunpoint if necessary, to ride this thing to its designated destination. Aside from this flaw, the MX appears, to this layman's eye, like good engineering. I am happy to report that it will probably do its job, and if ours doesn't theirs will.

William Faulkner once wrote a story called "Turnabout." The hero of the story is a World War I combat pilot in the Royal Air Force; he sees many good men die, and near the close of the tale his best friend, a gunboat commander, is also killed. Faulkner's character takes these deaths badly, becoming bitter. The story ends with the hero about to bomb and strafe a château in France where some German generals are billeted. As he dives his flying crate toward the building the pilot thinks, "If only they all were there. All the generals, all the admirals, *theirs, ours, all of them. . . .*" A turnabout. Good idea, I'm thinking. If we must have one more war let it be a simple and direct encounter between Kremlin and Pentagon, one deft surgical strike removing simultaneously two malignancies from the human body politic.

Mankind will not be free until the last general is strangled with the entrails of the last systems-analyst. As my sainted grandmother used to say.

Perhaps some boring statistics are necessary at this point. The Pentagon's current plans call for two hundred MX mobile missiles, each loaded with ten hydrogen bombs (one, we may recall, was enough to vaporize an entire Pacific island near Bikini). Each missile hauled about by a 750-ton TEL—transporter erector launcher—these nuclear dinosaurs would creep back and forth at a cruising speed of ten miles per hour (thirty mph in case of fear) among the forty-six hundred hardened missile shelters over a new road system of twelve thousand linear miles dispersed over some twenty thousand miles of desert valley and mountain range, an area the size of Pennsylvania. In the event of Soviet attack on the MX system, the area would serve as what Air Force publicists call a "nuclear sponge" capable of "absorbing" the Soviet's estimated four thousand H-bombs. This sponge, however, could not retain the radioactive dust and debris that such an onslaught would hurl into the atmosphere. Borne on the prevailing westerly winds, the resulting radioactive plume would drift eastward across the United States and perhaps all the way back to Moscow. Human bodies, massed in our proliferating multimillions, would serve as the ultimate nuclear sponge. It's hard but it's fair.

Most of us assume that the leaders of the Soviet Union have no desire to commit national suicide; there should therefore be no attack from that quarter, at least not by human volition. The *pax atomica* might then continue indefinitely, or until some array of silicon chips in an orbiting space computer—either theirs or ours—misinterprets signals from another electronic android. The functional drive-force behind the MX project is not so much military defense as intellectual inertia—the natural institutional tendency to continue along familiar grooves. The nuclear arms race has been in progress for thirty-five years; why stop now? Furthermore, there are financial motives—eight principal motives have already been mentioned: Thiokol, Aerojet, Hercules, Rocketdyne, Autonetics, Northrop, Honeywell, General Electric. There are other sensitive institutions involved here, including the U.S. Air Force itself, now obliged to compete with the superiority of nuclear submarines.

The effect of MX on the balance of terror appears vague, unpredictable; as usual the experts disagree. What is neither vague nor unpredictable is the impact of the project on the farms, ranches, small towns, the water supply, the land and landscape and people, the life both animal and vegetable of the present inhabitants of Nevada and western Utah.

Contrary to the apparent belief of the military, this region is fully inhabited. It is not empty space. Wide, free, and open, yes, but not empty. The mountains and valleys are presently occupied to the limit of their economic carrying capacity by ranchers, farmers, miners, forest rangers and inspectors of sunsets, and by what remains of the original population of Indians, coyote, deer, black bear, mountain lion, eagles, hawks, buzzards, mice, lizards, snakes, antelope, and wild horses. To make room for MX, its thirty thousand construction workers, and its glacier of iron, steel, cement, and plastic, many of these creatures, both human and otherwise, would have to be displaced.

So much for background briefing.

Time for a firsthand look at the impact area. A friend and I loaded bedrolls, wine, cheese, beans, and bread into a pickup truck and launched ourselves into Utah's West Desert. We followed the route of the Pony Express, southwest from Salt Lake City into the back of beyond. I wanted to see for myself, smell, taste, touch, and divine for myself the sagebrush and juniper, the dry lakes and arid mountains, the color of the light, the feel of the place. Too much proximity to folly tends to make it seem normal; we thought it time for a return, however brief, to the prehuman sanity of the desert.

So we passed the Great Salt Lake, the burned-out ruin of Saltair, once a famous resort. We turned south into a valley green with irrigation farming where old Mormon villages lie between snow-covered mountains. Two-story pioneer homes line the streets of Grantsville, St. John, Clover. Potential boom towns: lots of room here for trailerhouse slums, prefab school buildings, motor pools, sewage lagoons, truckyards, and the other usual benefits of development, such as a bullish alcoholism, a flourishing divorce industry, and a booming crime rate. Familiar social phenomena to most Americans by now, part of the price we have agreed to pay for progress and prosperity. But to the backward populace of these hick hamlets, still living out their lives in nineteenth-century dreams of peace and stability, the changes may come as a shock.

The pavement ends; we follow the dirt road into the Sinai of this Mormon Zion, through rocky hills covered with a pygmy forest of juniper and piñon pine, across valleys of greasewood, sagebrush, bunch grass. Cow country. Beyond Johnson's Pass and a ranch called Willow Springs we find ourselves at a fork in the road. The Pony Express rode south from here; we go west right to the entrance of Dugway Proving Grounds, where we have no business and no official permit to enter. Curiosity is sufficient motive. I want a glimpse of the Pentagon's nerve gas plantation, home of the Wet Eye bomb. And of anthrax. Botulism. Basic research. We get nowhere. Politely but firmly the young soldiers at the gate deny us entry. I inspect the name tag on one man's combat uniform. "German," it says. What army is this anyhow?

We back off and turn around, intimidated. We drive south into the open desert toward distant blue mountains. The Dugway Proving Grounds, a vast area in itself; as a glance at a Utah map will show, might seem like the proper place for the military's new *Star Wars* toys, a handy deployment area for two hundred missiles. But the Army doesn't see it that way. Too many unexploded bombs scattered about among these "target grids," they say, too many duds buried in the sand. This is forbidden and haunted real estate, a land condemned. DANGER, proclaim the signs on the fence; NO PUBLIC ACCESS.

Very well, we're law-abiding folk, we'll keep out. If the war establishment will leave me alone I'll leave it alone. But it must be a two-way, genuine, reciprocal agreement; after all, if the Sierra Club and the Odd Fellows can get by on voluntary contributions, *why can't the Pentagon?*

We drive on into the shimmering April afternoon. Grand, arid, primeval country opens before us, range after range of purple mountains, each separated from the next by a broad open basin. Sparsely inhabited places, to be sure—but not *un*inhabited. Cowboys, sheepherders, prospectors, miners live and work out here, plus a few vagabonds and hermits, and no doubt some Russian spies.

The Air Force promises that most of the MX range will remain open to public use. But security measures will surely be taken, surveillance must be severe, guards and helicopter assault teams will be stationed near each of the two hundred missile road-grid systems. How could it be otherwise? Big investments.

You may still be free to wander around in this region, to camp almost anywhere you wish; but heat sensors and electronic eyes will be tracking your movements. Many Americans, we know, do not object to this; only the guilty and those with illegal or immoral intentions, they feel, could possibly resent being watched, supervised, policed everywhere they go, by day and night. "True freedom," argued the Teutonic philosopher Georg Wilhelm Friedrich Hegel, "lies in willing obedience to law." The Germans and the Russians and the Japanese, among others, have made a state religion and a religion of society based on such a doctrine. Our ancestors came to America to escape that sort of thing. Building the MX would mean building another wall.

But there is no escape. Only interludes of illusion. I drive on, indulging the reveries of a solitary wanderer, keeping one eye peeled for topaz, amethyst, opal, beryl, tourmaline, obsidian, agate, crystal-loaded geodes. This is rock-hound country—a place for hounding rocks. But I am satisfied to look and touch and leave each stone where it belongs, *in situ.* Every rock should be regarded as what some call "leavitrite": leave it right where it is. The same holds for what's left of original America: love it or leave it alone.

We roll on, up one hill and down the other side, across wide valleys where the deer and the sheep and the antelope roam. And the wild horses. We stop many times to check out springs, stone ruins, abandoned mines. We study our maps and read the wonderful names, that anarchic nomenclature of the early wanderers that fits so well this wonderful desolation. Skull Valley (bordering the Proving Grounds), Black Knoll, Death Canyon, Sapphire Mountain, Cedar Mountains ("a wild horse area"), Lookout Mountain and Lookout Pass, Camel's Back Ridge, Pyramid Peak, Castle Mountain, Antelope Ridge, Pismire Wash, Slow Elk Hills (slow elk?), the Little Sahara ("sand dunes"), Fish Springs (a wildlife reserve), Deep Creek Mountains (visible from sixty miles away, glowing with snow), the Goshute Reservation, where the Goshute Indians live, Blood Mountain, Topaz Mountain, Whirlwind Valley, Cricket Mountains, Notch Peak, Conger Range, Confusion Range, Disappointment Hills, Snake Valley, Rainbow Valley, the Drum Mountains and the Little Drum Mountains, Lady Laird Peak (who was she?), Cowboy Pass and Rattlesnake Bench and the Wah Wah Mountains. Miners' lore, cattlemen's hopes, and Indian lairs are contained in these names on the land, all to be included in the proposed MX electronic battlefield. And all in one portion of western Utah; we have not even reached the Nevada border, beyond which the major part of the MX system would be constructed, deep in the ancestral hunting and gathering grounds of the Shoshone Indians. Lands, by the way, that never were ceded to the U.S. government.

We pause for an hour at a place called Simpson Springs. Here stand the stone walls of a Pony Express station. Three men once lived here: the station keeper, in charge of the horses; a blacksmith; and an extra rider. Upslope I find the spring, a seep of potable water flowing from a small reedy marsh. The water is hard but cool, drinkable. What will become of this spring and many others like it if the MX is built? Construction and maintenance of the MX system will require billions of gallons of water, so much water that the Air Force is even considering the diversion of water from the Columbia River, water now "wasted" because it is allowed to flow into the sea. But the politicians of the Northwest will never consent to such a scheme; they have their own plans for that water; after all, to their way of thinking, there is still plenty of room for more growth in Oregon and Washington.

The military will have to go *down* for water, therefore, into the aquifers beneath the Utah and Nevada desert. Deep wells may or may not supply sufficient water for the project; no one can know until the effort is made. But in any case the current water table will fall and many of the springs, seeps, ponds, and shallow wells on which wildlife and domestic livestock now depend will dry up.

We go beyond Simpson Springs a few miles and camp for the night at a place we call Eagle's Nest, after a giant bed of thatched sticks we find on a nearby stone outcrop. A series of craggy hills roll toward the sunset; on the skyline rises a cloudlike apparition—the Deep Creek Mountains. In the middle ground, past a dark ridge, the marshes of Fish Springs National Wildlife Refuge shine under backlight. We walk through a lavender twilight along an obscure mining road, past the stakes and cairns of forgotten mining claims. KEEP OUT, says a rusty sign, sagging on a two-by-four in a pile of stones, surrounded by an immense expanse of lifeless sand, gravel, bare rock, the desert pavement. I pull a broad-tipped felt pen from my pocket and revise the sign to read KEEP OFF THE GRASS.

Darkness floats in. The constellations emerge one by one from the cloudless sky, blazing like chandeliers in this still clear, clean, unpolluted sky. We slide into sleeping bags and sleep like children. But once after midnight I come awake, startled by the sound of a distant cry. Coyote? Mountain lion? Banshee? Staring up at the Corona Borealis, I see a ball of fire glide beneath the crown of heaven, trailing green flames. "A screaming comes across the sky," wrote Thomas Pynchon in the opening lines of *Gravity's Rainbow*. Humanity has entrapped itself, he seems to be saying, in the burning spendor of *technikos*.

We make a cheery breakfast of coffee and oranges and leftover beefsteak. We load and lurch off, on dust-dripping wheels, into the curious and threatened oasis of Fish Springs. Curious because there is so much water here, under hills like burnt iron, in the midst of this sun-scorched desert. Threatened because the MX system, if built, will transect part of these marshes with a railway, and very likely drain away the water as well.

But today the threat seems remote, implausible, trivial, like any nightmare remembered in the grace of morning. We walk along dikes which the U.S. Wildlife Service has erected between the marshes and lakes. The water comes from springs in the grim limestone mountains nearby; the surface of the water is absolutely still, reflecting perfectly the cliffs beyond. A resort home for birds. We see herons, Canada geese, mallards, pintails, green-winged and cinnamon teal, ruddy ducks, a marsh hawk, rails, coots, killdeer and sandpipers, avocets and stilts and terns and dozens of species more. The long-billed, long-legged, elegant waterfowl stand and stalk among the reeds, waiting, listening.

We linger for only an hour, then drive on and around the next range of hills to the west. Immense alkali flats, dry lakebeds, extend to the north. A burned-out motorbus lies in the middle of the white glare, patiently oxidizing. Near this skeletal wreckage we find mineral springs, sapphire pools of steaming water. An old sign leans against the bus: DANGER KEEP OUT, SURFACE MAY BREAK ANYTIME, ANYWHERE. We soak for a while in the nearest of the pools, dry off in the breeze and the sun, regroup, and drive toward the magic mountains in the west.

We stop at the Bid Boyd [sic] Pony Express station, so named for the hermit who once lived here, years after the station was closed and the Pony Express made obsolete by telegraph and railway. This is a hot, dry, intensely silent place; I can hear the crazy keening of locusts out there in the scrub. One small whirlwind, a spinning dust devil, dances across a dry lakebed flat as a floor. What would happen to one of those 750-ton TEL missile transporters, I wonder, if it had to be driven across or even near one of these lakebeds after a good rain? Might sink to the chassis frame in oleaginous muck. I hope.

Approaching the Deep Creek Range, we enter the village of Callao. It looks like the America of fifty—even a hundred—years ago: old cottonwoods and irrigation ditches parallel the dirt road that serves as the main street. Shaded by the trees are handsome, sturdy log homes where the ranching families of this community live. Children ride their ponies bareback through shady lanes; women in long dresses and sunbonnets tend the big gardens behind each house. Dogs bark dutifully and unfenced chickens, liberated, search the grounds for bugs and worms and seeds and insects—high protein egg food. A redtail hawk patrols the air, keeping a sharp eye on but respectful distance from—beyond shotgun range—the hens. One rooster shatters the stillness with his barbaric yawp. This little town lies in the shadow of MX.

Here in Callao lives a rancher named Cecil Garland—a good man. His opinion of the MX project is as follows (I quote from a letter he sent me):

> The MX would destroy the small-town way of life. It would destroy the spirit of a place like Callao and desecrate the beauty and health of the land. Worst of all, it would surround us, for a generation, with reminders of all that is evil in the soul of man.

Mr. Garland is not alone in his feelings. The people of Utah and Nevada are as patriotic as the rest of us, and most of them, according to the polls, oppose the MX. Some because of its probable effect on the land and water, many more because of its threat to a traditional way of living, and almost all because of a painfully acquired fear and distrust of the federal government. The rising incidence of leukemia in southwest Utah followed years of assurance from the Atomic Energy Commission that the atmospheric testing of atomic bombs would do no harm. When Air Force officials promise that the MX will bring more good things than bad, their listeners tend to suspect that they are being lied to. Even the politicians of Utah and Nevada, usually eager to accommodate military and industrial expansion, have raised some timid questions about this project, even going so far as to request that the Pentagon produce a thoroughgoing environmental impact statement before commencing construction of roads and bases.

We departed Callao, a place without gas station or even post office, for the town of Baker on the Nevada line. Got there, and paid $1.35 per gallon, regular, and looked at the silent female croupiers sitting behind inactive blackjack tables; business was slow today. The MX would certainly help things along in here. But even in Baker, an extremely conservative little town dedicated to such fine old conservative institutions as Ronald Reagan, gambling, alcohol, and prostitution, even in Baker there is an active group of the Great Basin Citizens Alliance Against MX.

Tank filled, running full, cool and collected, we bear eastward into Utah again, through more potential MX country, through Marjum Pass in the massive limestone walls of Notch Mountain and onto high and golden grasslands beyond. A bunch of pronghorn antelope races away to our left, swift and elegant as gazelles. The MX would not displace these creatures, not directly and immediately. But there will be ten times as many sportsmen in radio-equipped Jeeps, Broncos, Toyotas, Powerwagons, Blazers, and trailbikes out gunning for them.

We fill our canteens at Painter Spring, under a group of spring-green cottonwoods with shivering leaves. Would this little spring survive the drawdown of a falling water table? Probably not. We cook our supper on a bed of juniper coals, watching distant storm cells trail curtains of rain across the tawny uplands. Lightning flickers deep in the massy clouds. We explore a little side canyon spangled with flowers—pentstemon, larkspur, lupine, Indian paintbrush and skyrocket Gilia—where the sheep have not yet come. Wedged in an alcove in the canyon wall we find what looks like a medieval stone cottage, the stones the color of rock candy. Like the witch's house from Hansel and Gretel. A wizard's house, a hermit's retreat, long abandoned. Someday, perhaps, the original owner of this canyon will return, tootling on Pan pipes, I suppose, and scratching his ribs with a hairy hoof.

My friend and I smile at each other across the glow of the fire; she passes the wine. Common nighthawks appear, beaks gaping as they plunge through space, scooping up gnats. The usual little bat arrives, *die Fledermaus,* oh mouse with wings, and with it comes twilight and stars and the ancient peace of the desert. Here is one place, surely, where the human world's confusion and hatred will never reach. But such a naïve optimism comes too easily to a man eating baked beans from a can with a whittled stick for a spoon.

Another day, another circle. Way off to the east, sixty, seventy miles away, the lights of the city of Delta blink through the troposphere. Still farther away we can see the broad illuminations from Ogden, Provo, and Salt Lake City, where the people of Utah, most of them, mostly live, secure in their homes, safe for the night. No doubt.

Author's Note: In October 1981 President Reagan, apparently in response to regional opposition, announced that the MX system would not be deployed in the Utah-Nevada desert—at least not in the immediate future. Since the U.S. Air Force insists, however, that the project is necessary, the final outcome of the issue remains in doubt. In the meantime the President suggests that MX missiles be installed in what are now Titan missile bases, such as those surrounding the city of Tucson, not far from where this author currently resides. I find a rough justice in this proposal.

7

Of Protest

Rocky Flats, Colorado; November 1978

A canvas tepee straddled the railroad tracks, clearly obstructing passage. The railway—a spur—curved across a field of tawny grass and basaltic rocks toward a distant complex of buildings, towers and lights enclosed within a high-security fence topped with barbed wire, patrolled by armed guards. Occasional wisps of steam rose from the short stacks within the plant, fading out in the chilly blue as they drifted toward the rich brown haze of Denver, sixteen miles to the southeast. West of the railroad and the highway nearby stood the foothills of the Front Range of the Rocky Mountains.

A steady stream of truck and auto traffic moved on the highway, but few of the drivers of these vehicles paused to wonder at the strange sight of a wigwam erected across a railroad track. Mostly local people, they had grown accustomed to this oddity; the archaic tent had been standing here for most of the last six months.

Two flags and two young men attended this structure and the scatter of camping equipment around and within it. One flag was the blue, red, and white of the United States; the other bore a golden sun on a field of green, representing—what? Some adventurous new nation in the human community? A nation within a nation? A gesture toward another form of independence? Aspen poles twenty feet tall carried the flags well above the peak of the tepee; the cool November breeze rolling down from the mountains stirred both flags with separate but equal nonchalance.

One of the young fellows was a student at Denver University. He wore a wool shirt, a light blond beard, a shy but friendly smile—I failed to catch his name. The other looked like a pirate: bandana for a headband, gold earrings, black beard, skin darkened by sun and wind. He wore a green sweat shirt, baggy gray sweat pants, the canvas sneakers of a jogger, the fingerless wool gloves of a rock climber—or of a golfer. He admitted with a grin to a touch of Irish in his genes; his name was Patrick Malone.

Patrick Malone had been here, like the wigwam, for most of the previous six months. He said he planned to stay through the winter—blizzards, ice, subzero temperatures notwithstanding—until that quiet but industrial-looking installation at the end of the railway spur was shut down forever, or converted perhaps to the manufacture of something different—of solar heating devices, let us say, or skis, or mopeds, bicycles, plowshares.

An electric power line on wooden poles paralleled the railway and led into the factory. Wooden poles: it occurred to me that one resolute man with a chain saw could put that place out of business for a short while, easily and quickly. Such a suggestion would not be welcome here; Malone and his friends were opposed both in principle and in practice to violence in any form. Even to moderate violence, technically restrained, tactically precise, against mere inanimate property.

They did not consider their wigwam on the tracks, barring the right-of-way near a sign that read U.S. PROPERTY NO TRESPASSING, to be a form of violence. Once a week, when the train came, the short train of specially designed armored cars marked FISSILE MA-TERIAL—RADIOACTIVE, Malone and helpers dismantled the tent and carried it out of the way (saving it from confiscation and the security forces from unnecessary paperwork). Then he and friends, a series of them totaling about two hundred so far, returned to the railway and sat on the tracks, offering only their bodies to the advancing engine. The train always halted, or had so far, and the people on the rails were taken away by the police, booked for trespass and obstruction of traffic, and jailed or released on their own recognizance.

This scene had been repeated more than twenty times since April 29, 1978, when some four thousand people, mostly from the cities of Denver and Boulder (nine miles to the north), gathered in a well-organized and peaceful assembly at the gates of the Rocky Flats nuclear weapons plant to make their feelings known to whoever, or whatever, might be in charge. There had been so far no fights, no bodily injuries of any kind on either side. Demonstrators, protesters, security guards, and the Jefferson County sheriff's deputies who made the actual arrests had all been on their best behavior. The world was not watching, but a small part of it had been here, including the local press.

After saying goodbye to Malone and his mate—they were now being visited, interviewed, and photographed by a German professor of American literature from the University of Hamburg—we attempted to enter the plant itself. We were turned back at the gate. The guards were polite but firm: No entry, they said, without a pass from Rockwell International Corporation, which manages the plant under contract with the U.S. Department of Energy and the Pentagon. What Rockwell makes here is no longer a secret, if it ever was, though it was only gradually revealed to the public after 1952, when the plant was established. Rockwell is making an essential component—the plutonium "trigger"—of what the government calls thermonuclear devices. Hydrogen bombs. The trigger, which itself is an atomic detonating device equivalent in explosive power to the atomic bombs dropped on Japan, is shipped from here to another factory near Amarillo, Texas, where the actual H-bombs are assembled.

Our government has been in this business, operating through various private corporations (Rockwell was preceded by Dow Chemical here at Rocky Flats), for thirty years. The total number of atomic and hydrogen bombs now available for use is a state secret; but everything leaks, eventually. Careful students of the matter, such as Daniel Ellsberg, estimate the size of the American stockpile at something between eleven thousand and thirty thousand nuclear bombs. Since a few hundred of these weapons could obliterate most mammalian life from Dublin to Vladivostok, that should be, from a layman's point of view, a sufficient number. But production continues, a $1.7 billion annual business.

The government justifies continued production on the grounds that bombs made ten, twenty, and thirty years ago are no longer reliable or adequate, and that ever more sophisticated refinements in design and delivery make regular model changes desirable. Furthermore, the Russians are doing the same thing. And the Chinese. And the English, and the French. And maybe the Israelis, the Indians, the South Africans, the Brazilians. All governments need enemies.

We have lived for so long under the umbrella of Mutual Assured Destruction (MAD) that perhaps we would feel uncomfortable, even defenseless, without it. It is certainly arguable that the threat of nuclear devastation has helped prevent a major war. When presidents and premiers, commissars and commissioners, generals and admirals are compelled to share the dangers of war with ordinary citizens and common soldiers, then we are all a little safer. We hope.

We drove on to the town of Golden, seat of Jefferson County, State of Colorado, where the trial of the railway trespassers was taking place. An arch across the main street proclaimed WELCOME

TO GOLDEN—WHERE THE WEST BEGINS. (If so, this must also be where the East begins.) We found the courtroom packed, the proceedings under way, with thirty-one-year-old Judge Kim Goldberger presiding over his first criminal case.

Several days had already been spent in selecting the six-member jury, a touchy and difficult process, and in the presentation of its case by the prosecution, a much simpler affair. The defendants freely confessed to being present on the tracks at the time alleged, freely admitted their attempt to block rail traffic into the weapons plant. But they did not plead guilty; they pleaded not guilty, using as their defense an old Colorado "choice-of-evils" statute that allows the intentional commission of an illegal act when the purpose of such act is to prevent a greater harm or a greater crime. For example, the law allows you to violate speed limits when your purpose is to save a life, or to escape imminent danger.

Unfortunately for the defendants and their lawyers, the judge had ruled that only he, and not the jury, had the right to determine if the choice-of-evils defense was "applicable" in this instance. The defendants were obliged, therefore, to present their case without being heard by a jury of their peers; the jury had been excused, forbidden to hear the defense, read about it, or talk about it. Since trial by jury in criminal cases is supposed to be a constitutional right, the judge had already given the defense firm grounds for appeal to a higher court. Which *might* have been his purpose, since he had been quoted earlier as saying that the issues involved were too important to be settled in a county court. But as will be seen, Judge Goldberger would make no secret of his prejudgment of the defendants.

The defense went ahead with its case, jury or no jury, calling a number of experts to the stand to testify to the reality of radiation hazards imposed on the residents of Boulder, Denver, and environs by the Rocky Flats installation. One witness came from England, another from Georgia, another from California; the remainder were recruited locally. All traveled at their own expense and gave their testimony without monetary compensation.

The seven Denver attorneys working for the defense were

doing the same thing; they had volunteered their time out of sympathy. The defendants, though presumed innocent until proved guilty, are not allowed, under our system of justice, any form of reimbursement for their loss of income or livelihood, even if they should finally be acquitted. The judge, meanwhile, and the prosecuting attorneys (including a couple of lawyers on loan from the U.S. Department of Energy) continued to receive their pay without interruption. Since the trial dragged on for eleven days, the defendants and their counsel were effectively punished even before the judge pronounced sentence. But nobody questions this way of doing things. Perhaps, in a rationalized society like ours, there is no better way. As Hegel concluded in his 457-page *Philosophy of History*, stealing a line from Leibniz, Whatever is—is right.

The defendants and their legal counsel did not appear to share my sense of the injustice already imposed on them. They were busily and happily engaged not so much in defending themselves as in prosecuting the adversary, putting on trial the Rocky Flats weapons plant itself, and by implication the Department of Energy, the Department of Defense, the U.S. government, the Russian government, the nuclear arms race, the freight train of history, the complacency and cowardice of us all in meekly accepting, like mice in a laboratory, the miserable nightmare that statesmen and scientists, industrialists and technologists have laid upon our lives, without our consent, and upon the lives of our descendants (if any) for thousands of years to come.

The first witness that I heard was Karl Z. Morgan, a professor at Georgia Tech of what is called "health physics." Dr. Morgan, age seventy-two, is an old-timer in the nuclear enterprise; he took part in the origins of the Manhattan Project, when the first atomic reactor was built under the stadium at the University of Chicago during World War II; he served for twenty years as director of safety operations at the nuclear laboratories at Oak Ridge, Tennessee, before returning to teaching. He has published many books and papers on the subject of radiation-induced illness and is considered to be one of the world's authorities on the subject.

In a soft, gentle voice, with a slight Southern accent, Dr. Morgan reviewed for us what should be familiar stuff by now: the invisible and insidious effects of low-level radiation, intangible to the senses, measurable only by instruments, but potentially fatal all the same, given sufficient exposure, to any organism unlucky enough to inhale or ingest even the most minute particles of plutonium or its derivative, americium. There is no such thing, he maintained, as a safe or "permissible" dose of internal radiation; the slightest quantity can be enough, in a susceptible human, to cause some form of cancer.

He is not, said Dr. Morgan, against nuclear power, nor would he support unilateral nuclear disarmament; but he thinks present safety standards are dangerously inadequate. Accidents are inevitable, he said, given human fallibility, and he mentioned (over objections from the county attorney) the three deaths at Los Alamos and the three at Idaho Falls that resulted from nuclear mishaps. People living near or downwind of Rocky Flats are subject to a 3 to 6 percent greater risk than those in other areas; he accused the Environmental Protection Agency of failure to enforce uniformly even its present inadequate safety standards; the Rocky Flats installation should never have been built so close to a city, and should be shut down or relocated as soon as possible, "preferably deep inside a mountain."

Did he think the dangers posed by Rocky Flats justified the demonstrations, protests, and railway sit-ins staged by the defendants? Since ordinary political means have so far failed to produce the needed changes (Colorado's governor and Congressional delegation have been advocating removal of the Rocky Flats plant for years), Dr. Morgan thought that yes, any nonviolent action that served to publicize the problem was probably justified—even though, he added, the railway trespass would not "miraculously" decontaminate the estimated eleven thousand acres stretching from the plant grounds toward Denver that were already poisoned by plutonium leakage from waste-storage barrels.

Dr. Morgan's testimony required three hours for its detailed elaboration. Two more days of similar testimony by other defense witnesses followed. Dr. Alice Stewart from Oxford University, an epidemiologist by trade, and Dr. John W. Gofman of the University of California at Berkeley, a specialist in physical chemistry and, like Dr. Stewart, an M.D., reinforced Dr. Morgan's fears of the long-range effects of nuclear contamination in the Denver area. "Protest is always justified," said Gofman, "when it is the only means to make a deaf government listen."

Local scientists from the University of Colorado, the Colorado Department of Health, and the Atmospheric Research Center appeared on the stand to back up Drs. Morgan, Stewart, and Gofman. Dr. Anthony Robbins testified that he had "serious concerns as to whether one could believe or trust the statements of the Department of Energy" about radioactive emissions at the plant. Dr. Edward Martell, a nuclear chemist, said that Rocky Flats officials had "resisted suggestions" that they make tests for nuclear contamination in the soil beyond the plant boundaries. Therefore Dr. Martell made the tests himself and found, in Jefferson County and the Denver area, concentrations of plutonium—"hot spots"—more than 250 times greater than normal background levels of radiation.

Dr. John Cobb, a member of a governor's task force appointed to investigate the safety of the plant, said that he had made sixteen recommendations for improving safety operations, but that none, so far as he had been able to find out, were put into effect. As for nuclear power in general, Dr. Cobb said that he was in favor of it, but only if reactors were confined to a safe distance from human habitation, "about 93 million miles away . . . on the sun."

Like the other witnesses and most of the defendants, Cobb opposed unilateral nuclear disarmament, given the present state of international affairs, but did think it would be worthwhile, from the point of view of human survival, for the U.S. government to take a significant initial step toward such disarmament; world opinion, he felt, as well as its own best interests, would compel the Russian government to follow. The present course, he said, is one of premeditated suicide.

The trial was adjourned for four days of official Thanksgiving. After the recess some of the defendants were allowed, through a constant barrage of united objections by the judge and prosecution, to make their statements directly to the three men and three women of the jury. Said Roy Young, age thirty, a Boulder geologist: "I was on those tracks not to commit trespass but to prevent random murder on the population of metropolitan Denver." [Objection, your honor! Objection sustained.] "And if I thought," continued Young, "that by staying on those tracks . . . I could close that plant tomorrow, I would be willing to stay there for the rest of my life." [Objection! Sustained.]

Said Nancy Doub, age forty, housewife and child-care worker from Boulder, who with her seventeen-year-old daughter had been arrested on the night of May 8: "It was a pretty far-out thing. I'm not accustomed to going out at night in two feet of snow to stop a railroad train." They waited two hours for the train to emerge from the plant. "When we saw the light we walked up the tracks together . . . singing 'We Shall Not Be Moved.' " [Objection! Sustained.]

Skye Kerr, age twenty-three, a registered nurse and student at the University of Colorado, said that she had received her training at the Boston Children's Hospital and was familiar with the effects of radiation-caused cancer and leukemia. She said, "There were three-year-old children with their hair falling out. They were getting sick from the medicine they were taking and didn't understand." [Objection! Sustained.] She said, "The children keel over and die. They gush out blood from all over." [Objection! Objection! Inciting sympathy in the jury, Your Honor! Sustained.] "It happens years later. You can't see or feel or touch radiation, but it's as real as a gun." [Objection! Sustained.] "I felt the only thing I could do . . . was to bodily put myself on the tracks. I knew that laws much, much higher [than trespass] were being broken." [Objection! Sustained.] What kind of laws? she was asked. "Laws of human—of life. You know—violations of rights you have as a human being." [Objection! Objection sustained.]

The defense rested its case a day later, after a summation by chief defense attorney Edward H. Sherman that appealed to the jury as "the conscience of the community." (The ancient and traditional role, in Anglo-Saxon law, of any jury.) The prosecuting attorney, Steve Cantrell, summed up his argument by saying that this was "a case of simple trespass. We are not here to change the policy of the U.S. government. . . ."

The judge read his instructions to the jury. It took him twenty minutes to guide—or delimit—their deliberations. He reminded the jury that he had ruled as irrelevant the choice-of-evils defense, as well as a defense based on the First Amendment right to assemble peacefully for redress of grievances. The members of the jury were to disregard "emotional appeals" and consider only, and nothing but, the formal charges of obstruction of traffic on a public right-of-way and trespass against U.S. government property.

The jury went into deep seclusion. It emerged five hours later to confess inability to reach a decision. The judge excused the jury for the night but put it back to work next morning. After another five hours, the jury announced its verdict: All defendants guilty of trespass, innocent of obstructing traffic.

The jurors explained that though in sympathy with the defendants, they could not, under the judge's instructions, acquit them of the trespassing charge. One juror wrote a note to the defendants: "My support and prayers are with you all." Another, Diana Holman, said to defendant Jack Joppa, "We support you and your cause." Another juror tried to explain her decision to reporters, faltered in midsentence, left the courtroom weeping.

The judge looked glum and a little bored. The defense attorneys looked weary, sad, disappointed, the prosecuting attorneys tired and exasperated.

Both sides claimed a moral victory but the divided verdict satisfied no one. No one, that is, but the defendants and their supporters; they alone seemed pleased by the results of the trial—not jubilant, but serenely happy. Linking hands and arms they sang "We Shall Overcome," about seventy of them there in the crowded little courtroom, while the flashbulbs flashed, the high-intensity video lights glared, the cameras clicked and clashed.

The judge set a later date for sentencing; penalties up to six months in jail and/or a fine of $500 were possible. The defense attorneys announced, as expected, their plans for appeal to a higher court.

I spoke briefly with a few of the defendants, including Daniel Ellsberg, who now lives in San Francisco and makes his living, he told me, as a writer and lecturer, devoting most of his efforts to the antinuclear crusade. I met Steve Sterns and Ellen Klaver, both students at the University of Colorado; the latter supports herself by working as a seasonal Ranger with the National Park Service. I met Peter Ediger, about age fifty I would guess, who is the minister of the Mennonite Church in nearby Arvada, another Denver suburb.

The defendants impressed me not so much with what they had to say as with their manner. They are happy people, these crusaders, at ease with themselves and with others, radiant with conviction, liberated by their own volition from the tedious routine and passive acquiescence in which most of us endure our brief, half-lived, half-lives. One single act of defiance against power, against the State that seems omnipotent but is not, transforms and transfigures the human personality. At least for a time. For a while. Perhaps that is enough.

I had come to the Rocky Flats affair in a state of mind vaguely sympathetic with the protesters, but basically skeptical, burdened by the resigned cynicism that passes for wisdom in contemporary America. Like some people I know, I could sometimes settle for the belief that our most serious problems are finding a place to park the car, the ever-rising costs of gasoline and beefsteak, and the nagging demands of the poor, the old, the disinherited.

Now I felt a guilty envy of the protesters, of those who actually act, and a little faint glow of hope—perhaps something fundamental might yet be changed in the nature of our lives. Crusaders for virtue are an awkward embarrassment to any society; they force us to make choices: either side with them, which is difficult and dangerous, or condemn them, which leads to self-betrayal.

While the glow lasted, one of the defendants—Robert Godfrey, transplanted Englishman, mountaineer, filmmaker, writer—and I walked down the streets of Golden (golden Colorado!) to the Coors Brewery where visitors are always welcome, for the free beer. We had been denied entrance to the Rocky Flats nuclear-weapons plant; here we were admitted by cheerful ladies wearing red-and-white uniforms and genuine simulated Disneyland smiles. Which was gracious of the Coors Corporation, I thought; people like Godfrey and myself have never felt or said anything nice about Adolph Coors and Company—a highly influential right-wing force in Rocky Mountain and now national politics.

We took the official "short" tour of the plant, direct from front door to free-beer dispensary, and sampled the product, generously offered, liberally taken. If we could not celebrate exactly a victory, then—as César Chavez has said—we would celebrate our defeat. The beer tasted fine, I am happy to report, despite what seemed to me a strange, Day-Glo phosphorescence in the foaming head.

Yes, I had come by now to imagine particles of plutonium 239 and americium 241 everywhere I looked, floating on the air, settling on my shoulders like microscopic flecks of dandruff, lodging in my lungs, where they—the particles—could carry on, undisturbed, their peculiar half-life of twenty-four thousand years. Nevertheless, we drank the beer.

Drank the beer and carried on. Driving home to Boulder that evening, Godfrey and I were happy to see Patrick Malone and his wigwam, flags flying, still firmly and symbolically obstructing traffic on the nuclear railroad. Can one man derail a train with nothing but his will? Can a few thousand human beings armed with nothing but audacity and purpose bring to a halt the mighty freight train of government, industry, power, war, that overwhelming vision of a future charged by pride and ambition?

The only answer we know is the most comforting and terrifying of answers: anything is possible.

Author's Note: The defendants received six-month suspended sentences. Patrick Malone maintained his stand, violating probation, and served three months of a six-month jail sentence before friends paid his fine. In April of the following year, fifteen thousand people took part in the protest at Rocky Flats. The nuclear-weapons plant remains in operation.

8

Thus I Reply
to René Dubos

In his recent book, *The Wooing of the Earth,* René Dubos describes
with pride the transformation of the European landscape, during
recent millennia, by human labor, human need, human thought. I
understand and sympathize—indeed, I empathize—with his feeling of reverence for the pastoral scenes of his boyhood. I too was
born and raised on a farm, though not in France but in Pennsylvania, and my deepest emotions—those so deep they lie closer to
music than to words—were formed, somehow, by intimate association in childhood with the woods on the hill, the stream that
flowed through the pasture, the oaken timbers of the old barn, the
well, the springhouse, the sugar maples, the hayfields, and even
those cultivated fields of corn that my father and brothers and I
planted in April and hoed (not without some coercion) through

summer, and later cut, husked, and loaded, ear by ear and bushel by bushel, into a wagon pulled by a team of horses, during the haunted finality of October.

Who would deny the beauty as well as the utility of well-tended fields, close-cropped pastures, barns, farmhouses, stone walls, small dams, waterwheels, winding dirt roads lined with poplars, any and all things built with care by human hands, nourished and nurtured into fruitfulness by human love? Who could deny it? Poets have busied themselves since the days of Vergil and Horace, for two thousand years, in praising the bucolic scene. While ten thousand painters, from Watteau to Constable to Inness, have portrayed in glowing colors the peace and plenty, as they saw it, of agrarian life. It is a staple of the picture-postcard business. American politicians from Thomas Jefferson through Franklin Roosevelt to Ronald Reagan (to list them in declining order) have spoken of the family farm as the backbone of the nation. Jefferson even meant it.

Today the staunchest defenders of agriculture in its traditional mode, are conservationists. The true conservatives. I need mention by name only two: Aldo Leopold, whose phrase "the land ethic" is now part of the basic vocabulary of the conservation philosophy; and Wendell Berry, himself a farmer as well as poet and writer, whose bold, brilliant essays in such books as *The Long-Legged House* and *The Unsettling of America* make the best case yet for the preservation of the family farm and the independent farmer, for the complex of economic, political, spiritual, and esthetic values—farming as a way of life—still to be found in the ancient art of agriculture. I cannot imagine any conservationist so "pure" as to object to farming—by freeholders—in its traditional style. Such farming is indeed under heavy attack in our time but not by conservationists. The object of dispute between René Dubos and myself is not farming but what we call industrialized farming, or "agribusiness."

Farming as a way of life is a self-sustaining, symbiotic relationship between man and earth resulting in the harmonious, beautiful, and fruitful cultural environment praised so eloquently

by René Dubos. Agribusiness, on the other hand, means industrialized, mechanized agriculture, the mass production of food and
fiber obtained through the mining—not the wooing—of the land.
Agribusiness is a modern phenomenon, developed in response to
the urgent needs of a rapidly expanding human population.
Whether this kind of large-scale agriculture, dependent as it is on
water diversion projects, fossil fuels, chemical fertilizers, and other
forms of heavy capital investments, can long survive remains to be
seen; its future seems dubious. From a jet plane at thirty thousand
feet over Kansas the vast fields of brown and green below present a
reassuring appearance; close up, on the ground, not so pleasing.
This kind of farming—monoculture—involves a gross simplifica-
tion of the natural order, satisfying perhaps to the taste of a ge-
ometer, but not to the livestock grower, or the traditional farmer.

The high plains of the American West are not, as Dubos
thinks, a deforested region but a semiarid natural grassland; as everyone knows, they once supported enormous herds of bison. Later,
before the coming of the plow, the plains supported great herds of
domestic cattle. Those parts of the grasslands not yet broken by the
plow—or destroyed by strip-mining for coal—are still devoted to
cattle ranching, a century-old free enterprise; the native grasses of
this region make it one of the most productive rangelands in the
world.

Which form of agriculture—farming or ranching—is best
suited to the high plains environment? Which is better in the long
run for human beings as well as for the land? (Remember the Dust
Bowl.) And if beauty is also a concern, then what kind of use,
which way of life, best combines utility, long life, and beauty?
These are the questions, seldom considered by those in power, that
should be asked. The answer, on reflection, becomes as clear as the
difference between a busted-sod, abandoned homestead down
there on the flat and beef cows and antelope at home on the range
over yonder.

Utility and beauty are inextricably intertwined in human affairs. The useful is always attractive to us, the beautiful in some
sense always useful. The beauty of agriculture lies primarily in its

usefulness, and where the human population has grown large and dense within a given area, agriculture (in some form) becomes a necessity.

The development of agriculture made possible the exponential growth of human population: the latter in turn made—and makes—the continuance and intensification of agriculture vital to survival. I would not question the argument that this reciprocal functioning of man and earth has led, in much of Europe and other parts of the world, to an attractive humanizing of the landscape. But it might be interesting to remind ourselves of what has been lost in this process, and to review, once again, the values inherent in wildness and wilderness, now in so parlous a state.

I can claim some acquaintance with the surface aspects of Europe, having sojourned there twice, once as a soldier, later as a student, for a total of three years. One of the most vivid images on the scroll of my life so far is the memory of that first view of Gibraltar, from the troopship *La Mariposa*, as we entered the ancient womb of the Mediterranean, and the spectacle, three days later, of Capri and the Bay of Naples. To me it was a vision of delight, augmented soon afterward by visits to Amalfi, Sorrento, and those other sweet towns on the coast of southern Italy, where humankind and the landscape have been wedded so well, for so long. Or so it appears from a certain esthetic distance.

Seven years later, as a student, I toured Spain, France, Austria, England, and the Scandinavian countries by train, on a bicycle, on foot. Again my first impressions were of the harmonious integrity of farm and village, town and landscape, and the pleasures, little known in America, of living cheaply on good bread, cheese, wine, almost anywhere I traveled.

But my second visit to Europe followed five years of life in the American West, years that spoiled and corrupted me forever. This time, despite its delights, Europe seemed to me a constrained, constricted, crowded world, and I became conscious, everywhere, of the long dark centuries of forced labor, of serfdom and slavery, that went into the creation of Europe's historic beauty. Over each quaint village hangs the black shadow of the castle, the château, or the manor house—symbols and reminders of a thousand years of injustice.

Through revolution and progress that heritage of evil has been partly transcended, but its memory lingers in the air, in the atmosphere, a somber undertone to "the still, sad music of humanity." And this dark note reminded me of things that I had failed to understand during my earlier travels in southern Italy. The landscape that had seemed, from a ship, so charming and lovely, turned out on close inspection to be heavily burdened by human need. Hardly a square foot of surface was left unused; the terraced hillsides smelled of human dung, the fields were cultivated to within inches of the roads, the most barren peaks cropped to stubble by the ubiquitous flocks of goats. When I walked in the villages of Spain, Majorca, Italy, so picturesque from a distance, I discovered the smell of poverty, the smell of fear, the oppression of invisible but all-too-confining walls.

It may be true that the deforestation and intensive cultivation of the Mediterranean world actually improved its appearance. (From a landscape architect's point of view.) For a time, no doubt, as Dr. Dubos says, the destruction of the forest may even have contributed to a sunny liberation of the human spirit. But over the long run (again!) that excessive use resulted in a general impoverishment of life, from which many southern Europeans eagerly sought escape when the opportunity became available. And they still seek to escape it. As for the esthetic quality of this man-made landscape, it would be easier to judge its beauty if at least a little of the original landscape, say a third or so, had been allowed to survive. If we had something left there to measure it by. But we do not. A certain diversity, vital to the highest art, as it is to the freest life, is lacking.

The benefits of agriculture are common knowledge. We wear and eat them. Not only did agriculture enable us to multiply, many times over, the total numbers of our race, but it has also led to the creation of the city, of written literature, history, law, philosophy, and from there to science, technology, and industrialism on the grand scale, as we know them today. But sacrifices had to be made.

We gave up the free, spacious, egalitarian, adventurous life of the hunting-gathering societies. (See Peter Farb's *Humankind, The Tender Carnivore* by Paul Shepard, or *The Imperial Animal* by Robin Fox and Lionel Tiger.) We submitted to the organization required by the first great social machines, machines that were made, as Lewis Mumford has pointed out, not of metal but of flesh, human blood and bone, of living men and women—and children. An army, for example, is a machine with men for its component parts, each part subordinated to the working of the whole. The same is true for a royal household, the pyramid construction gangs, the field hands of plantation or manorial estate.

With the order entailed by complex organization came class and caste, the establishment of elaborate social hierarchies in which, as customary, a few enjoyed the benefits of well-organized work while the majority provided the sweat, the blood, the servitude, and the raw material. The laborers and serfs, in fact, were themselves the essential raw materials.

Somewhere in his *Essays* (circa 1560, "On Cannibals"), Montaigne mentions an American Indian who was brought to France and shown around; asked to give his opinion of the civilized glories he had seen, the Indian, reports Montaigne, wondered how a few rich men could keep so many poor men in subjection, and why the poor men did not cut the rich men's throats. What the Indian failed to see was that the poor were trapped by their dependence on agriculture, their escape foreclosed by the spread of dense human populations and the enclosure of free, wild, unoccupied lands. With the forests cut down, most of humanity submitted to slavery in one form or another in order to survive. It must have seemed to most of them, before they ceased to think about it, before they ceased to think, that they had no choice (Sherwood Forest now was gone); it was either serve the lord of the manor or starve. The disciplining of the earth required and led to the disciplining of human beings.

Robin Hood, not King Arthur, is the real hero of English legend. Robin Hood and his merry rebels were free men, hunters, woodsmen, and thus—necessarily in their lifetime—outlaws. Doomed. While King Arthur and his armored goons functioned as the politburo of a slave state: Camelot. Of all who have written on the Arthurian matter, from Chaucer to Malory, through Spenser and Tennyson to Thomas Berger, only Mark Twain could see this. But Mark Twain was a great writer.

The discovery of America gave some release to the people of Europe, loosened the feudal bonds. The wealth brought about by the Enlightenment, by science, industry, and political emancipation, seemed to promise a new age of freedom—the advantages of what we call "modernization" without the corresponding injustices associated with the historical past.

But that freedom now seems likely to be short-lived. We emerge from one nightmare only to find another threatening to engulf us: the technological superstate, densely populated, centrally controlled, nuclear-powered, computer-directed, firmly and thoroughly policed. Call it the Anthill State, the Beehive Society, a technocratic despotism—perhaps benevolent, perhaps not, but in either case the enemy of personal liberty, family independence, and community sovereignty, shutting off for a long time to come the freedom to choose among alternate ways of living. The domination of nature made possible by misapplied science leads to the domination of people; to a dreary and totalitarian uniformity.

If the chrome-plated world of the futurologist becomes real there will be no room for the family farm of either Thomas Jefferson or Wendell Berry, and less and less room for the gently humanized landscapes so loved by René Dubos. What we must expect, it seems, is a planet where the entire surface, water as well as land, is subjected to intensive economic exploitation. The sea will be farmed, all deserts irrigated, whole mountains pulverized, the last forests turned into pulpwood plantations, in order to satisfy the ever-growing needs (no doubt as desperate as in the past) of a human population much larger than at present. We will live to see a ruling priesthood of administrators and technicians still trying, after five thousand years, to build a pyramid of power up to the stars. And this pyramid, like those of Egypt, will be based on the subjugation of human beings.

Only a bad dream? Maybe. Probably. But our worst fantasies have an alarming way of becoming realities; the events of the twentieth century may serve as illustration. Without necessarily rejecting either science or technology, it seems to me that we can keep them as servants, not masters, only by doing our best to preserve the variety and openness of life on earth. This means, especially in America, defending the family farm against the mechanized monoculture of agribusiness; defending the family ranch against the strip-mining company; defending the selective cutting of sustained-yield forestry from the clear-cutting of quick-profit wood products corporations; defending the small town against the spreading BLOB of suburbia; protecting our surviving rivers from the dam-building mania of the politicians; saving our hills and fields, mountains and deserts, roadless areas and wild areas from the aggrandizement of the extractive industries.

Wilderness complements and completes civilization. I might say that the existence of wilderness is also a compliment to civilization. Any society that feels itself too poor to afford the preservation of wilderness is not worthy of the name of civilization. A completely man-made environment would not be a civilization at all but merely another kind of culture, in the anthropological sense of that word, merely another *village,* though it be of global dimensions.

Europe was saved from becoming a permanent prisonhouse by the opening up of America. (And the forcible displacement of America's original inhabitants.) But suppose we in America surrender our last remnants of wilderness to the demands of industrialism? With most of arable Asia, Africa, Latin America exploited by the urgent needs of their vast populations, only the United States, Canada, Australia, perhaps Siberia, and a few portions of far northern Europe are left as reserves of undomesticated nature, of ample regions where man, in the words of the Wilderness Act, "is a visitor who does not remain." Even in the forty-eight contiguous United States only 2 percent of the total land surface has been given official status and long-term protection as wilderness. The fate of the remaining roadless areas, some 200 million acres, mostly in the West, remains in doubt, subject of contention between those who would save them for future generations and those who want to *get in there and drag something out right now.*

How much wilderness is enough? And what is it good for anyway? Who needs it? as they say in Moab, Utah. We might answer these questions with counter questions. How many cities are enough? How large a human population do we really need? How much industrial development must we have to be content?

This is not to suggest that our race should efface itself from planet Earth, or that humanity is an "excrescence" on the map of Nature. Nobody believes such things except certain Hindu and Gnostic philosophers, and metaphysicians like Pierre Teilhard de Chardin, for example, who urge us to discard the biosphere (the realm of physical life) for the noosphere (the realm of divine ideas shared in telepathic unison), whereby we transcend our carnal existence to become disembodied spirits rising and converging upon a metaphysical point where, at last (as before), All Become One. The totalitarianism of the divine.

But the woods, the hills, the rocks: how much Nature is enough? Enough to go around, I'd say, or about one square mile per human—with a little surplus left over. By a "little surplus" I mean wild areas where through general agreement none of us enters at all. An absolute wilderness, we might call it, justified by our recognition of the rights of other living things to a place of their own, a role of their own, an evolution of their own not influenced by human pressures. A recognition, even, of the right of nonliving things—boulders, for example, or an entire mountain— to be left in peace, alone, for a few centuries now and then. A foolish, utopian idea, no doubt; I advance it merely as a suggestion of what is possible were the human consciousness, and the human *conscience,* ever to reach so generous a level. It is not enough to understand the natural world; the point is to preserve it. Let Being be.

How defend the ideal of wilderness? The wilderness idea

needs no defense—only more defenders. It cannot be defended by promoting the complacement, traditional, orthodox, and institutional view that anything man-made or human is, by definition, superior to the other-than-human. (This attitude, if not soon modified, may get us in trouble with explorers, developers, and tourists from other worlds, those nonhuman entrepreneurs from deep space with whom our astroscientists are attempting, recklessly, to establish premature contact. Why should we assume that superior beings from a foreign galactic shore, if alerted to our existence, would treat us any better than we treat those in *our* power?)

In any case, the beauty and existence of the natural world should be sufficient justification in itself for saving it all. If this argument fails to interest the exploitative and cannot convince the indifferent, then we must appeal to deeper emotions than the ecophilosophical. We need an appeal to the Indian, to the Robin Hood, to the primordial in every woman, every man—in all who are still emotionally alive. Such an appeal exists; I formulate it in this manner:

The chief reason so many people are fleeing the cities at every opportunity to go tramping, canoeing, skiing into the wilds is that wilderness offers a taste of adventure, a chance for the rediscovery of our ancient, preagricultural, preindustrial freedom. Forest and desert, mountain and river, when ventured upon in primitive terms, allow us a sort of Proustian recapture, however superficial and brief, of the rich sensations of our former existence, our basic heritage of a million years of hunting, gathering, wandering. This elemental impulse still survives in our blood, nerves, dreams, and desires, suppressed but not destroyed by the mere five thousand years of agricultural serfdom, a mere two hundred years of industrial peonage, which culture has attempted to impose on what evolution designed as a feeling, thinking, liberty-loving animal. I say culture, not civilization; civilization remains the ideal, an integrated realization of our intellectual, emotional, and physical gifts which humankind as a whole has nowhere yet attained.

The modern urban-industrial world—like the feudal world—offers adventure and freedom to a certain elite, the aristocracy of our time: to the rich, to the scientist, the star athlete, the big-time entertainer, the techno-warrior, the artist *arrivé,* the successful politician, a few others. But most, the overwhelming majority, seem condemned to the role of spectators, servitors, dependent consumers. Consider our politics, for example: the right to choose once every two or four years between Party A and Party B, Candidate C and Candidate D is a pitiful gesture in the exercise of freedom, hardly deserving of the name of citizenship.

But one exception remains to the iron rule of oligarchy. At least in America one relic of our ancient and rightful liberty has survived. And that is—a walk into the Big Woods; a journey on foot into the uninhabited interior; a voyage down the river of no return. Hunters, fishermen, hikers, climbers, white-water boatmen, red-rock explorers know what I mean. In America at least this kind of experience remains open and available to all, democratic. Little or no training is required, very little special equipment, no certification of privilege. All that is needed is normal health, the will to do it, and a modicum of courage.

It is my fear that if we allow the freedom of the hills and the last of the wilderness to be taken from us, then the very idea of freedom may die with it.

Thus I refute René Dubos. Ever so gently.

PART III

Places and Rivers

9

Running the San Juan

Bluff, Utah

Not another river trip? Yes. This time it's the San Juan in southeast Utah. We have twenty plastic rowboats, the kind known as Sportyaks, lined up on the beach, plus two rubber support rafts. Since this is a commercial tour, outfitted by Wild & Scenic Expeditions, Flagstaff, Arizona, we have three paid professional river guides with us, plus two cook's helpers and swampers, and myself; I have been invited along in the capacity of "wilderness philosopher." The pay is not very good—nothing—but it's a good job. As near as I can figure out I am not expected to do anything but look wise, keep quiet, and stay out of the way. I accept.

My daughter Susie, age twelve and three-quarters now, is coming with us. Not her first river trip—she rode the Green through Desolation Canyon last year—but the first in which she will be in sole charge of a skiff, a Sportyak II, all her own. She is elated by this advancement and understandably excited. She packs her waterproof ammo can and her waterproof river bags with care, secures them inside her boat with line and the proper half hitches, and fastens on her Mae West life jacket.

Head boatman and trip leader Randy Tate assembles the customers and gives the customary prelaunch lecture: how to handle the Sportyak, the rudiments of rowing, the push, the pull, the ferry, the pivot-turn. He demonstrates the right way to don and adjust the life jacket. Very important; the San Juan is the fastest major stream in the United States, dropping an average of eight feet per mile over the eighty-four miles of our projected journey. He talks, at length, about the "Groover," the camp toilet, a device and subject of great interest to everybody or nearly everybody. He concludes his talk by stressing the importance of keeping baggage firmly lashed to one's boat; in case of a flip or upset, the loss of sleeping bag or food or other gear could be the source of much distress.

We customers and philosophers listen to it all; though some of us have heard the lecture already, we are engaged as before by Randy's wit and charm. He likes to talk and he does it well, with authority. He's an attractive man, about thirty, brown, muscular and athletic, with sandy hair and beard, intelligent eyes, and a small gem of turquoise set in the lobe of his right ear—the Californian touch, although he has lived in Utah now for several years, wintering at Snowbird near Salt Lake City, summering on the Utah rivers.

Randy's fiancée, Marilyn Rivas, stands nearby. She too is a professional river guide, a member of our crew. A slender woman, with long flowing brown hair and warm brown eyes, she moves with the grace of a dancer.

The third guide is Gary "Silvertip" George, a native Utahn and "wild Mormon," as he calls himself, who stays mostly in the background, smoking his hand-rolled Bugler cigarettes and puttering about on the big raft with his dog Teddy. Gary is both a boatman and a cowboy, equally at home on the rivers or on the range, as familiar with oars and rapids as with horses and cattle. His dog is a good mutt, well behaved and alert, but with a wary, haunted look in the eyes; Teddy once spent four days and nights in a #5 coyote trap and has the stump of one hind foot to show for it. Knowing his story, you are not tempted to call him Hopalong. Teddy sleeps at his master's feet every night and rides the raft through the rapids by day—with ease, with nonchalance.

We put in, push off, row into the current. The San Juan is a muddy brown, cool but not cold on this day in June, fast but not high: it's been a dry winter in the San Juan Mountains in Colorado, the river's source. The water hisses past the mud banks, swirls toward the main channel, and rolls under the blue sky toward the Sea of Cortez and the Pacific, the "cold mad faery father," which it will never reach. Like many rivers these days the San Juan is bound for practical ends, condemned by industrial agriculture to expire in a thousand irrigation ditches, transmogrified from living river into iceberg lettuce, square tomatoes, celery, onions, Swiss chard, and radishes. Not an entirely unworthy end, I suppose, since we Americans do like to eat and God only knows there are so *many* of us, but—it makes me sad. If I think about it. Like fish, chickens, cows, pigs, and lambs, the rivers too are penned and domesticated and diverted through manifold ingenious ways—some which will not bear witnessing or thinking about—into the bottomless gut of the ever-expanding economy. There must be, somewhere, good reasons for our collective gluttony, but if there is a Judgment Day and a God of justice we humans are going to have much to answer for. If I were a good Christian I would dread that day.

Don't think about it. Nobody else does. Except animal liberationists. And vegetarians—those murderers of zucchini! those bean sprout killers!

Randy takes the lead in the smaller, fifteen-foot rubber raft, looking back anxiously at the twenty bright orange rowboats bobbing behind in a long, wavering, straggly line stretched over a quarter-mile of river. The Tupperware navy. I'm in the middle—

plastic man in a plastic boat—trying to keep my daughter in view. She seems so small in her seven-foot Sportyak; only her straw bonnet shows, and her bare arms rotating the oars with a regular and expert beat. Like a pro, like a true-born river rat. Only her second float trip and she's addicted already, hooked like a trout on the lure of flowing water. May she never run out of rivers.

Far in the rear, as planned, Gary George, with Teddy for company, rows the eighteen-foot raft. He is the sweep man, meant to pick up the pieces and gather in the strays if anything goes wrong.

I'm rowing a Sportyak III, eight feet long. Like the others, it's made of a tough and durable orange plastic, a double-hull construction partially filled with foam, "virtually" unsinkable. I can see by the dents in the gunwales that it's been bounced off a few rocks. One oar is wrapped with duct tape but seems sturdy enough; I have a spare oar slung to the side. Weighing about fifty pounds, this ridiculous-looking little toy boat can carry up to four hundred pounds. It is highly buoyant, riding the top of the waves, and easy to handle; with one cross stroke of the oars I can turn it 180 degrees. The Sportyak does not have the elegance and beauty of a dory, or the utility of a rubber raft, but—it's workable. A river trip in Sportyaks is the only kind of commercial tour that offers the passengers an opportunity to fully participate in the delights and hazards of wild-river boating.

An old-time river runner named Dock Marston, I recall, went down through the Grand Canyon in a Sportyak. At low water levels, to be sure. And only once. But he did it. One of these days . . .

Floating backward, looking upstream (the déjà view), I see the green cottonwoods of Sand Island wheeling slowly out of sight around the river's bend. No return. The temperature on shore was in the nineties, but here on the river the heat seems tolerable, even pleasant, and if it were not I could easily make it so by pouring a little water over my head and shirt.

At any minute now, among the veteran boaters, the water battles will begin. My Susie is one of the worst of the troublemakers. But I also have to keep an eye on Scott Frezza, a young fellow from Philadelphia, and on Berna Hahn, the glamour girl from San Diego, and on Jim Ferrigan, the gentleman from San Francisco, and on Honest Bob Reeve, a car salesman from Michigan. Nor do I like the sly smile on the face of Marilyn Rivas. In fact you can't trust any of these Sportyak types, they're all inclined to mischief. I pull my big hat down low over my eyes, hoping they won't see me. Like any honest riverman, I detest getting wet. But I've got my bailing bucket close at hand and full of water, ready for action if an aggressor strikes.

Scott comes gliding near, rowing a bit faster than necessary. He pretends to be looking at the scenery but has something—probably his bailer—clutched between his knees. As he comes alongside, starting to pass, I empty my gallon of muddy water down the neck of his shirt.

The battle immediately becomes general. Through waves of flying water I hear shouts and screams, see my daughter jumping out of her boat—bailer in hand—and into the river. Ferrigan shouts, "Stand by to repel boarders!" amid the splash and crash of bodies falling overboard. I am besieged by Scott on the portside and his girl friend Lynne on the other, both of them hurling water by the bucketful into my face. Randy stands on his raft fighting off two or three Sportyakkers circling round him like Indians. Within minutes everybody but Silvertip and his dog Teddy, far in the rear, is soaked to the socks. The battle fades, the swimmers struggle back into their boats. The sun blazes down and we begin at once to dry out; the evaporative cooling effect, in this intense heat, is doubly refreshing.

Thus we while away the time while drifting at the rate of seven or eight miles per hour toward the Raplee Anticline and the first gorge through the world of rock. Rock the color of rusted iron, rock the color of sand, rock that resembles the formal patterns of a Navajo rug. Old stuff to my unjaded eyes and always new. But in quirky ways. After thirty-five years of contemplating this bizarre landscape I can still find no human significance in it and remain emotionally unmoved—though intellectually persuaded—by the geologists' involved theories. What do I care whether these cliffs and buttes and clines, these synclines, anticlines, and monoclines have been here a billion years or only for a geological moment? Deep time is too shallow for me, about as interesting as charts in a textbook. What matters is the strange, mysterious, overwhelming truth that *we* are *here now,* in this magnificent place, and never will know why. Or why not.

The cool water flows between my fingers. My kid-daughter plies her oars three boat lengths ahead, serenely delighted by everything. My friends lie sprawled on their boats beyond, floating and sunning and dreaming. The fiery sun beams down. A great blue heron sails ahead. A beaver noses upstream close to the willow banks. Three black ravens yawp at us from the crags above and Jim Ferrigan yawps back at them, setting off a lengthy and repetitive dialogue. The crystalline blue dome of the sky turns with us, turning, still turning. And the fiery sun beams through it.

We go ashore to inspect some petroglyphs and the cliff-bound ruins of an Anasazi masonry village. The Ancient Ones were here, of course, until eight hundred years ago, tilling their fields of maize, squash, beans, and melons on the river bottoms, and whiling away the ample leisure of *their* hot afternoons in the making of pottery—the fragments are everywhere—and the chipping of arrowheads, the painting and carving of pictures on the panels of the canyon wall. They too had their scientific explanations for everything, no more and no less mythical than ours will appear to our descendants a thousand years from now. The ladies ground corn with mortar and pestle, the naked gentlemen convened in sacred committee meetings down in the kivas, smoking their sacred joints, and the swarms of children romped in the river, climbed the stony walls, chased lizards, and tormented the village dogs. I can hear the children shouting even now.

And then one day they all left. Departed. *Vanished.*

The world dissolves around us, hour by hour. Whole ranges of mountains come and go, mumbling of tectonic vertigo. Nothing endures, everything changes, and all remains the same.

I could be wrong about this.

We stop again, farther downriver, to climb the old Mormon

wagon trail that leads around the base and over the hump of a giant monocline known as Comb Ridge. In 1879 a party of pioneers—men, women, children, babies—left the town of Escalante in south-central Utah to establish, under orders from Brigham Young, a new settlement at the site of Bluff in extreme southeastern Utah. After six months of toil and travel, almost within sight of their goal, they came up against this five-hundred-foot-high sandstone barrier that reaches unbroken for fifty miles from the Abajo Mountains to the river. There is no pass, no gap, no natural passageway through it that is accessible to livestock and wagons. Therefore they forced a way through the rock with hammer and drill steel and blasting powder, and constructed a crude track up which their wagons could be hauled. The track is still here, modified by weather and erosion, impassable now even to a Jeep with four-wheel drive. Near the summit we find an inscription in the rock:

Oh God
We Thank Thee

Four years after their arrival the Mormons abandoned their mission at Bluff. No one could make a living there. The climate was too dry for farming, the Indians were troublesome, and the San Juan River, always flooding and then receding, filled their irrigation ditches with sand. Bluff was revived later by the cattle business and survives today on tourism, mining, and the sale of alcoholic beverages to the Navajo Nation.

We make Camp One by midafternoon. Jim Ferrigan, master flagman, designer and retailer of flags, plants a twelve-foot pole in the beach and hoists a black banner with a strange device: one red monkey wrench. The lords of misrule are here. Later that evening, joining the circle around the campfire, he tells a long shaggy story which begins, "Is it true that in a clearing somewhere deep in Africa, Tarzan paints white stripes on black zebras, black stripes on white zebras, and black and white stripes on plain zebras? And if so, why?" The answer comes half an hour later: "Yes. Tarzan stripes forever."

Birds sing in the gray dawn. Off in the brush the pheasants—chukar—are cackling. A lean and hungry coyote stalks through camp, weaving among the sleeping humans on the beach. Teddy growls a warning; the coyote trots away, stopping now and then to look back over one gaunt hip. Teddy goes back to sleep.

Rising early, I step to the river's edge. A small beaver swims toward me, within a foot of the bank, only its nose showing, followed by a slender wake. The beaver seems unaware of me. I freeze, watching. The beaver swims by, goes under the first raft floating on the water, under the second, and right past the nose of Teddy, who is sleeping with his head twelve inches from the bank. The dog fails to notice. The beaver swims steadily on, direct and purposeful.

The penitents from last night's party sag around the fire, red-eyed, hungover, sipping hot coffee. Kevin Briggs, a black-bearded young literary scholar, also from San Francisco, chants his morning pledge, paraphrasing Chief Joseph:

"From where the sun rises and the river now runs, I will drink no more forever. . . ."

This pledge like most pledges is guaranteed good for at least six hours.

Ferrigan arrives, demanding coffee, and immediately begins a new story: "Three hippies are discussing the meaning of Easter. . ."

We clamber into Sportyaks and hit the river. We float through the ancient cut in the anticline, through the great up-warping of the earth's crust. Here we see not sandstone but cliffs of pink and gray limestone rising in tiers, benches, and ledges toward the crest. The walls of this canyon resemble the interior of a grotesquely oversized Roman Colosseum, the seating arrangements designed for patrons fifty feet tall. Along shore and in the river are fallen chunks and slabs from the walls, boulders of blue-gray limestone inset with fossil crinoids and brachiopods.

We approach the fine white noise of troubled waters. The first rapids. We ride through in style. Nobody flips a boat. Even the rankest beginners make it look easy. The old-timers watch with mixed amusement and chagrin; what's the pleasure in feeling superior if you're not?

That was Four Foot Rapids, where the river drops four feet over a length of fifty yards. Next we come to Eight Foot Rapids. We beach our boats on shore above the rapids and walk close to plot a course through the waves, suckholes, and rocks. Nothing difficult, really. Back to the boats. We launch. I follow Susie through the big waves, we ship a little water, but have no trouble. She maneuvers her Sportyak like an expert, gliding into the center of the tongue, facing the waves, pushing over them, pulling away from the rocks, straightening into the glittering riffles in the tail of the rapids.

When in doubt, straighten out, that's the boatman's motto. Never broach on a rock. Always face the danger. Keep a three-boat interval between your own boat and the boat ahead. Would never do to tangle oars in the middle of a rapid. And watch that downstream oar—don't crab it on a hidden rock. Avoid the big holes if possible or, what the hell, go for the gusto and run right through them. But maintain momentum—if you get caught in a keeper you're in trouble. Watch the bubbles and the drift, follow the current, look for sandbars and gravel shallows, read the river. Read the river like a book. And if still in doubt—?

Jump out. Stay home. Read a book.

We pause on a beach for lunch. The air quivers with heat, with albedo reflectivity from the radiant canyon walls. Must be close to a hundred degrees in the shade and the sand is much hotter than that. Gary unloads the cooler, the crowd goes for the drinking water and the Tang. The hardcases among us snap the tabs from cans of beer, kept cool like catfish in gunny sacks trailed in the river. *Fssst!* The others stare. Impossible to muffle that sudden release of CO_2 under pressure, the conspicuous *pop!* Sounds like a grenade attack. *Incoming!* Nobody here flinches but everyone knows who is drinking the beer. And who's been hoarding it. Would be helpful if some clever lad invented a more discreet, a

more genteel mode of opening beer cans. A soft, susurrant, suspir-
ing sort of . . . *s i g h* . . . might serve nicely. A sound that could
pass, let us say, for the relaxed, simple, artless fart of a duchess. Ingenuous. But our technology continues to lag behind genuine
human needs.

Onward. On through the gorge. On down the river. How
come it's always *down* the river, never up? A good question, and I
am willing to offer an answer. The answer is that some do go up
the river. In July 1960 a New Zealander named Jon Hamilton
drove a high-powered jet boat from Lake Mead upriver through
and over Lava Falls and the other great cataracts of Grand Canyon all the way to Lee's Ferry, the usual put-in point for a Grand
Canyon voyage. His was the only successful uprun of the Canyon;
other attempts had been made, and one jet boat was lost at Grape-
vine Rapid. The Park Service forbade upriver runs thereafter. Too
much downriver traffic.

Hamilton's stunt was impressive but I am more impressed by
Bert Loper, one of the pioneer river runners, who *rowed* a boat,
alone, not once but several times, 150 miles upriver from Lee's
Ferry through Glen Canyon to his river home near Hall's Crossing
on the Colorado. Now that was not a stunt but a feat, an achievement, a labor of oarpower, finesse, and love.

And no man, or woman either, ever loved the river more than
Bert Loper. In 1949 he took his final voyage—the last of hundreds—down the river and died while running 24½ Mile Rapid in
Marble Gorge. His wrecked boat was found in an eddy a few miles
downriver. His body was not found. Bert Loper was seventy-nine
years old at the time of his death.

We emerge from the anticline. Mexican Hat appears, a
mighty slab of sandstone resting like a sombrero on a dark, head-
like pedestal. A few miles farther and we come to the original
hamlet of Mexican Hat itself: the highway bridge across the river,
a gas station, café, motel, and picnic supply store. Nothing more
here, although there is a post office and other establishments a
quarter-mile up the highway. We stop to replenish the beer supply.
Last Chance Oasis. Salvation Station. There will be nothing more

in the grim and thirsty wilderness ahead. The boys come stumbling and sweating down the dusty road through transparent waves of heat, shouldering their cases of Budweiser, Millers, Olympia, Michelob, and the sweet green Coors. Six cases of angel piss. Everybody knows there's hardly a decent beer, aside from homebrew, made in the United States anymore. The last good American beer I ever tasted was Iron City Pilsener, brewed in Pittsburgh. The death of local breweries was the death of good beer. Although, by general agreement, some American beers are worse than the mediocre norm. At a ballgame in Tucson—Toros leading Dukes 3–1 in the fourth—I called down to the vendor for more beer. The boy looked in his bucket, shouted back, "Sorry, sir, all I got left is Schlitz."

As I always say, capitalism sounds good in theory but it just doesn't work.

We plunge at once into a new canyon, the beginning of the Gooseneck meanders, leaving Mexican Hat out of sight out of mind in an instant. The river rushes down into the limestone bowels of the Monument Upwarp, heedless of the ignominious fate that awaits sixty miles ahead, the gentle commergence of this mad stream with the bland, soft, clear, stagnant reservoir of Lake Powell. Better known as Lake Foul, or Government Sump, or the Gangrene Lagoon, or Glen Canyon National Recreation Slum, property of the Del Webb Corporation, Inc. We never give it a thought.

I think instead of my previous journey down this river, two years before, in a cold rainy week in March. The river was high then, surging with power, and the banks were strewn with giant cakes of ice coated with frozen mud. We read the river with great interest then, you can bet your life on it. We wore rain suits or wet suits—hypothermia was only minutes away without such protection. And one poor devil did flip his boat, submerged himself in the icy river. We rushed him onshore, stripped him, wrapped him in an unzipped sleeping bag, built a big fire. The man came out of it well, although, as he admitted, his bones stayed cold for the next three days.

But now in June it's quite different. Making camp Number Two in late afternoon, just below another rapid, some of us leave our boats and walk upshore—wearing life jackets—to a point above the rapid, wade into the river, and go bobbing like corks down over the big waves. This is the way to truly feel and know the power of a fast river. Facing downstream, feet and legs lifted to act as shock absorbers in case you hit a rock, guarding your tailbone, you flounder into the current and are suddenly, helplessly swept away. The waves soar above your head, blotting out the sun. You gasp for air just before the water wallops you in the face, rise into the light at the crest of the wave, and descend like a duck into the next trough. Cheap thrills.

We ride to the bottom of the rapid, backstroke hard out of the current and into the peaceful eddy at the beach.

A few go trotting up the beach and over the boulders for a second body-run, my daughter Susie among them. I still get nightmares when I recall that day last year, on the Green River in Desolation Canyon, when we discovered that Susie's life jacket had a pinhole in it. Swimming the rapids nearly every day, she came out of the tail of one choking and gurgling and blue in the face. She complained that her life jacket seemed too heavy, that it was taking her through rather than over the waves. Checking it, we found that one of the four kapok flotation pads in front had somehow been punctured, probably by cactus, had soaked up water and turned hard as a stone. Susie was wearing what river folk call a sinker.

Ferrigan the Flagman sets two driftwood poles in the beach this evening. Up the first he runs the expedition flag, the one we've seen before. Kevin Briggs makes a bugle of his fist, playing "Salute to the Colors." On the second pole Ferrigan raises another exotic totem, a dark sun edged in gold on a field of royal blue. The meaning? He shrugs: "A literary allusion." Beer cans pop like pineapples; we salute the flag-maker. The two flags whip smartly in the evening breeze.

How to run this rapid. Randy Tate kneels on the sand, smooths it off, makes a diagram. This is the wall on the outside of the bend. This is the first rock. This is the big rock and the hole below it. This is the shoals beyond. This is the beach below. He draws his pliers from their holster on his belt and sets them on the sand at the head of the pictured rapid. The pincer end stands for the bow of your Sportyak, the handles for the stern. Okay. You push into the center of the tongue, stern foremost, facing downstream. (In any rowboat the oarsman faces the stern, his back to the bow.) You go down the tongue, ferry right (across current) facing the wall, follow wall around bend, go right of first rock, let current bear you left of big rock and suckhole, then go right of shoals and pull left to the beach. Everybody get it?

Everyone but Susie nods. We know that once in those heavy waters we'll forget the plan; some of those waves you can't even see over anyway. Susie plays with a twig, drawing her own pictures in the sand.

Susie? says Randy. She fails to hear him. Earth to Susie, Randy says. She looks at him. You get the plan? he says.

Got it, she says.

Good, he says, smiling at her. You follow me and go where I go.

We run the rapid. Only one boat flips, and it isn't Susie. Nobody hurt, no baggage lost. Though the river is fast the rapids are easy, if always unpredictable.

I find and mount a horse's skull on the bow of my Sportyak. The toothy grin bodes well for all.

We see a white egret. Another blue heron. Beaver, buzzards, and bullfrogs. White clouds passing beyond remote red walls.

From deep in the entrenched meanders of the endless Goosenecks, looking upriver, I catch a glimpse of Muley Point on the rim of Cedar Mesa, three thousand feet above.

We round Mendenhall Bend, where the river winds eight linear miles to advance one-half mile on the map. On the neck of the stone goose is a little stone cabin, built by a gold prospector named Mendenhall eighty years ago. Nobody lives there now.

Looking at petroglyphs on a rosy mural wall, I think of the legend of Kokopelli, the hunch-backed flute player of the Anasazi, who visited—when the men were away at war—all the villages of Indian America, from the Yukon to Tierra del Fuego, and left behind a spawn of syphilitic mutants. What is the secret meaning of that story?

Drifting close to a cranny in the vertical canyon façade, not rowing, half asleep in the heat and the shade of my hat, I see a sleek little garter snake coiled beneath the broad leaves and coarse white wilted flowers of a sacred datura. The snake is watching me as I flow slowly, silently by. How did it get there? I stare at the snake. The snake stares at me. Drops of water fall one by one from the blades of my motionless oars.

We stop one morning, deep in the canyon, to climb the Honaker Trail, built in 1904 by another gold seeker. Henry Honaker, like others, thought he could make a fortune in placer gold from the San Juan. The gold was here but of so fine and floury a grade that it proved more trouble to sift out of the sand than the gold would pay. He recovered $3,000 worth and, like Mendenhall, gave up on it and went away. But his trail, a remarkable job of doughty determined pick-and-shovel engineering is still in place; you could take a horse over it, probably, if you blindfolded the horse. It does traverse some breathtaking ledges. One-third of the way up one of our party succumbs suddenly to acrophobia. She stops and presses her back to the wall, staring down at the river four hundred feet below, chewing on the knuckles of both hands. She cannot go forward, she cannot go back, she cannot move. A member of the crew consoles and comforts her, as the rest of us pass blithely on, and leads her patiently back down to the beach.

We climb to a projecting ledge of rotten limestone called Horn Point, twelve hundred feet above the river. The ledge is ten feet broad and thirty long, tapering to nothing. To reach the extreme edge—Acrophobe Point—you step across a crevice only three feet wide but a hundred deep; enough to make one pause. From the edge we look down almost directly on the river and our bright little orange skiffs lined up like toys on the sand. We can see Kevin Briggs lying there, sleeping another one off. Perhaps we should drop a few boulders down his way, wake him up, make sure he's all right?

That suggestion is tabled but the urge to violence and destruction on the part of some cannot be wholly suppressed. One member of our party, followed soon by two others, leads a scramble across loose talus to a better promontory upriver. There they sweat and grunt for a while until they succeed in dislodging a half-ton block of limestone; they nudge it off the brink, it falls, revolving lazily in space, and explodes on impact far below. The boulder-size fragments bounce on toward the river and splash into the water. There is a cheer from the spectators, followed soon by reverberations from below. The sound is like that of distant artillery, echoed by further salvos from the cliffs across the canyon.

We roll a few more but the results are the same: a satisfying drop, a pleasing detonation, but the disappointing fragmentation at the terminus of the fall. This cheap sedimentary rock never was much good.

Downstream. In the morning sunlight the silt-loaded San Juan looks like red-eye gravy. In the shade it takes on a bluish, metallic sheen. In the afternoon, squinting toward the sun, floating into the wind, my eyes two feet above the surface of the water, I see the river as a desert Congo with golden scales.

The wind dies away. In the glassy, smooth, pooled water above Government Rapids, looking down at my hand in the stream and at three willow leaves floating nearby, all of them, relative to my boat, quite motionless, my impression is one of perfect stillness. An absolute and perfect stasis. And then I raise my eyes and see the hurried shore of the river, the willow and tamarisk and boulders rushing past.

Sue Bennett, a professional photographer, sits in the stern of Marilyn's boat, a camera in her hands, facing Marilyn as the latter guides her Sportyak over the waves and among the rocks of the rapid. Miss Bennett is making a photo-essay on "Women of the River." Marilyn Rivas, boatperson first class, performs her usual perfect run.

Berna Hahn overturns in this one, hangs onto her boat

through the tail of the rapid, gets it righted by herself and climbs inboard. The oars are still in place, attached to the oarlocks, but she sits in water up to her waist. She starts bailing.

Mike White, a customer from Connecticut, lies in his boat almost flat on his back, gazing up at the sky and the canyon rims, while rowing placidly, gently, down the stream.

Bill Hunter, white-bearded old gent from Louisiana, comes gliding close to my boat. He has been on more river trips than any of us except the crew. As always he is smiling from ear to ear, the same expression of serene delight I see all day on the face of my Susie. We call him Happy Bill. Another anarchist.

"Bill," I say, "what are you so happy about?"

"Nothing in particular," he says. "Everything in general."

I know exactly what he means. The magic of a boat. The splendor of a flowing river. The freedom of the desert. But of course a happy man's true paradise is his own good nature.

We pass the mouth of John's Canyon, a hanging canyon, as Major John Wesley Powell would have labeled it; the pour-off is a limetone ledge fifty feet above the grade of the river. In a few thousand more years, perhaps, John's Canyon may corrade its way down to river level. Two years ago in March there was a double waterfall pouring from that ledge; this time barely a trickle.

We stop a few hours at Slickhorn Gulch for lunch and a swim in the deep clear cold pools near the entrance. I watch the beautiful swimmers, then climb a trail to an old drill site on the first big bench above the river. From there an antique wagon road, laboriously constructed by hand and powder, leads to the high country beyond. At the site are the ruins of a massive ore wagon, loops of rusty cable, a cast-iron centrifugal pump for drawing water from the pools below, and one disintegrating board shack. An iron casing stands up from the drill hole. Welded on it in figures of iron is the legend

DON DANVER'S NO. IX
NW ¼ NW ¼ Sect. 15
T 40 S R 16 E
067829

Which may be read: "Don Danver's Claim Number Nine, northwest quarter of the northwest quarter of Section 15, Township 40 South, Range 16 East, County Recorder's File Number 067829." There is no date but it must be fifty years old.

I consider the wreckage, the road, the work. So much back-breaking, heartbreaking labor—to what end? Why, in hope of riches and a life of pleasure, what else? And anyway, for something interesting to do.

Hey, Zeb, whatcha doin' this fall?

I dunno, Don, what're you doin'?

Oh, I dunno. Maybe build forty miles of road across the mesa and down over them cliffs to that there San Jew-ann River, drill a few holes, get rich, I dunno. Find some gold, oil, uranium. Wanta come along?

What the hell. Why not?

We go on through the rapids below the mouth of Slickhorn. The half-submerged boulders rush toward us through a glowing phosphorescence of turbulent waves; each rock reminds me of Captain Nemo's submarine *Nautilus* as he comes to ram another enemy ship. Death to all Sportyaks! I can hear the captain mutter, his lips twitching in a neurotic grimace (he resembles the actor James Mason). Afterward he seats himself at the grand pipe organ in the master saloon and, while drowning sailors float past his marine picture window, plays Bach's *Tocatta and Fugue in D Minor* in the manner of E. Power Biggs after a trying day at the tabernacle. A fierce, tortured compassion for all beings, especially himself, wracks Captain No-Man's tormented soul. He plays on and on, twenty thousand minor chords under the sea.

We camp this afternoon at the mouth of Grand Gulch. Camp Number Five—our last evening on the river. Seem to have missed a couple of camps somewhere. But here we are.

"Say," shouts Ferrigan, "anybody know what day it is?"

A customer checks his supradigital quartz crystal silicon-chip chronometer. "June fourteenth?"

"Right!" shouts Ferrigan. "Flag Day!" And as always a man

of generous, magnificent gestures, he opens his duffel and passes out crisp bold new boat-size American flags to everybody. To everyone but Susie. She swallows her disappointment as Ferrigan rummages through his bag. He emerges in a moment with another bigger flag, the gayest, loveliest flag I have ever seen, a rainbow flag with seven broad horizontal stripes: red, orange, yellow, green, light blue, dark blue, purple. He presents it, with a flourish, to Susannah.

"A flag for all people, all nations," he explains, "symbolizing the neutrality of the high seas, standing for international peace and brotherhood, based on a design first suggested by Thomas Paine in 1789." (A good year.)

Again he gropes through his magically bottomless bag. He comes up with the black and red of anarchy (it's a grand old flag), the blue and black literary standard, and another big flag, spanking bright and crackling fresh, the red, white, and blue of our United States. Kevin Briggs has been digging holes meanwhile, and setting driftwood staffs; in a moment the three big flags are run up their poles, the national flag on the right as etiquette requires (viewed from the river). Right on cue a stiff upcanyon wind blows in, the three flags unfurl and flutter bravely on our golden beach. The beer cans go *pop!* like kraut potato mashers and we all hoist a salute to James Ferrigan, gentleman, historian, river rat, raconteur, and master flagman.

That night, over the driftwood fire, Ferrigan tells once more the story of Ned and Fred, the twin racehorses. It's a long story and a great one and I remember it all but the punch line.

Last day on the river. A river slowing down, losing force, as it sinks toward the reservoir. We pass the narrow opening of Steer Gulch and its tributary Whirlwind Draw. Alluring side canyons but there is no time to stop and explore. Ann Zwinger describes them both, as well as John's Canyon, Slickhorn, and Grand Gulch, in her excellent book *Wind in the Rock*. Someday I'll get in there.

But we must row on. If a headwind comes up now we're in for a long and dreary ordeal, rowing across flat water to our takeout

point at Clay Hills Crossing. (Where the Indians crossed the river.)
I come alongside Susie, who rows slow but straight, steady as she
goes. She gives me a cheerful smile but looks a trifle weary. Her
eyes, despite the straw hat, are red from the glare of sky and water;
her nose is peeling, her lips chapped, her hands sore and cracked
from five days of sun, water, mud, and rowing.

"Susie," I say, "don't you wish this river went on forever? An
endless river through new and always grander canyons?"

"Not really," she says.

The canyon walls are coming down, dipping into the lowlands
ahead. Looking over my shoulder I can see the Clay Hills not more
than two miles westward. The crossing and the road should be
within half a mile. We're getting there. We pause for a drink of
water—no more beer—and row again.

The pale sandstone bluffs come down to the water's edge;
there is no shore. We're on the reservoir. I can see the high water-
line on the rock: the Lake Powell Bathtub Ring. We approach a
lean and lanky fellow squatting on a ledge close to the water. He's
got a fishing pole beside him, a small fire going, a coffeepot, two
catfish frying in a skillet. I row in close.

"Hello there."

"Howdy."

"How's the fishing?"

"Not half bad."

"Where's the crossing?"

"You're there."

"Yeah? Where's the road?"

"About ten feet below you."

"Well, I'll be damned. Two years ago it all looked different."

"Well," he says, "two years ago there was still a river here."

"Well, I'll be damned."

"Yeah," he says, "it sure is."

10

~~~~~~

In the Canyon

Those who love it call it "The Canyon"—*the* canyon—as if there were no other such topographic feature on the earth's face. But we know better. There is Hell's Canyon in Idaho and Barranca del Cobre in Sonora, each of which may be deeper than Arizona's Grand Canyon, when measured in a certain way, from certain points. The Barranca, including its branches, is certainly much longer. There must surely be canyons coming off the Andes Mountains in South America, and off the Himalayas in central Asia, which are as long and as deep and perhaps as dramatic as Grand Canyon. The photo-astronomers have found a canyon on Mars said to be twice as deep as our local ravine in northern Arizona. I hope to mosey about in that Martian one someday, when the shuttle fare is reasonable, and if I keep hanging around long enough. But none of this world's great canyons, nor that on Mars, much resembles the Grand Canyon of the Colorado. Or even, so far as I have been able to ascertain, even slightly resembles it. Ronald Reagan would have been speaking truly if he had said, "See one Grand Canyon and you've seen them all."

Meanwhile, there it is, in my own backyard, waiting for me all these millions of years—the Canyon. I am tempted to write "my canyon," so possessive can that place make one feel. But the Canyon is not mine, nor anyone's; the Canyon belongs to all—and to no one. The Canyon belongs to itself, to the world, to God, for whatever those grand abstractions are worth. And so far as the term "possession" has meaning, it would be more accurate to say that the Canyon possesses us. Those who love it are possessed by it. We belong to the Canyon, having known it a little and loved it too much, as indeed all those who love the land, who love the earth, belong to it and consign themselves to it and finally return to it.

"The land was ours," said Robert Frost, "before we were the land's." But that attitude is changing. Must change. The entrepreneurs and the engineers must learn a new vocabulary of values. Not for the earth's sake—the earth will outlast human folly—but for our own.

To know the Canyon is to love it? Not necessarily. Crawling up the Tanner Trail some moonlight night in August, without food or water, you will hate the Canyon. Bitterly. That pale rim so far above, higher than five Empire State Buildings piled one upon another, seems inaccessible as Heaven, remote as salvation. But if you survive, if you make it, you learn to despise not the Canyon but your own fear and foolishness, in being unprepared, and return again and again, ready to risk everything for one more intimate encounter with the most sublime place on the planet. Who could ask for a finer place than our Canyon in which to taste life deeply by risking life? By hanging it over the edge?

To die in the act of love—every lover's fondest fantasy. As to the truth of that, we can learn only once. The truth may be different from the fantasy. "Behind the tender neon," wrote Jack Kerouac, "stands a red brick wall." No doubt. And beyond the hallucinating purple deeps of the Grand Canyon waits . . . we don't know what. Hours of pain and despair, perhaps, lying in sand, on unyielding rock, under a craggy cliff dark and evil as Hell, where only the vultures and the beetles gather to comfort you.

Very likely. Even so I hope now, as I have always hoped, that my own last vision, through fading eyes, will not be a window in a strange room, nor even the face of friend or lover, but the spectacle of distant canyon walls, the profile of a mesa against the sky, the gleam of a river far below. Those are the things I want to take with me in my dying moments, if I too must die, and taking them with and within me, all the way, become a part of them.

But this is morbid, idle talk. Better to think DO NOT LITTER, neither the Canyon nor the trails, with gum wrappers, beer cans, emergency underwear, frazzled socks, or the bodies of worn-out decrepit useless literary romantics seeking a picturesque death with a view. Dead bodies sprawled along the Hermit Trail would soon become a public nuisance, leading to more Park Service regulations. PERMIT REQUIRED FOR DYING HERE. ADVANCE RESERVATIONS NECESSARY. Therefore let us be discreet, considerate of others, and do our untidy final business well away from any trail, on some little pinched-out deadend ledge where only the lizards will ever find you.

These suggestions are made as a public service, for it is true, as those who work at the Canyon know, that every year a number of folks come here to die. Most arrive with no such conscious purpose on their minds, fated to die by accident, as it were, but some, I suspect, do it by design. During each of the four seasons that I worked at Grand Canyon at least one human being disappeared. I mean—*disappeared*. Was never seen again.

Meanwhile, let us live and enjoy the Canyon, in moderate numbers and with some restraint. The Park Service, I am delighted to learn, has finally got around to a proposal to phase out the motorized boating traffic on the river, down through the living heart of the Canyon. A small step but a good and essential one. The next step should be the banning of motorized aircraft over and within the Canyon, especially those obnoxious air-tour services, and the helicopters that the Park Service itself is often guilty of employing for "administrative" and rescue operations.

Search and Rescue is itself a nuisance. Let each person who enters the Canyon, whether on foot, on mule, or by boat, clearly understand that some risk is involved, some rather elementary and fundamental risk, and that nothing can guarantee your safety but your own common sense. Nor even that. Nothing should be guaranteed. Nothing can be.

Some say we're loving the national parks to death. Maybe so. Therefore let us install a few simple screening devices, like a ten-mile walk to the Canyon's rim. Outlaw motorized traffic on the roads along the rim. Tear down the man-made structures that now clutter up the Bright Angel trailhead—the hotels and gas stations and laundromats and jails and administrative offices and visitor centers and curio shops and Native American dance studios and hospitals and residential quarters—remove that *dreck,* which has no business being in a national park anyway, and rebuild it, if it must be rebuilt, back toward Flagstaff, at least ten miles back in the woods, at the terminus of the highway, before a great steel barricade reading HUMAN BEINGS WELCOME; MACHINES KEEP OUT.

That should help.

Next: Glen Canyon Dam, upriver from our Canyon. Take care of it. How? We can leave that to the engineers. They built it, they can unbuild it. With the dam gone, we can save and restore the natural riverine ecology of the Canyon, bring back the great spring floods that used to flush out the channel every year, clear out the tamarisk, bring back the driftwood, rebuild the sand beaches (now being eroded away and not replaced), and make the river, as it used to be and should be, warm and violent and golden and full of catfish—*muy Colorado!* The red-brown god.

Fantasy, you say. Perhaps. But if we don't do it Nature will. In a few more centuries the dams will be filled with mud and sand, will become great waterfalls and then, as erosion does its work, will be reduced to polished stumps of concrete and re-bar, foaming rapids full of vee-waves and suckholes, a challenge to boat people, nothing more. Any river with the power to carve through the ancient limestones, granites, and schists of the Kaibab Plateau will have little trouble with the spongy cement deposited here, once upon a time, by some dimly remembered clan of ant-folk known as the Bureau of Reclamation.

Meanwhile—the Canyon is still here. A national and international treasure. Go down that river, get down those trails, and watch the flat-bellied water *nixies* playing under waterfalls. Behold the river roar among the basaltic fangs of Upset Rapids. See the blue and gold twilight walls soar above you, out of shadow into morning sunlight. Smell the old-time smell of river mud and cottonwood and willow. Hear the feral burros cough and bray as they chew the prickly pear down to bedrock and piss in the bighorns' scattered waterholes. (Shoot a few burros if you get the chance.)

We are so many, the Canyon is but one. We are so busy, the Canyon so passive and slow. But that too will eventually change. Order will be restored. Harmony and peace and the slow evolution of the eons will come back. Must come back. Pray for peace. Fight for peace. Peace be with you.

11

Down There in Sonora

Where is the true country of men?
—B. Traven,
The Death Ship

Starving cattle stumble across the cow-burnt range. Above the cattle the vultures swarm like flies, attracted by the sight and smell of dying meat. (Always, you see more vultures once you cross the border; where life is abundant and inexpensive, crowded and cheap, as in Mexico, or Egypt, or India, you find a thriving business among the scavengers of death.) Giant mule-ear jackrabbits leap from the cactus and hurl themselves like kamikaze heroes into the grille or under the wheels of your car. Racing over a Mexican highway, especially at night, the thump and crunch of impacted bodies becomes a sound as familiar as the mariachi music on the radio. Those fur-covered roads . . .

Mariachi—the sound of fever. Every song is based on the same phrase: *mi corazón.* My heart. Your heart. Lunacy under the Mexican moon. That crazy music of sunlight, and murder, dust and blood and drunkenness, love, anguish, hatred, honor, passion, fear, stupidity, but fueled on by an inexhaustible hunger for life. For more life. Never say *demasiado.* Never say *bastante.* There is never enough. There cannot be too much. Not down here where the Spanish melded with the Indians, where every cop has a bandit brother, where the cactus mountains meet the wrinkled blue sea. Where the basic insanity of Mexico, like a river dying on a delta, spends itself on the immensity and emptiness and mystic nothingness of the desert.

Sonora. Northwest Mexico. Land of the open-air beer joint and the shade-tree mechanic. More old cars upside down than right side up. On the outskirts of the town of Sonoita I saw once a solitary pig leaning out of the broken window of an abandoned 1947 Plymouth sedan. The pig watched me, with casual interest, as I drove by in my 1962 Dodge carry-all. Someday that pig, if it survives, will probably be living in this truck.

We drive through villages baking under a sun without mercy. No trees anywhere. The *campesinos* can't afford trees. They cut them down long ago. Streets without a single tree, yards and courtyards and fields without a blade of grass. Around every house, every building, lies a glittering field of broken glass, painful to the eyes. Though the barefoot kids, snot-nosed *muscositos,* dash across it without a moment's hesitation. Can an entire nation, even a poor one, take on the appearance of a garbage dump? Yes, easy, every yard, street, and roadside is littered with broken glass, rusted tin cans, shards of plastic and shreds of rope, rubber, paper. Laundry hangs out everywhere, providing the only shade. Why are poor folks always doing the laundry? Pride, I guess, and lots of children. On the west wall of the little *iglesia* in the hamlet of Cobabi, as on the four walls of the cathedral in Hermosillo, you may see these words stenciled on the plaster in whitewash and official lettering:

SE PROHIBE HACER AGUA AQUI!

It is forbidden to make water here. Nevertheless the smell of urine is acute. Pungent. Poignant. The whine of flies, those flies that swarm like microcosmic buzzards above each little pile of Mexican dung down in the alleyways, pervades the hot air with a vibration constant as the murmur of bees.

This is a country of quick, easy friendships, sworn in *cerveza* and tequila, sealed with dazzling smiles in faces the color of good saddle leather. *Muchachos! Compadre! Compañero de mi vida!* A friendship, a love, too deep for thought, transformed in an instant, by one careless word, into a sudden flashing hatred sharp and violent as the thrust—*chingazo!*—of a knife blade. Romantic Mexico . . . carefree colorful Sonora. . . . It looks like his real and final home to the average suicidal gringo motherfucker, drinking his way from cantina to cantina along the dusty roads toward a colorful carefree death in a ditch behind a sheet-iron whorehouse ten miles south of Tubutama.

Eastward stand the Sierra Madres. Those mother mountains again, riddled with old silver mines, inhabited by Indians who still refuse to wear pants, and carved by vigorous if intermittent rivers into canyons more extensive, perhaps deeper, and almost as precipitous as the Grand Canyon of the Colorado. This primitive country, little known, poorly mapped, is transected from Ciudad Chihuahua to the Gulf of California by one railway but not a single paved highway. A few Jeep and truck roads, rock here, hub-deep in dust there, wind into the mountains to lose themselves and the careless *turista* in a maze of tracks known only to local ranchers, lumbermen, miners.

Despite the great canyons, however, and waterfalls that plunge—when it rains—three thousand feet, and Indians whose culture has still not been completely broken, the Sierra Madre Occidentale is not on the whole a very attractive place. The mountains do not rise above ten thousand feet, there are no dramatic peaks, and the forests and benchlands are being exploited to the limit and beyond by the beef, mining, and timber industries, and by the urgent needs of a human population growing at the rate of 3.5 percent per year—a rate of increase greater than that of any

Asian or African nation, including India and Egypt. Mexico City will soon be the biggest city in the world. By the year 2000 the nation's population will have doubled. Nobody seems concerned. As a recent pope said, "Welcome to the banquet of life, my children." Eat hearty—if you can fight your way to the table.

When I find myself in Sonora, waking up off a dirt road deep in the cactus outback—how did I get here?—I veer toward the sea. I buzz through towns, stopping only for gas, beer, *bolitos*, fruit, avoid the cities entirely, and keep bearing westward. For the sea. We drive through the passes between desert hills, past one *ranchito abandonado* after another—crumbling adobe ruins in the scant shade of a dead cottonwood, dry well, broken-down windmill, hollow-log water trough full of sand and tumbleweed—until a change transforms the horizon, until the skyline beyond the bony peaks and ridges becomes a curving plane of blue melting in mist with the sky. Beyond the last of the coastal hills, we follow the forest of giant *cardón* cactus—bigger than saguaros—down to the beach and make camp behind the dunes, close to mesquite for firewood and within sight and sound and an easy walk of the restless waves.

No one lives here. Probably no one, white man or Indian, has ever lived here. This is an arid coast, a barren desert seashore, with no water available but that from the bitter, salty, snot-green, scrotum-tightening sea itself. When I come here I bring my own drinking water—five gallons, ten gallons, enough for a week or so. We live by beans, wine, green chiles, and bacon, as usual, and fish for yellowtail and triggerfish from a rocky spit, lose whole days wandering alone, like Robinson Crusoe, up and down the desolate beach. I inspect the driftwood, the castaway garbage from fishing boats, the dying jellyfish, the bluish bottles containing indecipherable messages, the shell and wrack and pelican skeletons. I watch the birds, the dolphins, and hope for sight of a pod of whales. Wading in the water, I glimpse stingrays scudding flat and ghostly across the rippled sand. Evenings I spend by a little bed of mesquite coals, under a growing moon, listening for coyote, horned owls, poorwills, things that go bump in the night. For magic. Witchcraft. Wizardry. And find it, too—all in my own head.

When the drinking water runs low, as it finally does, we tend to depart. Pack up our gear and steal away, back to the other world, out of the dream of desert and shore. That separate reality. The dream will not last long anyhow. Sooner or later the Mexicans, aided by hired experts and capital from their oil, from Japan and from the North, will find a cheap way to desalinate seawater, will line this empty coast with Cancuns, Vallartas, agribusiness Mexicalis, transforming the desert valleys between the mountains into truck farms, cement plants, commercial-industrial slums, making what is now rare and irreplaceable into a smog-veiled simulacrum of a thousand other places. Yes, the Mexicans have good reasons. They want to survive, as we do. Industrial development will defer the inevitable disaster, the needed revolution, for another ten years. Maybe for twenty or thirty. After that—*el diluvio.*

Back to the border. Back through the towns and cities packed with hungry people like myself, climbing over one another in the struggle for existence. I hear laughter, music, screams, and gunfire on the outskirts of Nogales but do not pause to investigate. I know what it looks like. I was a military cop in Naples, Italy. I've worked as a welfare caseworker in Brooklyn and Jersey City. I know a little of that world, having been there several times. Once was enough.

But there is no escaping it. The empire of industry and social combat closes around us. B. Traven said it right, I'm afraid, near the end of his novel *March to the Montería:*

"This is the world, muchachos. This is the real world, and you are in it."

12

Aravaipa Canyon

Southeast of Phoenix and northeast of Tucson, in the Pinal Mountains, is a short deep gorge called Aravaipa Canyon. It is among the few places in Arizona with a permanent stream of water and in popular estimation one of the most beautiful. I am giving away no secrets here: Aravaipa Canyon has long been well known to hikers, campers, horsemen, and hunters from the nearby cities. The federal Bureau of Land Management (BLM), charged with administration of the canyon, recently decreed it an official Primitive Area, thus guaranteeing its fame. Demand for enjoyment of the canyon is so great that the BLM has been obliged to institute a rationing program: no one camps here without a permit and only a limited number of such permits are issued.

Two friends and I took a walk into Aravaipa Canyon a few days ago. We walked because there is no road. There is hardly even a foot trail. Twelve miles long from end to end, the canyon is mostly occupied by the little river which gives it its name, and by stream banks piled with slabs of fallen rock from the cliffs above, the whole overgrown with cactus, trees, and riparian desert shrubbery.

Aravaipa is an Apache name (some say Pima, some say Papago) and the commonly accepted meaning is "laughing waters." The name fits. The stream is brisk, clear, about a foot deep at normal flow levels, churning its way around boulders, rippling over gravelbars, plunging into pools with bright and noisy vivacity. Schools of loach minnow, roundtail chub, spike dace, and Gila mudsuckers—rare and endemic species—slip and slither past your ankles as you wade into the current. The water is too warm to support trout or other varieties of what are called game fish; the fish here live out their lives undisturbed by anything more than horses' hooves and the sneaker-shod feet of hikers. (PLEASE DO NOT MOLEST THE FISH.)

The Apaches who gave the name to this water and this canyon are not around anymore. Most of that particular band—unarmed old men, women, children—huddled in a cave near the mouth of Aravaipa Canyon, were exterminated in the 1880s by a death squad of American pioneers, aided by Mexican and Papagos, from the nearby city of Tucson. The reason for this vigilante action is obscure (suspicion of murder and cattle stealing) but the results were clear. No more Apaches in Aravaipa Canyon. During pauses in the gunfire, as the pioneers reloaded their rifles, the surviving Indians could have heard the sound of laughing waters. One hundred and twenty-five were killed, the remainder relocated in the White Mountain Reservation to the northeast. Since then those people have given us no back talk at all.

Trudging upstream and over rocky little beaches, we are no more troubled by ancient history than are the mudsuckers in the pools. We prefer to enjoy the scenery. The stone walls stand up on both sides, twelve hundred feet high in the heart of the canyon. The rock is of volcanic origin, rosy-colored andesites and buff, golden, consolidated tuff. Cleavages and fractures across the face of the walls form perfect stairways and sometimes sloping ramps, slick as sidewalks. On the beaches lie obsidian boulders streaked with veins of quartzite and pegmatite.

The walls bristle with spiky rock gardens of formidable desert vegetation. Most prominent is the giant saguaro cactus, growing five to fifty feet tall out of crevices in the stone you might think could barely lodge a flower. The barrel cactus, with its pink fishhook thorns, thrives here on the sunny side; and clusters of hedgehog cactus, and prickly pear with names like clockface and cowstongue, have wedged roots into the rock. Since most of the wall is vertical, parallel to gravity, these plants grow first outward then upward, forming right-angled bends near the base. It looks difficult but they do it. They like it here.

Also present are tangles of buckhorn, staghorn, chainfruit, and teddybear cholla; the teddybear cholla is a cactus so thick with spines it glistens under the sun as if covered with fur. From more comfortable niches in the rock grow plants like the sotol, a thing with sawtooth leaves and a flower stalk ten feet tall. The agave, a type of lily, is even bigger, and its leaves are long, rigid, pointed like bayonets. Near the summit of the cliffs, where the moisture is insufficient to support cactus, we see gray-green streaks of lichen clinging to the stone like a mold.

The prospect at streamside is conventionally sylvan, restful to desert-weary eyes. Great cottonwoods and sycamores shade the creek's stony shores; when we're not wading in water we're wading through a crashing autumn debris of green-gold cottonwood and dusty-red sycamore leaves. Other trees flourish here—willow, salt cedar, alder, desert hackberry, and a kind of wild walnut. Cracked with stones, the nuts yield a sweet but frugal meat. At the water's edge is a nearly continuous growth of peppery-flavored watercress. The stagnant pools are full of algae; and small pale frogs, treefrogs, and leopard frogs, leap from the bank at our approach and dive into the water; they swim for the deeps with kicking legs, quick breaststrokes.

We pass shadowy, intriguing side canyons with names like Painted Cave (ancient pictographs), Iceberg (where the sun seldom shines), and Virgus (named in honor of himself by an early settler in the area). At midday we enter a further side canyon, one called Horsecamp, and linger here for a lunch of bread, cheese, and water. We contemplate what appears to be a bottomless pool.

The water in this pool has a dark clarity, like smoked glass, transparent but obscure. We see a waterlogged branch six feet down resting on a ledge but cannot see to the bottom. The water feels intensely cold to hand and foot; a few tadpoles have attached themselves to the stony rim of the pool just beneath the surface of the water. They are sluggish, barely animate. One waterbug, the kind called boatman, propels itself with limp oars down toward darkness when I extend my hand toward it.

Above the pool is a thirty-foot bluff of sheer, vesiculated, fine-grained, monolithic gray rock with a glossy chute carved down its face. Flash floods, pouring down that chute with driving force, must have drilled this basin in the rock below. The process would require a generous allowance of time—ten thousand, twenty thousand years—give or take a few thousand. Only a trickle of water from a ring of seeps enters the pool now, on this hot still blazing day in December. Feels like 80° F; a month from now it may be freezing; in June 110°. In the silence I hear the rasping chant of locusts—that universal lament for mortality and time—here in this canyon where winter seldom comes.

The black and bottomless pool gleams in the shining rock—a sinister paradox, to a fanciful mind. To any man of natural piety this pool, this place, this silence, would suggest reverence, even fear. But I'm an apostate Presbyterian from a long-ago Pennsylvania: I shuck my clothes, jump in, and touch bottom only ten feet down. Bedrock bottom, as I'd expected, and if any Grendels dwell in this inky pool they're not inclined to reveal themselves today.

We return to the Aravaipa. Halfway back to camp and the canyon entrance we pause to inspect a sycamore that seems to be embracing a boulder. The trunk of the tree has grown around the rock. Feeling the tree for better understanding, I hear a clatter of loose stones, look up, and see six, seven, eight bighorn sheep perched on the rimrock a hundred feet above us. Three rams, five ewes. They are browsing at the local salad bar—brittlebush, desert holly, bursage, and jojoba—aware of us but not alarmed. We watch them for a long time as they move casually along the rim and up a talus slope beyond, eating as they go, halting now and then to stare back at the humans staring up at them.

Once, years before, I had glimpsed a mountain lion in this canyon, following me through the twilight. It was the only mountain lion I had ever seen, so far, in the wild. I stopped, the big cat stopped, we peered at each other through the gloom. Mutual curiosity: I felt more wonder than fear. After a minute, or perhaps it was five minutes, I made a move to turn. The lion leaped up into the rocks and melted away.

We see no mountain lions this evening. Nor any of the local deer, either Sonoran whitetail or the desert mule deer, although the little heart-shaped tracks of the former are apparent in the sand. Javelina, or peccary, too, reside in this area; piglike animals with tusks, oversized heads, and tapering bodies, they roam the slopes and gulches in family bands (like the Apaches), living on roots, tubers, the innards of barrel cactus, on grubs, insects, and carrion. Omnivorous, like us, and equally playful, if not so dangerous. Any desert canyon with permanent water, like Aravaipa, will be as full of life as it is beautiful.

We stumble homeward over the stones and through the ankle-bone-chilling water. The winter day seems alarmingly short; it is.

We reach the mouth of the canyon and the old trail uphill to the roadhead in time to see the first stars come out. Barely in time. Nightfall is quick in this arid climate and the air feels already cold. But we have earned enough memories, stored enough mental-emotional images in our heads, from one brief day in Aravaipa Canyon, to enrich the urban days to come. As Thoreau found a universe in the woods around Concord, any person whose senses are alive can make a world of any natural place, however limited it might seem, on this subtle planet of ours.

"The world is big but it is comprehensible," says R. Buckminster Fuller. But it seems to me that the world is not nearly big enough and that any portion of its surface, left unpaved and alive, is infinitely rich in details and relationships, in wonder, beauty, mystery, comprehensible only in part. The very existence of existence is itself suggestive of the unknown—not a problem but a mystery.

We will never get to the end of it, never plumb the bottom of it, never know the whole of even so small and trivial and useless and precious a place as Aravaipa. Therein lies our redemption.

13

~~~~~~

Fool's Treasure

The approach to the old ghost town of Bodie, California, lies through some of the grandest scenery in the American West. My daughter Susie and I had come from the southeast, out of Nevada, across the great trench of Death Valley and north through Owens Valley—under the east wall of the High Sierra—to Mono Lake and the turnoff a few miles beyond. Here we left the paved highway for a thirteen-mile drive over one of the roughest *passable* dirt roads I've ever had the satisfaction of hating. I don't mind a true Jeep trail: parallel tracks winding through sand, climbing ledges of solid stone, skirting the edge of an abyss. But this is what they call, out West, an "improved" dirt road—that is, one straightened, widened, and scraped so often by bulldozers and graders that the dust is hub deep, the stones loose and hidden, the surface corrugated like a washboard. My little truck was rattling in every bolt and joint by the time we got there.

~~~~~~

But Bodie is worth it. We topped a pass on the south and drove down into a bowl in the sere brown desert hills. In the middle of this valley, straddling a narrow strip of green that is sometimes a flowing stream, are the remains of one of the West's most famous ghost towns.

Only the remains. Much of the original town, which housed twelve thousand people in the 1880s, was destroyed by a series of fires, the most recent in 1932. The last permanent inhabitants of Bodie then gave up—gave up the ghost—quit, shut down the school, the gas station, the general store, and left. The houses, cabins, shacks, stores, and other buildings that stand today make up only 5 percent of what once existed.

From a distance you might think Bodie still a plausible little country town. The buildings stand in scattered formation along the grid of streets. The mill, three stories high, where gold and silver ores were processed, has a functional appearance, with its tipples, smokestacks, and power-line poles still erect. But there is no activity, no traffic, no sign of smoke or dust, no hum of machinery. Like the remainder of the town, the mill is now a museum piece in an out-of-doors museum, preserved in arrested decay as a historic park by the State of California.

Quite properly, motorized traffic is not allowed within the present bounds of Bodie. Along with a half-dozen other tourists arriving that day, Susie and I leave our car in the lot at the outskirts of Bodie and proceed on foot, following one of the dirt streets that leads into the town. I almost wrote "into the heart of the town." But Bodie no longer has a heart. Nobody lives here but a couple of young park caretakers entrusted with the job of guarding the ruins from theft and vandalism.

There is much to protect, both within and without the brick, tongue-in-groove and board-and-batten walls of what once were private homes, saloons, workshops, a morgue, a firehouse, a hotel, a bank, a warehouse, a livery stable, a school, a jail . . . and others. Peering through the dusty glass of the windows, Susie and I see such things as a rusty typewriter, an antique piano, a pair of coffins (empty), tools, furniture, pots, pans, and horse collars hanging on spikes in a beam, and a thousand other nineteenth-century artifacts of wood and metal and leather and glass that must make the fingers of collectors tremble with desire. Most of these things, though well preserved by the arid climate, are covered with dust, in some cases draped with cobwebs. (The flies and spiders still live here.) Which is as it should be, as one would desire, in a ghost town.

Most of the buildings are locked, out of necessity. But two are open to the visiting public. The first is a little Methodist Church, built in 1878–79, abandoned in 1932. We enter and contemplate for a while the bare wooden pews, the two cast-iron heating stoves (one on each side of the ranked pews), a small foot-powered pipe organ like the one my mother used to own and play. The afternoon sunlight slants in through narrow, high, Gothic-pointed windows. On the wall above the pulpit, painted with gilt now flaking off, are the words PRAISE WAITETH FOR THEE, O GOD OF ZION. According to our guidebook (supplied by the State of California), there was once, hanging behind the pulpit, an oilcloth inscribed with the Ten Commandments, including the seventh, or is it the eighth: "Thou shalt not steal."

Susie and I stroll on down the quiet street. This being a weekday, there are few other tourists about. There are no commercial enterprises of any kind doing business here—no gas station, no hot dog stands, no curio shops—nor any form of official visitors' center. The caretakers (with their wives) live in two of the original Bodie homes, repaired and maintained but in no way—at least on the outside—modernized. We notice the immense stacks of stovewood by each house; winters are severe at this 8,500-foot elevation, with high winds, subzero temperatures and snowdrifts, so we are told, sometimes ten feet high.

We inspect the one other building where entry is allowed. This was once the home of a Mr. Dan MacDonald and family back in the 1880s. The dried-out wooden floors creak beneath us; the doorways are so low that I have to stoop to pass through. This house has four rooms—a parlor, a couple of bedrooms, a tiny kitchen—and, in the back, partially enclosed, a shed for the storage of firewood and next to the shed a pit toilet. All of the rooms seem badly proportioned to me—much too cramped for grown-up humans. But for Susie, my kid, the house is just right. I know well enough that the meat-eating Americans of a century ago were, on the average, no smaller than myself and my contemporaries. Bodie's miners built their houses small because they could not afford to build large.

The furnishings are meager as the rooms are small: wicker chairs, a shaky wooden table with oilcloth cover, toylike stoves of cast iron, faded wallpaper on the walls and ceiling. Somebody, probably Mrs. MacDonald, must have spent a lot of time chopping wood and splitting kindling for the little stoves.

We sit on the front steps and enjoy the October sun. Flies buzz in the background. In a half-acre vacant lot across the street, scattered in casual disarray, are a number of historic-looking wagons, two-wheel carts, steam engines, boilers, ore cars, and machines of unknown purpose. Some of the wagons are gargantuan. There is one with wheels higher than my head, wooden wheels with iron rims twelve inches wide. Two of the wagons have chutes or hoppers that open underneath; they must have been ore wagons. The flatbed wagons were probably used for hauling logs, timbers, maybe firewood. I think of the compound teams of mules and horses needed to pull these great vehicles when they were loaded. The slavery of the beasts. Susie once asked me why domesticated horses need shoes while wild horses do not. I explained: because domesticated horses have to work; wild horses roam, loaf, eat, and play.

Beyond the ruins stretch open fields of sagebrush, saltbush, chamiso, and rabbit brush, reaching toward the distant hills. The rabbit brush is still in bloom, rich with its millions of miniature, mustard-colored flowers. The drab, dun-colored hills are treeless except for clumps of tawny golden willow at scattered seeps. A local rancher's beef cattle graze on the dried bunch grass and cheat grass along the course of trickling Bodie Creek.

The great peaks of the Sierra Nevada cannot be seen from this basin in the hills; I wonder if anyone among Bodie's twelve thousand-odd population of gold miners, shopkeepers, bartenders, whores, journalists, housewives, children, managers, and executives ever cared about that little fact. Possibly; probably not. And yet in the parlor of one house we see a baby grand piano, cracked, warped, yellowed, with a withered fiddle resting on its lid. Somebody cared about music. Later, looking at a display of children's essays through the window of the schoolhouse, I notice one child's paper that begins:

"BODIE: Bodie isnt much of a town but us kids like it. If there was only a river with some fish in it running by so we could go fishing."

And a little girl, a century ago, had written in her diary: "Goodby God, I'm going to Bodie."

We continue our tour, up one street and down another. We pass a small sawmill used for cutting firewood, always an important chore for anyone living in Bodie. The guidebook tells us that many of the town's inhabitants died during the winter of 1878–79, poorly prepared in their flimsy shacks for mountain weather. The town's founder, William S. Bodey (or Waterman S. Body—accounts differ), who discovered gold here in 1859, died in a blizzard that same winter. The name Body or Bodey became Bodie two decades later when the town's citizens deliberately changed the spelling to ensure a correct pronunciation of the name.

The heavy winters account for the large number of derelict sleds, sledges, and sleighs we see here and there, travel on snow being inescapable much of the year. In one store window hang old snowshoes and the most massive pair of skis I've seen anywhere. They look like pinewood planks, an inch thick, five inches wide, at least eight feet long. They have no bindings except heavy leather straps that fitted over the instep.

We pass a dug well, full of stones. A frayed rope dangles from the hand-cranked windlass. A wooden bucket with rusted hoops sits nearby. Behind one little cabin is a privy with three holes, each a different size, in the seat. Communal living; there was little of our modern fastidious (or neurotic?) passion for privacy on the frontier.

The town has a crazy, cartoonlike quality. Its wooden shacks, cabins, houses, each with supporting assembly of sheds and outhouses, lean at various angles before the prevailing wind, canting to the northeast. A dance with time. If the State of California continues to keep these old buildings propped erect and intact, they could last for another century. Nothing rots in this dry, thirsty air; things fade in the sun, sag before the wind, are undermined by storm and flood, the erosion of the ground. But there is no organic decay. There are no odors on the air but the vague, slight scent of sunbaked earth, hot planking, the dried-out grass that crackles underfoot. In the desert the process of change is patient, slow and subtle, unless hastened by the work, creative or destructive, of humankind.

We take a look at the old mill but do not enter. HAZARDOUS AREA, say the signs, ENTRY FORBIDDEN. Supervised by my daughter, I tend to be law-abiding. Like most children she believes in the validity of rules and regulations. So we stare at the sheet-iron structures from a safe distance. They sprawl across the hillside southeast of town in a complicated welter of walls, pitched roofs, enclosed conveyor belts, cables, fifty-foot smokestacks, and dangling power lines. Within those buildings the ore was broken, crushed, pulverized, and run through a series of chemical processes, including an acid bath in cyanide, to separate the gold from its matrix. The pure gold was melted down, poured into molds, cooled, packed, and shipped out of town by Wells Fargo stage to the nearest railhead—Carson City, Nevada. Each shipment was accompanied by armed guards, for robberies and attempted robberies were frequent. Sometimes the gold was concealed in a suitcase, or inside a stagecoach driver's bedroll while the official Wells Fargo strongbox was filled with bars of lead—a ruse that worked only the first time. While the boom lasted, this mill and its associated mines produced an estimated total of $90 million in gold. By 1915 the original ore vein played out. Even the tailings dumps would yield little more.

During the boom period, the townspeople of Bodie enjoyed the usual delights of life in a Western mining camp. There were thirty-four saloons operating at one time, plus three local breweries producing the customary chaser. Despite the barren appearance of the area around Bodie, there is a spring on Potato Hill, four miles to the west, which produces pure, soft, high-quality water. Bodie was famous for its bad whiskey and good beer, for its weather—"the worst climate out-of-doors"—and for its general wickedness.

An unrecorded number of brothels lined two streets known as Virgin Alley and Maiden Lane in the obligatory red-light district. Among the many shady ladies were some whose names still survive—Eleanor Dumont (alias Madame Mustache), Rosa May, Emma Goldsmith, Nellie Monroe, French Joe, and one remembered only as The Beautiful Doll. Several of them eventually acquired enough money, property, and husbands to join the ranks of the respectable; the majority, as seems to be usual in their profession, died early of drugs and disease or faded into the background of history—whatever that vague phrase may imply in individual pain, suffering, pleasure, joy, anonymity.

The graves of a few of these working girls can still be seen near, though not in, the town cemetery—social legitimacy was required (even in Bodie) for burial within official grounds. The sign reads THIS CEMETERY STILL IN USE; PLEASE SHOW RESPECT. Little is left of the part of town where these women practiced their frisky trade; the buildings were lost in the various fires that raged at one time and another through the close-packed and highly flammable structures of Bodie.

Close to the red-light district was a cluster of hovels and stores called Chinatown, where the Chinese contingent supplied the good people of Bodie with various services: laundry, of course, and a seasonal trade in fruits and vegetables brought in from elsewhere (the climate of Bodie was too cold and dry for home gardens), and the cutting and hauling of firewood, usually piñon pine, an excellent fuel, hauled down from a considerable distance. We may be sure that there was as well a brisk dealing in opium and hashish and perhaps other exotic drugs—all of them perfectly legal at the time. As with Virgin Alley and Maiden Lane, Bodie's Chinatown was wiped out by fire in 1889, rebuilt and destroyed again in 1932.

Bad whiskey, good beer, prostitution, drugs—what else was

there to take pleasure in during the long winter nights when the miners, a characteristically rambunctious crew, were not down in the pits where they belonged? Well, there was fighting. The locally written histories of Bodie claim an average of one killing a day during the height of the gold rush. One a day comes to a total of 3,650 during the ten years from 1878 through 1887, which is probably an exaggeration. This form of truth-stretching (as Huck Finn called it) is typical of ghost-town histories. Those who write such informal, nonacademic chronicles (usually for sale to tourists) take pride in the lawless behavior of their ancestors; this is known as color. Thus fighting, robbery, prostitution, murder, hangings, and lynchings are transmuted by a short length of time—a mere hundred years—into what is called the colorful past.

Every former mining town in the American West has its fans and promoters who like to boast that *their* town was the wildest, meanest, toughest of all. (Tombstone, Arizona, "The Town Too Tough to Die.") Understandable and forgivable; we are all prone to glamorizing the remote, whether in space or time. Nor do I doubt for a moment that Bodie was indeed a rough place. "A sea of sin," the Reverend F. M. Warrington described it in 1881, "lashed by the tempests of lust and passion."

I am inclined to doubt, however, that this colorfulness was actually particularly enjoyable at the time. I suspect that to the people who lived here it may simply have seemed grim. Hard work, tedious chores, and boredom must have been the general rule (how else to account for the thirty-four saloons?), interrupted from time to time by fatal accidents in the mines; by epidemic outbreaks of disease, especially pneumonia and dysentery (those pit toilets behind every house); by heavy childbearing for the women and high mortality rates for the children; and by the occasional breakdown into violence among the men—a shooting, a murder—followed by flight or a trial, by public execution or hanging by a lynch mob. Hardly matters for comedy, or even romance. And where the work was hard, dangerous, the recreation crude and sometimes brutal, we might assume that those who lived here acquired personality traits adapted to their condition: a hardness of spirit, a relative indifference toward suffering. Those who did not would have left.

No? Yes? Perhaps? Such are my thoughts, anyway, as Susie and I amble through the empty streets of this empty town. Maybe the fault lies not with those people of Bodie now dead and vanished but in myself: a fastidious squeamishness; a sissified excess of tenderness, rendering me unfit for life in anything but the soft, sheltered, affluent cradle of twentieth-century middle-class America. Life in Bodie must have been much closer than mine to what has almost always been the human standard.

Well, we don't know, do we? We don't really know enough about *anything* of importance. I am left unsatisfied by this walk among the ruined vestiges of a hundred-year-old and transient town. I want to see, grasp, feel, *taste* the quality of daily life in this place, at that time. But it is impossible to recapture the past—even Proust failed at that. The past, as he showed, can be evoked; it cannot be re-created. We can imagine and remember; we cannot relive. Difficult enough, it seems to me, to fully experience the present.

Here's the old jail, a small building with heavy crossbeam walls, barred windows, worn floors of solid planking on which the sun shines with beneficent indifference. A homely place—or nearly homey. I've seen worse jails. Supposedly, only one man ever escaped the Bodie lockup. Another, a fellow named DeRoche, was dragged from here by a vigilante group and hanged at the intersection of Main and Lowe streets; he had evidently murdered a more popular citizen named Johnny Treloar (or Treboar). A local justice of the peace investigated the alleged murder. His report was brief: "Case dismissed, as defendant was taken out and hanged by a mob."

Not far from the jail is the fire-blackened brick vault of the Bodie bank—nothing else is left. This bank escaped the great fire of 1892, but not that of 1932. It also has the necessary distinction of having been robbed at least once; in 1916 four men blasted their way into part of the vault and fled with $4,000. They were never identified or captured. Inside the vault is a huge steel safe. Peering

close, I can read the embossed lettering on the door of the safe:
MANUFACTURED BY HALL'S SAFE & LOCK CO., SAN FRANCISCO AND
CINCINNATI . . . 1867.

We check out the remains of the livery stable and the adjacent
blacksmith shop. Here I find a more direct connection with the
past. I remember from my boyhood in rural Appalachia the sound,
smells, and sight of a smith at work: the clang of hammer on anvil;
sparks flying off white-hot steel, the fiery coals in the forge, radiant
from the pumping of giant leather bellows; the feel of iron tongs,
clamps, chains, the heavy blacksmith's hammer—twice the size of
a carpenter's hammer—in my hands.

On to the U.S. Hotel, Bodie's finest. Looking through the saloon windows, we see a dust-covered pool table with balls and cues
in place; the long and curving mahogany-veneered bar; an antique
slot machine; a roulette wheel; a big octagonal poker table covered
in green felt; stacks of red, blue, white, and golden chips still in the
players' troughs. The sight alone is enough to make my hands itch
for the feel of the cards again.

The smell of money. The smell of trauma and nervous sweat.
The smell of blood and gold and fear. What was the point of this
madness? William S. Bodey had come here all the way from
Poughkeepsie, New York—by way of South America and Cape
Horn—to end up dying in a snowstorm, two miles from the
safety and warmth of his cabin in this circle of treeless hills. For
what? Twenty years later there were twelve thousand humans here, drawn by the sweet smell of quick easy wealth. Thirty
years after that they were mostly dead or gone; today there are
none.

There is a lustrous, yellow mineral known as iron pyrite that
occurs in abundance as a native ore in many places in the American West. It looks like gold. It looks like gold should look: bright,
rich, flashy. It glitters, under direct light, with the conviction of the
miraculous and takes your breath away. But it is worthless. Prospectors call it fool's gold.

Fool's gold—the treasure of imbeciles. But is not all gold fool's
gold? Gold—*Au,* atomic weight 196.9665, atomic number 79—has

a few minor industrial and dental uses, was long popular as coinage, makes attractive jewelry. Otherwise it bears no intrinsic value, serves no human need, provides no essential standard even of monetary values. All human cultures could have survived easily without it, and most have.

Once during a debate on a land-use controversy a mining-claims speculator (not a miner, not an engineer, only a speculator) said to me, "If God hadn't wanted us to dig up that uranium, He wouldn't have put it there." To which I replied, "If God had wanted us to use that uranium, He wouldn't have hidden it underground." A silly basis for an argument that immediately became sillier. Thoreau, as usual, perceived the issue clearly: "They go to dig where they never planted," he said of the California Forty-Niners, "to reap where they never sowed." B. Traven, author of *The Treasure of the Sierra Madre,* put it this way: "The treasure which you think not worth taking trouble and pains to find, this one alone is the real treasure you are longing for all your life. The glittering treasure you are hunting for day and night lies buried on the other side of that hill yonder."

Ah yes. The real treasure lies in the human heart. Certainly. A few words from the wise should be sufficient. But there is something in the rest of us that resists such classic wisdom. A sullen impatience warms the cockleburs of my heart. My hands itch, staring at that old-time poker table in the dark interior of the Bodie saloon. Itch for the cards, for the game, for the risk, for the gamble, for the downright foolishness of it all.

There is something in us that refuses to be bound by the sensible, the humane, the rational, or even the tautological. "I say the proposition that two plus two equals four," wrote Dostoevsky in his *Notes from the Underground,* "and must *always* equal four, is an arrogant imposition."

We cling to our folly as we cling to our sense of freedom, though it lead us to destruction. Never mind how many philosophers and how many psychologists and how many sociobiologists tell us that free will is an illusion, we will not surrender to the claims of mere reason and science. And if we want to play the crazy game of treasure seeking, no matter what the treasure, we will play it—and to hell with the consequences.

Yes . . .

We walk down Main past the firehouse, the manually operated gas pumps in front of the Boone Store and Warehouse, the morgue, the Miners' Union Hall (social center of Bodie, place of balls, brawls, and square dances), the Odd Fellows' Hall, the old post office, and the county barn. Relics, all of them, crumbling and abandoned, with the leaning stone walls of the Union Hall shored up by telephone poles. We conclude with a visit to Bodie's recycling plant—the town cemetery. Interesting, but Susie finds the scene a bit on the musty side, overstressing the history at the expense of the story.

I'm inclined to agree. Though most of my mind and half my heart side with Traven and Thoreau, the rest belongs to the imbeciles. I, too, would have gone with the Forty-Niners. Who cares whether we found true gold or only fool's gold? The adventure lies in the search, whether today, tomorrow or in

Those days of old,
Those days of gold,
The days of forty-nine. . . .

PART IV

People, Books and Rivers

14

River Rats

One cold evening in February I checked into the Tri-Arc Travelodge in Salt Lake City, a respectable-type hotel in a decent, law-abiding town. I was dismayed to find the place swarming with hairy ruffians in cowboy hats, greasy down vests, wool shirts, boots. It looked like a bronc riders' convention, an assembly of lumberjacks, an upsurge from the rural underclass.

I adjusted my necktie. Nervously I consulted the desk clerk: Should I give up my reservation, find a safer place to spend the night?

The clerk smiled a reassuring smile. Don't be alarmed, he said, it's only another boatmen's jamboree. They'll all be in jail by midnight.

The clerk exaggerated. By twelve that night only one boatman had been arrested. The police caught him committing a public nuisance in the Tri-Arc parking lot. When they shone a spot-light in his face he gave them the finger, then ran for cover back into the bar. Forgot to button his fly. He was caught, charged with "Lewd and Obscene Conduct," and locked in the city slammer. His friends bailed him out—for $100—at two in the morning, letting him rot in a cell long enough to sober up.

Thus began, in traditional form, another annual meeting of the Western River Guides' Association, an organization of professional white-water boatmen and outfitters. These are the people—including some women—who, for a price, will take you by rubber raft, pontoon boat, Sportyak, kayak, dory, or canoe down the remaining free-flowing rivers of the American West: the Snake, the Salmon, the Owyhee, the Dolores, the Yampa, the Rio Grande, the San Juan, the Green, a few others, and—climax of them all—the Colorado in its thunderous course through Cataract Canyon in Utah and the Grand Canyon in Arizona.

The length of a river trip can range from one day up to twenty-two; the cost to the customer from $100 to $2,000. Most of these commercial river operators provide a complete service: transportation to and from the points of embarkation and debarkation; the boats, motors, oars; the special equipment, such as rubberized bags, life jackets, and waterproof storage cans, usually considered essential; food, cooks, and cooking gear; emergency first aid; and most important, the skill, experience, and knowledge of the boatmen themselves. It is no trifling matter to row a boatload of passengers through Satan's Gut in Cataract, through the Green River's Gates of Lodore (a canyon that might have been named, as well as imagined, by Edgar Allan Poe), or into and out of the rocks, whirlpools, and twelve-foot waves of Crystal Rapids and Lava Falls in the Grand Canyon.

You might think, all the same, that despite the hazards you would prefer to do a river trip entirely on your own, alone or with a few friends, rather than pay some expert a profit-making fee to do all the work—and have most of the fun—for you. A natural and wholesome feeling. For myself, I would rather paddle a washtub through the storm sewers of Los Angeles than merely ride along, one among a huddled pack of hapless passengers, on a thirty-three-foot motorized neoprene jumbo rig wallowing down the corridors of Grand Canyon. There'd be more satisfaction in it; greater spiritual rewards. But nature, commerce, and officialdom have placed obstacles in the course of self-reliance.

First you must buy the minimum equipment. Expensive. Then you must find the time to acquire the experience necessary if you wish to run the wild rivers successfully, without a series of upsets. Finally, and for the popular runs most difficult, you have to get a permit. A *permit?* Of course; you didn't think the rivers were there, free, public, and waiting, for any damn fool who thinks he can float in a plastic tub from Lee's Ferry to Hoover Dam's Lake Merde, did you? There are rules, restrictions, regulations, most of them desirable, some of them unavoidable, that come inevitably into effect whenever too many people crowd upon a limited resource.

I detest the word "resource." How could a wild river, part of nature's bloodstream, ever come to be regarded primarily as a damned *resource?* As if it were no more than a vein of coal, a field of cabbages, a truckload of cow manure?

Rhetorical question: we know how it happened. Human needs, human demands, human greed—alas, we must say it—have so expanded during the past half-century that we are compelled, like it or not, to look upon the world as a meat pie, to be divvied up according to the will of the strongest. No particular race or nation can be blamed for this sorry situation; it has arisen naturally; human beings, like other animals, obey the reproductive regulations: be fruitful, multiply, replenish and overplenish the defenseless earth. In a newly founded, relatively still rich society like the American, that which is not needed for food and survival is utilized for entertainment; a river becomes a "recreational resource" and fun, play, sport become among other things a business enterprise. An *industry,* in accordance with the carefully instilled belief that you can't have fun unless you pay for it.

As most everyone knows, the Colorado River was first followed for most of its length by Major Wesley Powell and his men in the year 1869. In the eighty years afterward no more than a few dozen others repeated their daring journey. Then in the 1940s and 1950s a few experienced river runners, such as Norm Nevills, Ted Hatch, Don Harris, Albert Quist, hired themselves and their boats out to those willing to pay for the experience of a white-water float trip. Commercial river running was born. The business grew rapidly as more and more boatmen set themselves up as outfitters; by 1972 they were taking some fifteen thousand customers per season through the Grand Canyon alone.

At this point the National Park Service, charged with the responsibility for preserving Grand Canyon in its supposedly wild and natural state, finally stepped in—too late—and set maximum limits to the volume of this new and burgeoning commerce, licensing boatmen and outfitters, and limiting use of the river to those permittees already established there. Ninety-two percent of the river traffic was allotted, in various proportions, to the twenty-one commercial outfitters, leaving only 8 per cent for everybody else, for those private citizens who preferred to do it on their own.

In 1972 this seemed fair enough; the demand for river-running permits by private parties was small. But this is no longer the case. As white-water boating becomes a more and more popular sport, the conflict between freelance boaters and the commercial outfits has grown intense, creating a legal and political issue still unresolved by the courts or the Park Service.

However the issue is finally settled, if it is, somebody is going to get hurt; when the demand for something far exceeds the supply there is obviously not enough for everyone. Attacked from all sides, as usual, the Park Service proposed a compromise that satisfied no one: doubling the annual visitor-day use of the river over a longer season and increasing the private-party allotment from 8 to 33 percent. The catch to this is that the river is a cold and difficult environment during most of the year; the water emerges from the depths behind Glen Canyon Dam at a temperature of 40 ° F. If the commercial operators are forced to share the three summer months (the favored season for a river trip) with a larger proportion of noncommercial boatmen then they, the commercials, fear that they will lose customers, lose business, lose money.

Another sensitive question is that of motorized boating in the national parks. Under pressure from conservation organizations like the Sierra Club, the Park Service has been trying for over a decade to include its portion of the Colorado River in an official wilderness system. Wilderness entails a ban on motors. Any proposal to ban motors in the Grand Canyon stirs up the wrath of the larger commercial outfitters, whose prosperity (a gross of half a million dollars per year in some cases) depends on the quickie trip—the rapid transport by motorized rubber raft of a large volume of paying passengers. Pack them in at Lee's Ferry, rush them through the Grand Canyon, hustle them out by helicopter. What should, by traditional standards, be a two-to-three-week adventure can be condensed by such means to a four- or five-day whirlwind tour. The passengers don't object; they don't know what they're missing; they don't know any better; and the operator becomes modestly rich. (One of these quickie-tour outfits was sold a few years ago to a group of investors for over a million dollars.) So far the large commercial outfitters have been able, through political finagling, to forestall wilderness designation for the interior Grand Canyon and thus defeat every attempt by the Park Service to manage the river in the general public interest.

But in the long run the big outfitters are on the losing side. As should be apparent to everyone by now, we are approaching a new age of frugality in the national economy; motorized recreation in its many forms (snowmobiles, trailbikes, dune buggies, off-road vehicles, motorboats, etc.) must sooner or later be phased out of existence. The commercial river outfitters will be forced by economics, if not by the Park Service, to junk their outboard motors, dispose of their giant rafts, use smaller boats and—sharing the profits—employ more oarsmen. They'll learn to live with it. All concerned will be better off because of it—the big outfitter, whose business will be reduced to the family-size enterprise that it should be; the boatmen, who will find more jobs available; and last and not of least importance, the paying passengers, who will see the Grand Canyon as it should be seen, at a leisurely pace, in quietude, as members of small groups.

Private river runners versus commercial river runners; motors versus oars; these are two of the hairiest, prickliest issues that boatmen and outfitters, the government, the politicians, and the general public must somehow deal with. But why should emotions be involved? the reader may ask; surely these things can be settled on the basis of common sense and equity, with the aid of an ordinary desk-top calculator. Not so; these are questions of profitability, of money, in some cases of big money—and therefore, quite naturally and understandably, blood is stirred and passions rise. (Some people get very emotional about money.)

Take the impossible question of fairness, for example: Is it fair that the small outfitter should be forced out of business by the big outfitter? Or fair that superior managerial ability should be penalized in some way so as to allow the small outfitter (perhaps less hard-driving as an entrepreneur but a *nicer guy,* offering his customers a more enjoyable experience, who knows?) to remain in business? Is it fair that currently established outfitters be allowed to keep a virtual monopoly, through the government's permit-franchise system, of the use of what is supposed to be a *public* river flowing through public property such as a *national* park? But would it be fair to open the rivers wide to one and all, on a first-come first-served basis, perhaps driving into bankruptcy some of the established river outfitters who may have invested not only money but thirty years of their lives in the business?

What is fair? Life is not fair, said ex-President Carter in one of his more brilliant unrehearsed spontaneous public statements. His answer was satisfactory to the winners but infuriated those who saw themselves as unjustified losers.

The river outfitters complain bitterly about the various agencies—Park Service, Forest Service, Bureau of Land Management, state boating commissions, even the U.S. Coast Guard, and of course the I.R.S.—that they must deal with, and of the maze of red tape and regulations they must grope their way through in pursuit of an honest dollar. (The pursuit of happiness.) And indeed the

constraints are many and complicated: the permits, the safety requirements, the sanitation and disposal requirements, restrictions
on wood fires, user-day quotas, number of passengers per boat,
minimum and maximum allowable days per trip, campsite restrictions, scheduling restrictions, allowable charge per customer, user-
day fees payable to the agency, and other variables create a nightmare of paperwork, logistics, penalties, and dubious rewards.

And yet the outfitters need these regulations, or most of them,
now that their well-advertised operations have attracted such
enormous numbers of people. Without regulation a few unscrupu-
lous operators could soon make a mess of things, fouling the camp-
grounds, drowning an occasional passenger, overwhelming the
river with crowds so large that a river trip would lose what vestiges
still remain of an actual "wilderness" experience. More important,
from the outfitters' point of view, is that unregulated river use,
without the protection of the permit system, would expose them to
unlimited competition. Any muscular young fellow with a couple
of Canyon trips to his credit, a boat and a pair of oars, could then
offer to take you or me down the river for a fee much below that
charged by the commercial operators—and be glad to do it. Might
even do it for nothing, if he was a friend, and make more of an adventure of it all to boot, since you'd be a participating member of
the trip and not a mere passive passenger. And save all partici-
pants a lot of money besides. (In 1979, for example, I took part in a
twenty-two-day share-the-expense trip through Grand Canyon for
$350. A commercial trip of equivalent value would have cost me at
least $1,000.)

These are the hot issues in the river-running business, and
should be discussed at every opportunity. I was surprised to discover, therefore, when I sat in on some of the river guides' meetings
at the Tri-Arc Travelodge, that they were mostly busy in wran-
gling with representatives of the Park Service and the BLM about
matters of secondary interest: amount of user-day fees, the sale and
transfer of outfitter permits, safety regulations, sewage disposal,
etc.

Well-meaning but innocuous resolutions were passed, urging

the federal government to designate this or that stretch of river as an official Wild and Scenic River, thus protecting it to some extent from the dam builders, power plant promoters, oil shale developers, and other good intentioned but wicked people. But when Howard Brown, director of an organization called American Rivers Conservation Council, suggested that the outfitters impose a $5 surcharge on each river-boating passenger to help finance wild river lobbying in Washington I could detect no support for the idea. (It should be said that the W.R.G.A. does contribute $1,000 per year to Mr. Brown's efforts, and that individual members of the group contribute more on their own.)

One of my favorite old-timers among the outfitters, Martin Litton, owner of Grand Canyon Dories, Inc., worked in a combined attack on the Bureau of Reclamation and the metric system:

> BE IT RESOLVED, That the Western River Guides' Association deplores the costly, misleading, confusing and dangerous trend on the part of the Bureau of Reclamation to report river flows in unfamiliar, nontraditional, unintelligible, unusable terms of cubic meters per second and calls upon the Bureau of Reclamation to stop it.

Passed, with only three dissenting votes. When I asked one of the dissenters if he really cared all that much for the metric system he admitted that he didn't, he just wanted to vote "against Martin." Why? "Oh—I always vote against Martin. Keeps him honest."

One B.L.M. official introduced another with the careless remark that "maybe you fellas would like to bounce a few questions off him." Voices in the crowd replied: "Questions? How about beer cans? How about rocks?"

The official, clutching the rostrum with tense hands, immediately got himself in more trouble with the rivermen by announcing that the B.L.M. was going to make it "tough" and "hard" for outfitters to sell or transfer river-running permits; those permits, he said, with incredible lack of tact, are not private property but the property of the U.S. government. He should have said "of the public" or "of the American people." But he didn't. More angry outcries: "Whose government? Who owns the goddamned government?"

Again Martin Litton rose to state the case for the outfitters. Litton, a former journalist, is a forceful speaker, not at all shy in public, always ready with well-thought-out opinions on any subject. "River-running permits," he argued, "like grazing permits in the cattle business, are essential business property. Possession of them gives us a legal right, established by custom and common law, to buy and sell them as we see fit." And he pointed out the obvious fact that a river-running business without the franchise to take paying passengers down the river is worthless.

Ken Sleight, another veteran river guide, who has been operating a family-size outfit for thirty years, stood up to make a plea for both a floor and a ceiling on the size of any one river-guiding enterprise. A floor is needed, he said, a certain minimum amount of user-day and passenger permits guaranteed by the government on a long-term basis, in order to provide an economic base sufficient to keep the small outfits (like his) in business. The ceiling is needed to prevent the large outfits from getting too large, stifling competition, buying out the small guide services, and establishing a complete monopoly. Many small outfits, said Sleight, can provide a more varied and therefore better service for the public than a few big ones.

The meeting concluded with the election of officers. Boatman Stewart Reeder seconded the nomination of boatman-outfitter Clair Quist for the board of directors. Reeder's speech consisted of one sentence: "Clair's been running rivers since he was a bucket-ass kid." Reeder paused for thought, said nothing more, and sat down. Clair Quist, "from the underworld of river guides," as another boatman told me, was elected by universal acclamation. What is a bucket-ass kid? I asked. Anyone not big enough to sit on a chair, I was told.

The best thing about the river-running business is the people in it. The worst thing is the business. I find it saddening to see good honest boatmen forced to become accountants, clerks, advertisers, lobbyists, managers, and executives in order to survive in what used to be, before the roads were paved, half the rivers dammed, and the crowds came, not a business but an adventurous trade.

Fourteen years ago a seasonal park ranger stood on the beach at Lee's Ferry, Arizona, on the Colorado River, watching an outfit called Grand Canyon Expeditions preparing to launch on a twelve-day river trip. The ranger had never been down the Grand Canyon himself. The wistful expression on his face must have been apparent to the owner and head boatman Ron Smith. "For chrissake, Abbey," says Smith, "don't just stand there like a sick calf. We need a number two nigger. Somebody to wash the pots. Go get your bedroll and come along."

"I'll get fired."

"Who cares?" Smith says, opening a can of beer with the pliers on his belt. So I gave my boss due notice—thirty minutes—and went along. Nor was I fired. When I came back two weeks later my job was waiting for me—only the boss was gone; the Park Service had transferred him to some cannonball park in Virginia. (A little mix-up in the paperwork.)

Good men, these boatmen. Generous, vigorous, competent types. The exasperating kind of people who can do and do well most anything: hunt and fish, naturally. Build a boat, a house, or a hogan. Repair an outboard motor in rapids or fix a truck engine in a sandstorm. Pitch tents, build fires, cook meals in driving rain. Great lovers? Of course. Truthful? Undoubtedly—drink you under the table any day. Sporting men? You name the game—poker, pool, craps, Frisbee, backgammon, macramé, Monopoly—they'll play it.

For instance:

A boatman named Hall is watching a couple of sharp California dudes playing eight-ball at a table in Flagstaff. They are good. Hall challenges the winner. The dude looks at him: Man, you're no pool player. Well, says Hall, I ain't too good with these here skinny *cue*sticks you got but if somebody'll bring me a long-handled shovel, why, I'll take you on. The dude sneers, the bets are laid, another boatman brings in a garden spade. Hall chalks the tip of the handle, breaks the rack, runs the table. (Of course he then had the problem of getting out of the poolroom with his winnings—always the hardest part of the game.)

There could be an element of bullshit in some of the stories. Boatman Al Harris tells me this one:

"We took this kayaker from Vermont along down the Grand. He done pretty good till we got to that Hance Rapid. There he tried to run the hole, ate it, got sucked under, came back up about half a mile downriver. After we pumped the water out of him and sewed up his head and he commences to come around, he says, Jesus, I'll never do that again; it hurts—you got any drugs? So I open up the old first aid kit and look over the pharmacy. Well, I says, we got morphine, Demerol, amytal, codeine, Percodan, Thorazine, Valium, Librium, Lithium, ether, Methadone, mescaline, LSD, peyote, and some of that what they call wacky tobaccy—you know, *mary-hoona*. Homegrown. I'll take them all, the kayaker says, and he did; he passed out for ten days but said he felt just fine when we got to the takeout at Diamond Crick."

In this story even the accent is suspect: Harris can talk like a Harvard graduate when he's not putting you on. Or when he is. As for vigor, I remember the time a friend and I were going through Cataract Canyon with Ken Sleight and Bob Quist (Clair Quist's brother). At the worst possible moment, entering a hellhole of rock and waves called the Big Drop, the outboard motor failed. (A Johnson Sea Horse.) Grab oars! yells Sleight, grabbing the spare oar on the right. Bob Quist—a very powerful young man—grabs the one on the left, jams it in the oarlock. A fang of limestone menaces the port bow. Bob takes a deep bite in the water and gives a mighty, a superhuman, heave. The oar, brand-new, never before used, snaps apart in the middle. We make it through the rapids anyway, right side up, pinballing off the rocks. One oar or two, one boatman or none, it didn't seem to make any significant difference. The true function of a boatman, on a river trip, is to provide *moral* leadership. Ask any boatman.

When a passenger, confused by the terms upstream and downstream, asked a boatman I know to explain the distinction, he tied a length of string to a cork and gave it to this—this person. Throw the cork in the river, he said, and hold on to the string; whichever way the cork goes, that's downstream, probably; unless you're in a eddy. The other way is upstream. But keep ahold of the string. What's the string for? the passenger asked. For the next time, he said; it'll last you for years.

One day Clair Quist was telling me about some rancher friends of his—these jolly cowboys climbing into his thin-skinned rubber boat with big spurs on their boots. I imagined I heard a note of envy in his tone. "Don't you wish," I said, "your father had left *you* a working cattle ranch?" (Certainly I was familiar with the wish.)

"No," Clair said, after a moment; "our old man left us something a lot better—Glen Canyon." (His father had been the first to operate a guide service there.) "But the politicians took it away from us."

Ah yes, that dam. That Glen Canyon Dam, and the 180-mile lake behind it that boatmen call Lake Foul. In all of the Rocky Mountain, Inter-Mountain West, no man-made object has been hated so much, by so many, for so long, with such good reason, as that 700,000-ton plug of gray cement, blocking our river.

Final anecdote. Ken Sleight and a few others are sitting around a campfire, on a beach, by a river that still flows. We're talking about *that dam.*

"Listen," says Ken, "it's not enough to talk about it. Let's do something about it." He holds out his hands to those on either side of him. "Grab hands. Tie in. Form a circle." We join hands around the fire. Ken closes his eyes and leans back a little. "Now concentrate," he says. "Concentrate real hard, all together, and let's see if we can't lift that dam. Just a few inches. Let the water out." Eyes closed, we concentrate and strain, visualizing the huge dam, trying to make it rise. "Oh," groans Ken, "it's so . . . heavy. It's so . . . goddamn . . ." *sigh*—"heavy. . . ."

On the evening of the last day of the Guides meeting, about to leave for the Salt Lake airport, I went into a bar for a final drink with some of these river rats. Through the smoke and whiskey fumes (this bar was the kind known, in Mormon Utah, as a "private club"), I saw a mob of them jammed around a long table. Sleight was there, of course, and the Quist brothers, and Al Harris, and Stew Reeder, and Dave Kloepfer, and Kim Crumbo, a few others, and Grant Gray with his wife Millet, and Pamela Davis, and the parking lot nuisance of course, I'll not mention his name, and Frogg Stewart—collectively the worst element, the most disgusting and disreputable crew in the whole river-running clan.

Naturally I hesitated a moment inside the door, then decided to chance it. What the hell, I was leaving in an hour. So I stayed for a bourbon or two, and listened to the talk. The time soon came for me to depart. Feeling relaxed, happy, foolishly sentimental, I began saying goodbye to these great people, shaking hands one by one around the table. My necktie, worn for prevention of disease only, was dangling in the drinks. Halfway through the process I started to feel a bit silly. Bob Quist, roaring above the babble, confirmed the feeling: "God, Ed," he yelled, "you look like a politician." Grinning at me through the smoke.

I stopped, turned, gave him the big finger. He jeered at me again, an unspeakable epithet which, nevertheless, he spoke. I slammed my left palm against the crook of my right elbow and sprang *two* rigid fingers on him—the deadly Neapolitano *double prong*, thrust right in to the hilt. Again, I turned and had almost reached the safety of the exit when I heard an augmented roar of clapping, laughter, and screaming in my rear. I looked back. Bob Quist had climbed on his chair and pulled down his pants. The son of a bitch was mooning me.

I fled at once. Never turn your back on a boatman.

15

Footrace in the Desert

Labor Day 1980: the Hopi town of New Oraibi, Arizona. Heart of the heart of Indian country.

One hundred and fifteen of us wait in a pack behind the starting line, about to begin the Seventh Annual Louis Tewanima Memorial Footrace. The course extends for seven long looping miles in the desert heat, over dirt roads, across the highway, and up a winding and sandy trail to the top of Third Mesa and the three-hundred-year-old village of Old Oraibi, and from there down another steep trail, another dirt road, to the starting point.

Pickup trucks line the street that forms the home stretch. Perhaps a thousand people, mostly Hopi and Navajo, half of them children, are gathered here to watch the beginning and the end of the race. There is much laughter, much talking, in the soft and quiet voices of the Indians. (Or Native Americans, as some of them prefer to be called these days.) My daughter Susie crouches beside me, raring to go. I'm neither raring nor ready myself—I hate running, and most other forms of physical effort, but here we are anyway. This race is open to everybody, of any age, all sexes and tribes, including the WASP. (White Anglo-Sexy Protestant.) The youngest runner is nine, the oldest fifty-eight. Susie, No. 23, watches the Hopi starter, Dr. Alan Numkena, a chiropractor from Oraibi, as he issues final instructions: no pushing, no shoving, no shortcuts. I'm still watching the crowd—the runners, the onlookers—when I hear Numkena shout "Go!"

There is a howl of joy from the runners and we're off, trotting easily down the dirt street toward the first turn a quarter-mile away. The route lies on a slight downgrade, here at the beginning, and having stationed myself close to the front of the mob, I have no difficulty in keeping the pace. At first. This is easy, I'm thinking, as we jog along, me, my kid, other children, with most of the crowd somewhere behind. Halfway to the first turn, however, moving very well it seems to me, considering the fact that we have a long way to go, I become aware of bodies floating past me on the left and right—young men, women, children, most of them still laughing and talking as I begin to labor for breath.

Getting serious here. With nearly seven full miles, mostly uphill, yet to run. At the first turn there seem to be more bodies, legs, and heads in front of me than behind. Madness. At the half-mile point I'm near the back of the last bunch. The runners—the genuine runners—are far ahead, fading out of sight. I'm having trouble just keeping up with Susie, who is no more a true believer than I. But unlike me, Susie means to complete the course, even if she has to walk most of the way and crawl the final mile.

Emmett Bowman, a short stocky Navajo from Phoenix, age fifty-eight—fifty-eight!—jogs steadily past me. He moves like he's treading on broken glass. But keeps moving. A moment later his wife Emma, age fifty-three, passes me. I find this discouraging. I drop out at the end of the first mile, armed with alibis. After all, I have journalistic duties to perform; I am here to observe and report, not to compete with 114 physical-culture addicts. I want to see the middle of this race, and the end of it, and already the main body of runners is far ahead, disappearing in the dust, sorting itself out for the long ordeal up the single-file trail that leads to the summit of the mesa.

Before quitting, though, I urge Susie to carry on. She agrees to uphold the family honor. As I turn back to town I see her little legs working, not fast but resolute, the last runner still running. A red van functioning as ambulance and pickup wagon, manned by two Hopis, follows her in low gear. A mile beyond, where the course diverges from the dirt road, Susie will be alone. But the trail is well marked with arrows of lime in the sand, and streamers of blue and yellow bunting tied to the desert shrubbery, the cliffrose and juniper and rabbit brush that flourish in this arid zone. I'm not worried about Susie. Or not yet. I unpin my number tag, walk back to the parking area, get in my car and drive to the top of the hill, near the midpoint of the course, to await the lead runners.

It's a clear bright sunny day, very warm. Nearby are the cliff-walled mesas of the heart of Hopiland. The small villages, built of local stone, blend perfectly with the color and forms of this dramatic landscape, which somewhat resembles that of Old Castile. To the southwest I can see the San Francisco Mountains near the city of Flagstaff, fifty miles away by line of sight. Those are sacred mountains to the Hopi, home of their many gods, the *Katsinas*. A few snowfields linger above timberline on the north face of the peaks. South and southeast stand the Hopi buttes, ancient volcanic plugs of blue-black basaltic rock rising into the sky. To the east is Second Mesa and First Mesa, each surmounted with its group of medieval-looking villages. They make strange names on the map: Shungopavi, Mishongnovi, Shipaulovi, Walpi, Sichomovi, Tewahano, and Polacca.

On the lower slopes of the mesas, and on the desert floor beneath them, are fields of corn, beans, squash, and melons cultivated by those locals who carry on the old Hopi way of life. Most of the fields are sandy, bowl-shaped; they look like the sandtraps of a golf course. In each field is a scarecrow flapping in the breeze. There is no irrigation system and little rainfall in this barren reservation; it seems a miracle that any kind of agriculture can be carried on here. But the Hopis must know what they're doing; they've been here for many centuries, and plan to stay for many more. And they believe in miracles.

Why here? As with all tribes, all peoples, the origin and wanderings and destiny of the Hopi tribe are veiled in myth, legend, visionary prophecy. The tribal tradition speaks of former worlds, former existences, and of their emergence into this world through the womb of the Earth—the *Sipapu*. Most archeologists believe that the Hopis are descendants of the cliff-dwelling people who built the magnificent stone cities of Mesa Verde, Chaco Canyon, Betatakin, and Keet Seel.

The written record begins with the advent of the Spanish during the sixteenth century, who made their customary effort to Christianize the natives. They failed. The Hopis took part in the Pueblo Revolt of 1680, when the Spaniards were temporarily driven out of their colonies in New Mexico and Arizona. The Spanish returned twelve years later, this time to stay and become a permanent part of the Southwest, but they failed to reconquer the Hopi nation. This year, 1980, is being celebrated by the Hopis and the other Pueblo tribes as the Tricentennial of their great rebellion—the only occasion in all of North American history when the Indians succeeded in organizing themselves into a large-scale force capable of defeating European invaders.

After the revolt, fearing the return of the Spanish, the Hopis built their stone villages on the mesa tops, the more easily to defend themselves. They were never attacked. The mesas, however, were too dry and rocky for farming; the cornfields were maintained below and sometimes miles away from the villages, scattered across the desert in the little sand pockets of tillable soil. (The sand acts as a mulch, helping to retain rainfall.) Networks of trails led from the mesa villages to the fields. The Hopi farmers commuted to work on foot—no horses, no pickup trucks in those days—and made a habit of running each way, sometimes for many miles. Running seemed for them as natural a mode of self-propulsion as walking. Running led, as it always does, to competitions. And here they are, once again, trotting through the desert, along with their Navajo neighbors and a number of white folks from various places.

A few other onlookers wait with me here on the hillside, some of them with binoculars, watching the long file of runners below. One small dark figure races along far in advance of the others. After the first come groups of two and three, then bunches, then the main body strung out like ants on the narrow trail. Borrowing glasses, I search for Susie. No sign of her but she's got to be down there somewhere, lost among the bushes, trudging forward I assume, as she had promised to do. Susie and I had walked out the course the day before; at the foot of the hill the race organizers had written, in letters of lime on the sand, KEEP GOING.

Two young men with paper cups full of drinking water wait by the side of the trail. We watch the lead runner approach, a bare-chested young man with a red bandana tied around his long hair. He has a bony, almost gaunt face, a small, lean, muscular, perfect body, and serious eyes. He runs steadily, uphill, breathing audibly but not, it seems to me, with any trouble. He is at least a quarter-mile ahead of everybody else. As he passes us he takes a cup of water without breaking stride, gulps it down, drops the cup and races on toward the highway that leads up another hill to Old Oraibi. Watching him go, on and on at that apparently easy, unflagging pace, I feel an emotion which I have not felt in a long time: a certain awe in the presence of ability and determination far beyond any ambition of my own, a surge of admiration for the physical beauty of a good athlete in action.

"Who was that?" I ask.

"Hoffman Shorty," says one of the men near me.

"Hoffman Shorty? You mean Shorty Hoffman?"

"No, Hoffman Shorty. He won the race last year too."

"That doesn't sound like a Hopi name."

The Hopi I'm talking to, a young man sitting on the tailgate of his pickup truck, smiles and shrugs. "Shorty's a Navajo."

The Navajos are old-time antagonists of the Hopi. But nobody here in Hopiland seems to mind that a Navajo is winning this

Hopi-sponsored footrace. Or if they mind they don't show it; the Hopis are a people of exquisite tact. The true root meaning of the name Hopi, I am told, is not "the peaceful people," as we used to think, but "the well-mannered people." And so they are. But beneath the gentle manners lurk the usual human hearts. Like every human society, the little Hope tribe of eight thousand people is murky with intrigue, obsessed with gossip, alive with internal as well as external conflict. To the Hopis it no doubt seems like merely one additional complication among many that an alien should win their Louis Tewanima Memorial Footrace.

Tewanima, now that is definitely a Hopi name, a famous one among the Hopis. And a name unjustly forgotten, I suppose, by most of the rest of the world. Louis Tewanima may not have been the greatest of all Hopi runners but he was certainly the most successful. So far.

Born sometime in the 1880s—the records are vague; another Hopi characteristic—young Tewanima was sent in 1907 under federal compulsion, in the fashion of the time, to the Carlisle Indian School in Carlisle, Pennsylvania. The purpose was to liberate him from the subtle and complex culture of the Hopi and make of him an educated, civilized, happy American citizen like the rest of us. At Carlisle, according to legend, this dark little runt of a youth approached Glenn "Pop" Warner, coach of the track team, and told him, "Me run fast good. All Hopi run fast good."

Which was true—a simple fact. Tewanima made the school team, along with classmate Jim Thorpe, and one year later they both were in London as members of the U.S. team for the 1908 Olympiad. Tewanima finished ninth in a field of fifty-six in the twenty-six-mile marathon. Four years later he and Thorpe competed in the Olympic Games at Stockholm. Tewanima won the silver medal in the 10,000-meter race, second by only a few paces to the Flying Finn, Hannes Kolehmainen. That was the high point in Tewanima's athletic career. Soon afterward he returned to his hometown of Shungopovi on Second Mesa and spent the rest of his life as a farmer, wool-grower, husband and father, and as a priest in the ceremonies of the Antelope Clan. Deep obscurity, by contemporary standards. But he had set a record in 1912 that was not surpassed by any American runner until Billy Mills, a Sioux, broke Tewanima's record at Tokyo in the 1964 Olympics.

Tewanima was never entirely forgotten by the world of athletics. In 1954, then in his seventies, he was flown to New York City—his first airplane trip—to join a gathering of the All-Time U.S. Track and Field Team at the Waldorf-Astoria Hotel. Wearing his Hopi finery of velveteen shirt, silver jewelry, scarlet headband, made much of by the New York press, old Tewanima enjoyed an honored guest's tour of the city. Shown the wonders of Manhattan from atop the Empire State Building, the old man said, "Not enough land for sheep." That was Tewanima's only lapse from Hopi good manners. He died in 1969, aged eighty-five or so. Five years later some Hopis got themselves organized—a difficult thing in this decentralized, noncommercial and extremely cautious tribe—and began a *new tradition,* the annual Louis Tewanima Memorial Footrace.

And here we are. More runners have straggled past now, all of them young men. I can hear the desperate panting of others laboring up the sandy trail. No sign yet of the girls, the women, the middle-aged, the old men, the children, or of my darling daughter. I can't wait here much longer if I hope to see the leaders cross the finish line.

I get in my car and start back toward New Oraibi. At a high viewpoint along the highway I stop for a look at the final downhill length of the race course. A mile away and five hundred feet below I see one small lone dark figure streaking among the corn patches, the bean patches, the garbage dumps, and burnt-out abandoned Chevrolets that lie between Old and New Oraibi. Hoffman Shorty is far ahead of me. And of everybody.

By the time I get back to the town and find a place to park the car and walk the two blocks to the finish line Shorty has crossed it and gone, disappearing among his friends. A few other runners have also finished the course. They stand around in the shade of the cottonwoods, eating free community watermelon and talking with their admirers.

One by one the majority of the contestants appear. Coming down the homestretch, most of them manage a heroic sprint for the ultimate fifty yards. Looking good for the spectators. Each finisher receives a polite patter of applause from the crowd. The first female appears, Cindy Bakurva, age twenty-four, from New Oraibi; she dashes to the finish line with a young man on each side holding her hands high in triumph, and receives a burst of applause and cheers from the home folks. I talk with her for a few minutes and learn not only that she'd been the winner last year, too, in the women's category, but that she is a niece of the great Louis Tewanima. Of course, like all Hopis, like all Indians, she has many uncles, many aunts. She had never met her famous uncle but had always admired him. (Older Hopis, I was told, were not aware of anything so special about Tewanima. "All Hopi run fast good.") Cindy Bakurva is bright-eyed, beautiful, calm and articulate despite her strenuous victory. She takes sports, especially running and basketball, quite seriously. "They make me feel good," she explains. That seems a sufficient reason; maybe the best reason.

The first boy in the thirteen-and-under category comes running to the finish. He is Gary Silva from Polacca; he too receives an ovation. A few other children show up but not my Susie. I see the red van-ambulance appear with a dejected-looking little girl in the rear seat—not my little girl, I'm relieved to discover. Or am I? I start to worry about that kid of mine.

Now the older runners begin to trickle in, an hour or more behind Hoffman Shorty. Winner in the fifty-and-over group is Guy McIntosh, fifty-four, a Bureau of Indian Affairs employee from Keams Canyon, Arizona. Member of the WASP tribe. Second in this group is another *Paháana,* or white man, Al Schauffler, fifty-seven, from Fort Defiance, Arizona. Schauffler is followed across the finish line by his dog Alex, sole finisher in the dog category. Schauffler places ninety-third. Alex ninety-fourth. "I am a boondock runner," Schauffler tells me, "and my religion is Nature." He was the first white back in 1975 to take part in the Tewanima races.

Old Emmett Bowman comes jogging in at exactly the same pace he had set at the beginning of the race, when I was thinking how ridiculously easy this sort of thing is. His wife Emma is waiting for him with half a watermelon. She'd beat him by ten minutes.

A few more runners come in, mostly children, finishers 101 through 113. Only two of the 115 entrants fail to be accounted for, myself and my daughter Susie. The footrace seems to be over. The scorekeepers and race officials have left their table by the finish line, preparing now for the best part of the race, the awards ceremony. Trophy cups and piles of medals in the colors of gold, silver, and bronze wait at the awards table. Plus the First Prize, a Hopicrafted, handmade, solid silver belt buckle for the overall winner. The race *is* over. Everyone is eating watermelon, waiting for the prize-giving and speeches to begin. No one but me still keeps an eye on the homestretch. Where is Susie? Time to look for that child.

I drive the car through town and as far as I can up the dirt road that had served as the last mile of the course. I get out and look up the winding trail toward Old Oraibi on top of the mesa. No little girl in sight. I drive out over the beginning of the course for the first three miles, thinking that Susie might have given up and turned back. I rupture the car's exhaust pipe on the high center of the dirt road but find no daughter. I turn and drive up the highway to Old Oraibi; the car brays like a dragster through its damaged pipe. I walk through the village, following the white arrows of the runners' route, to the ruined mission church at the tip of the mesa where the trail begins its descent. No Susie.

A white-haired old man beside a pile of piñon and juniper logs—this coming winter's fuel supply—greets me with a smile and the curling and uncurling of his fingers in lieu of a wave. I inquire about my daughter; he speaks no English. I drive back to New Oraibi and discover Susie under the trees, eating watermelon, only slightly worried about me. She had strolled across the finish line a few minutes after I'd left. She was the last runner to complete the course but she did complete it. I am proud of her.

We watch the awards. Hoffman Shorty wins the silver belt buckle, given to him by Joan Nuvamsa, Louis Tewanima's fifty-five-year-old granddaughter. The serious, shy, unsmiling Shorty receives a good round of applause from the largely Hopi crowd. His time for this race is 44 minutes and 59 seconds. Last year he'd won it in 46 minutes and 30.9 seconds, same race but following a somewhat different course. The length of this year's course is approximately, not exactly, seven miles.

I corner Shorty a few moments later, while he's still admiring his new belt buckle. How's it feel to be the winner? I ask him; a dumb question but *de rigueur*. Feels pretty good, he solemnly admits. He is twenty years old, lives near Farmington, New Mexico, began running two years ago, now runs fifty to sixty miles a week. For fun, he says. He competed in last year's Boston Marathon, doing the twenty-six miles in 2 hours and 50 minutes. Does he have Olympic aspirations? He's thought of it, he says. Parting, he lets me shake his hand, giving me the soft and diffident clasp of the Navajo.

Susie and I pick up our commemorative Louis Tewanima T-shirts, awarded to all entrants in the event, even nonfinishers. I talk briefly with Kedric Outah, Cedric Navenma, and Alan Numkena, prime organizers of this year's race. They feel it's been a success, attracting many more runners and a bigger crowd than the year before. Running, they say, is enjoying a revival among the Hopi young people, and maybe, they hope, one of these years, who knows?, there will be another Olympian from Hopiland. I hope so too.

Late in the afternoon Susie and I head for home. Three hundred miles to go. We pause once along the highway south to patch up the exhaust pipe with a beer can and baling wire. Now that the race is over, the weather has changed. The wind is blowing hard and a pall of yellow dust obliterates the horizon. The sun goes down behind moaning winds, leaving a cloudless, sinister, and lingering red glow across the entire Western sky. It looks like the end of the world.

Maybe it is. The Hopi prophecies call for such a termination. But they offer consolation too: this world, they say, like former worlds, will be succeeded by yet one more. Susie and I find this a comforting thought, but not one of crucial importance. In this world or the next our prime concern must be, can only be, the eternity of the moment—the joy of the race. One world at a time.

16

Reviewing *Zen and the Art of Motorcycle Maintenance*

When the editors of the late and lamented *Mountain Gazette* of Denver (probably the best magazine of its kind ever published in America—in fact the only one of its kind) asked me to write a review of Robert Pirsig's book, I agreed to do it but subcontracted the assignment to Dave Harleyson.

For two reasons: first, I had already written a favorable review of the book for the *New York Times*—I called it a "splendid psychomelodrama"—and wasn't about to praise another writer's work twice in the same year; second, I thought it appropriate that Pirsig's much-esteemed and best-selling book be subjected to critical scrutiny by an expert.

My friend Dave is an expert. He's been a member of the Southern Arizona Road Huns (a motorcycle social club) for fifteen years, makes his living as a dealer, pimp, and freelance mechanic, and has studied the arts of literary composition for two years at a state institution in Florence, Arizona. (Armed robbery, freshman English, aggravated assault.)

I met Dave the first time at the Ranchhouse Bar near Tucson, where he and his fellow Huns often convene on weekday afternoons. Dave is easy to spot: he's the large red-bearded gentleman at the pool table, a tattoo of a rattlesnake on his left arm, wearing purple shades, a sleeveless shirt, a Levis vest with a dragon embroidered on the back, original blue jeans dark with grease, and black engineer's boots. You don't see many of those any more. The fat leather wallet in his hip pocket he keeps chained to his belt.

When I gave him a copy of *Zen*, etc., to read he seemed at first reluctant—"What's this shit, man?"—but finally consented to take on the job if I kept his name out of the magazine. He was still wanted in Denver at the time. He would write the review, he said, but only for fun, not money. I had offered him my usual commission: one-tenth of 1 percent.

Six months later he produced the review. Good help is hard to find these days. This is what he wrote:

ZAMM

Sorry to be so fucking late with this here book report, man, but I been having trouble with my transmission. Can't get my ass in gear. Haw Haw. This here book Zen and the Art of Fucking Motorcycle Maintenance or I call it ZAMM for short has some interesting things to read about motorcycle maintenance but the trouble is the author don't give us much technical information about his own machine, just some little hints here and there, so I guess he was riding a Honda "Dream" of before 1970, probly the 250 cc. model, but no motorcycle I ever heard of and I been fooling around with bikes since 1950 needs all that fucking *obsessive*, man, obsessive fucking around with the rear chain and adjusting and oiling that this here Pirsig gives his rear chain. That was a sick bike. Some of his other ideas are funny too, man, like saying a seized-up engine comes from piston expansion caused by too much heat when what he should know is the cause is increased friction due to fucking lack of oil for chrissake. Too much oil on his chain and not enough in the motor, man. Jesus. There's lots more theory in ZAMM but not much practical fucking sense. He uses his bike headlight to light his camp at night to cook his supper and eat, man, but for chrissake with the tiny toy battery on the old Honda that was a dumb fucking idea, man. Later on this Pirsig writes for ten pages about how to remove a broken screw from the block but not once does he tell you about the simple easy way which is the old Ezi-Out screw remover. In fact as far as I could figure out, man, I don't think he ever did get that broken fucking screw out. Also there's something queer about his trouble-finding method which is he don't seem to understand that riding his bike from Chicago up into the Rockies in Wyoming and Idaho caused the overrich fuel mixture because of the high altitude which is a beginner's mistake. He writes a lot about a remedy for engine trouble called Gumption but the only product by that name I ever heard of was something my grandmother bless her holy gash used to clean the kitchen sink with, man, back in Perth Amboy and I wouldn't tell my worst fucking enemy, man, to put any of those gunks in his motor. If you take care of your motor you don't need any fucking artificial additives for chrissake except gas and oil. Sweet motherfucking jesus, man. Then he gives us tips on setting up your own home mechanic's workshop but forgets to tell you the most important of all which naturally is a fucking big shade tree in your backyard and a good trained hungry fucking Doberman attack dog to rip the head off any cocksucking motherfucker lays a hand on your tools. The way he uses to judge how tight a bolt is is not very good when he writes a bolt is either *finger-tight* or *snug* or *tight*. That's crude, man. Somebody should maybe tell that poor fucker about torque wrenches. All in all I'd say though this ZAMM has some useful stuff for you if you are a biker, man, that it is scattered out through too many pages and there's a lot of fuzzy philosophizing and too much half-assed mystical fucking ancient history, man, keeps getting in the way of the book as a fucking whole. If you are serious about reading a book about motorcycles you should get a regular service manual for your particular bike and stick to it and if you want a general information book on how to do it with machines this guy Abbey who hangs around here a lot says a good book is the Velvet Monkey Wrench, and the Guide, man, for the Complete Idiot by John Muir and A Bleak Week at Tinker Creek by Annie Dillard, man, and the Decay of Lying by Oscar Wilde but I ain't got the time to read any more books myself and don't recommend any of them.

17

Paul Horgan's
Josiah Gregg

Josiah Gregg? Who was he? I'll confess that I never heard of him either. But here he is, resurrected and fully rendered in the round by Mr. Horgan, and a superb creation he is, too. Josiah was a child of the American frontier, says our author, born in 1806 in a village in Missouri. A sickly but precocious boy, avid for book learning, he grew up to become a "frontier intellectual." He studied law, medicine, botany, and the literary arts. When only a youth of twenty-three he was invited by the town officials of Jonesborough, Missouri, to deliver the principal Fourth of July speech for the year 1829. The young man's reply to this invitation, though lengthy, is worth quoting in full; if style is character, and manner reveals the man, then his letter explains much of what would happen to him in his remaining twenty-one years.

GENTLEMEN:

Your polite note of yesterday,—informing me of your design to celebrate the Anniversary of our Independence, on the 4th prox. at Jonesborough, and requesting me to deliver an appropriate address on the occasion,—was received last evening. It is, Gentlemen, with sentiments of emotion, that I acknowledge the respect shown me, in thus requesting me to become the "Speaker of the Day"; and I should be "thrice happy" did I think myself, in any degree, adequate to the task: But I fear—aye, I know—that those of you with whom I have had the honour of an acquaintance have greatly over-rated—and those with whom I have not, have been misinformed of, my talents and acquirements—else you would never have selected me to deliver your sentiments to an enlightened audience; when there are so many others of your fellow-citizens, who could (and, I presume, would) discharge the functions of an orator, infinitely more to the satisfaction of, not only to yourselves, but the contemplated auditory.

Yes, Gentlemen, were I ever so competent—and, what is more (with regard to my compliance), were I ever so self-conceited—I should feel an extreme diffidence in undertaking the performance of such a task, at this late hour,—engaged as I am in a business which occupies nearly all my time; and which it would neither be my interest, nor, I presume, the will of my employers, for me to dismiss. Moreover, I have never delivered an address on such an occasion, nor do I make the least pretensions to oratory of any description. Therefore, I trust you will select some one else, whose leisure and talents may enable him to acquit himself with more honour than I should have it in my power to do. In the mean time, however, I will prepare such an address as my business may permit me to compose; which, should you fail (the time being short) in procuring another speaker, I will endeavor to deliver. It would be a very great gratification to me to be excused, for the reasons above, even after having written it—I shall not consider the time occupied idly spent.

I will endeavor to be at Jonesborough next Saturday, when we can make some further arrangements; yet, should I not, you may be assured, Gentlemen, that nothing which you would conceive would be conducive, in the slightest degree, to the enjoyment of yourselves and the company, *will be too arduous to be attempted (though I fear not consummated) by one, who would be happy to be styled,*

Your Friend, and
Most ob't. Servant,
Josiah Gregg
[Flourish]

P.S. You did not mention, or even intimate, in your note, that there was any other person in contemplation, to be my co-adjutor. I should be very glad, should I eventually have to deliver an address, that I could have a fellow-labourer, as mine must needs be short. Mr. P. W. Nawlin—or probably others with whom I am unacquainted—would, I have no doubt, deliver an address on the occasion.

It is a letter such as only an Ebenezer Cooke, protagonist of John Barth's *The Sot-Weed Factor,* or maybe a nineteenth-century Inspector Clouseau, of *Pink Panther* fame, could have penned. The ruling dignitaries of Jonesborough were much impressed, as we can imagine; then as now, now as always, their kind place supreme value on public speech as periphrasis—the fine art of saying as little as possible in the greatest possible number of words.

Unfortunately for young Gregg, the American frontier was mostly populated at that time, as in the best of times, by a common, ignorant, vulgar, and ill-bred sort, congenitally lacking in respect for the sort of oration, rotund and orotund, that Gregg delivered on the date appointed. His address, while well received by the notables in the front row, was interrupted several times with hoots of crude laughter from "surly ruffians" lurking at the back of the crowd, whose animosity "puzzled" our hero.

No matter. Gregg persevered, in all things, and soon became an esteemed member of his community, making his mark primarily as a businessman. In the 1830s he joined the fur trade between St. Louis and the far western town of Santa Fe, then a part of Mexican territory. With others he transported wagonloads of manufactured goods to that remote mountain capital, exchanged them for beaver pelts, and returned to the American city, where he could sell the furs for a tidy profit.

Modestly successful in this business, Gregg gave it up, after nine years of trekking back and forth across the Western plains, to write a book about his adventures called, in full, *Commerce of the Prairies: or, Journal of a Santa Fe Trader, during Eight Expeditions Across the Great Western Plains and a Residence of Nearly Nine Years in Northern Mexico, Illustrated with Maps and Engravings.* The book was published in 1844, becoming a "classic in Western historiography" according to our author Mr. Horgan, "fashioned with high literary skill, the ablest account we have of the Western adventure. Other accounts were possibly as accurate . . . but what other one has the sensitivity which turns observation into vision, and feeling into art?"

High praise indeed, in support of which Mr. Horgan offers us samples from Gregg's book, such as the following:

> Merchants conveying their goods across the prairies in wagons . . . should be entitled to the protection of the Government, as are those who transport them in vessels across the ocean.

> We were encamped at noon, when a murky cloud issued from behind the mountains, and, after hovering over us for a few minutes, gave vent to one of those tremendous peals of thunder . . . making the elements tremble, and leaving us stunned and confounded . . . I was deeply impressed.

> A heap of buffalo bones stretch upward to the height of several feet, so as to present the appearance of so many human beings. Ravens in the same way are not infrequently taken for Indians, as well as for buffalo; and a herd of the latter upon a distant plain often appear so increased in bulk that they would be mistaken . . . for a grove of trees. This is usually attended with a continual waving and looming, which so often writhe and distort distant objects as to render them too indistinct to be discriminated.

Strange and singular observations. I am intrigued for example by that "murky cloud," waiting in ambush, as it were, *behind* a mountain, emerging suddenly to hang above the travelers for several minutes, then start bellowing at them. Or Gregg's description of mirages, resembling none ever seen or heard of since; perhaps Gregg needed a pair of spectacles. But of this kind of prose Mr. Horgan writes, "What is the curious flavor of intimacy in this? He has encompassed a vast act of nature as if he were a painter, able to command the elements in a little square of canvas."

Canvas prose, all right; is Mr. Horgan perhaps pulling the reader's leg a bit here? These quotes, mind you, were chosen by Horgan, not me. Let us consider another excerpt from the writings of Josiah Gregg, this time in his role as Prophet of the Future:

> The high plains seem too dry and lifeless to produce timber; yet might not the vicissitudes of nature operate a change likewise upon the seasons? Why may we not suppose that the genial influences of civilization—that extensive cultivation of the earth— might contribute to the multiplication of showers, as it certainly does of fountains? Or that the shady groves, as they advance on the prairies, may have some effect upon the seasons? May we not hope that these sterile regions might yet be thus revived and fertilized, and their surface covered one day by flourishing settlements [all the way] to the Rocky Mountains?

Sterile regions? Where the grass grew belly-high to a horse, where the bison roamed by the millions, where the plains Indians had created the most colorful, happy, and adventurous culture to appear in all of North America, far superior to anything the white Americans have since supplanted it with? As for Gregg's odd notion that agriculture would stimulate rain, that was later taken up by land speculators and real estate sharks in the lying slogan "Rain follows the plow!"

What actually followed the plow, as we know, were swindled sodbusters stumbling over ox turds, and dust bowls, and Secretaries of Agriculture like Ezra Benson and Earl Butz, and Secretaries of the Interior like James G. Watt.

Let us continue with the epic saga of Josiah Gregg, frontiersman, businessman, scientist, prophet, poet, and the first great Ichabod Klutz of Western folklore.

One morning, Gregg reports, "Our campfire was permitted to *communicate* [my italics] with the prairie grass. As there was a head

wind blowing at the time, we soon got out of reach of the confla-
gration; but the next day, the wind having changed, the fire was
again perceived in our rear approaching us at a very brisk pace."
Gregg and his fellow traders had to run for it, chased across the
landscape by their own campfire. The scene suggests a great new
film: *Inspector Clouseau in the Wild West*.

One more quote from Gregg's book:

> Returning home from our first New Mexican journey, we had
> an opportunity of experiencing a delusion which had been the fre-
> quent subject of remark by travelers on the Prairies before. Accus-
> tomed as we had been for months to our little mules [*little* mules?]
> and the equally small-sized Mexican ponies [burros?], our sight be-
> came so adjusted to their proportions, that when we came to look
> upon the commonest hackney of our frontier horses, it appeared to
> be almost a monster. I have frequently heard exclamations of this
> kind from the new arrivals [Gregg's teamsters]:—"How the Mis-
> sourians have improved their breed of horses!"—"What a huge
> gelding!" "Did you ever see such an animal!"

(Exclamations we doubt ever got exclaimed, especially by to-
bacco-chewing, moonshine-drinking, hard-bitten mule-skinners
returning from an eight-hundred-mile wagon drive across the
plains.) But Mr. Horgan says, "It is these curious and unexpected
details that reveal the observer and the man inclined to share his
odd knowledge." He concludes his summary of Gregg's book with
this, as announcers say on the Tee Vee: "Where poetry and truth
meet: there is always the heart of a human character; and, in literary terms, the source of energy in a great book; and that is what we
may call *Commerce of the Prairies*."

So much for the book within the book. Far more interesting is
Mr. Horgan's account of the life of Josiah Gregg. As indicated by
the evidence of that Jonesborough letter, by his book, and by the
letters and journals later discovered, Gregg was an exceedingly stiff
and humorless man, rigid with his sense of self-importance. He
never drank, hated smoking, and avoided women—never married,
never had amicable relations with any woman, or comfortable relations with any man. And something in his manner seemed to

arouse the meanest impulses in his social inferiors. Everywhere he went, he reports, he found "unaccommodating" innkeepers, "insulting" clerks, and "annoying" steamboatmen. Although his book met with fair success, going through several editions, he left the United States in 1847 for temporary exile in Mexico, where, he hoped, he would be free from "continued annoyance."

On the way, however, war broke out, and Gregg joined the Texan-American invasion of Mexico as interpreter and liaison man, "with the status and perquisites of a Major"—although, as he confided in a letter to his brother, he secretly felt he should have been given the rank of a lieutenant colonel. Riding along with his surveying and botanical equipment piled behind him on the saddle, holding a red silk parasol above his head, Major Gregg found himself, once again, subjected to catcalls and jeers from the common soldiers, whereby he was "a little annoyed. . . ." Collecting botanical specimens on the march, he was forced to endure "taunting and insulting expressions; the naturalist has to pass an ordeal in laboring among ignorant people, who are wholly incapable of understanding the utility of his activities."

His mishaps continued, on to the end. As Mr. Horgan tells us: "He lost his keys by dropping them somewhere. Bending over a pool, he lost his Colt revolver out of its holster and saw it vanish in the water. The same thing happened again. . . ." (Again? Yes, again.) In a journey along the Gulf Coast he took berth on a ship that lacked keel or cutwater and therefore "slid over the water sidewise" before the wind. Who but Josiah Gregg could have found such a vessel? After the war he lived for a time in the Mexican city of Saltillo, among a colony of Americans, and attempted to improve their morals by giving classes in Spanish in the evenings, in order to educate the officers and "break up . . . card parties." Only a few came for the first lesson, and none for the second. Prowling around the historic castle of Chapultepec, Gregg was questioned by a guard in what he thought an insulting manner, answered "with asperity," and was promptly arrested, reviled, kicked out. Gregg protested to the U.S. minister at the capital, demanding punishment of the offenders. Nothing was done.

He journeyed to the west coast of Mexico, meeting with the usual "ill breeding and rascality" on the way, such as that from farmers who loudly objected to his blundering through their corn-fields with his train of pack animals. Reaching the coast, he predicted that all of Pacific Mexico would and should fall under the rule of America and its Manifest Destiny. "In this," writes Mr. Horgan, "Gregg echoed the popular idea of his time, which seems *so foreign to our regard* [my italics] for the independent integrity of the other republics of the hemisphere."

In Mazatlán, our hero Josiah took ship for San Francisco on the barque *Olga*. In Gregg's opinion it was a generally pleasant voyage for a change, highlighted for him by "an agreeable ser-mon" from a "Rev. Mr. Bull." He was puzzled though by the pres-ence on board the *Olga* of "three lone females" who seemed "not wholly destitute, as they sustained a character of virtue and un-ceasing industry." What their industry consisted of, Gregg could not figure out; but the year was 1849, and the "three lone females," like Gregg himself, were bound for the newly discovered gold fields of California.

Now begins the last act of Josiah Gregg's obscure career. As with Don Quixote, what begins in comedy ends in pathos. Some-how Gregg found himself at a place called Rich Bar, in the Trinity Mountains of northwest California. A remote place by overland routes, it appeared that what was needed to bring the delights of American industry to this spot was the discovery of a shortcut through the mountains to the nearby seacoast where, the Indians said, there was a bay suitable for shipping. Gregg volunteered to pioneer the route and induced seven men (they did not know him very well) to go with him. The season was November, and the rain, as it always does in this part of California, was falling. The Indians warned Gregg that rain in the valley meant snow in the moun-tains. "But Gregg," as Mr. Horgan reminds us, "rarely abandoned a course of action once decided upon."

Halfway up the first mountain they encountered snow, as the Indians had foreseen. Undaunted, Gregg led his men, with their pack string of horses, straight up the steepest slope "in order to reach the top more quickly." They stumbled on, over ridge after ridge, for weeks; every time Gregg, the amateur surveyor, took readings with his sextant, the party seemed to get more surely lost. Game was hard to find, and the crew often went hungry. When they finally reached the coastal redwoods Gregg, always botanizing, called on members of the party to assist him in making measurements of the great trees. They answered his calls with "shameful abuse," and when he led his horses into a bog and got them mired, the men refused to help him. As Mr. Horgan says, "a collapse of character overtook the whole party."

Nevertheless, they eventually reached the sea, after more than a month of wandering, in a journey that the Indians had said should take eight days. They found the bay, which Gregg named Trinity, and started the long march down the coast toward the Sacramento Valley. While they straggled through the rain forests a sea captain named Ottinger cruised into the bay, discovering it a second time, and named it Humboldt Bay, which is the name it bears today. Josiah Gregg, meanwhile, had fallen off his horse and promptly died, probably of exposure and exhaustion. His companions, all of whom made it back to civilization, buried him, they *said,* "somewhere near" what is now Clear Lake, California. Gregg was forty-four years old.

When the news of his death came in due course to Mrs. Gregg, Josiah's mother, she remarked, "Well, he overtaxed his energies that time." Mr. Horgan sums up Gregg's short life by writing: "Gregg was of the order of men who create literature out of their most daily preoccupations. . . . He might be called the intellectual frontiersman of the natural world. There is high poetry in the quality of his achievement. . . . His story is part of a great conquest, in which his particular weapons were curiosity and a batch of little bound books with blank pages. . . . No chronicler who loved the truth ever needed more."

Long before I read the final pages of this book I had smelled something shaggy, doggish, fishy. Was our Mr. Horgan capable of a little hoax, having some fun at the expense of the gullible? I opened the biographical section of my dictionary; as I'd suspected no "Josiah Gregg" was listed there. I checked in my *Ranger Rick Complete Outdoors Encyclopedia*—again, no "Josiah Gregg." I mentioned my suspicions to my wife and she suggested an even bolder fraud. "Who," she asked, "is Paul Horgan?"

"Well," I said, "according to the op-title page of this *Josiah Gregg* book, Paul Horgan is the author of such works as *Memories of the Future, The Return of the Weed, Great Reefer, One Red Rose for Christmas, Maurice Baring Restored, A Distant Strumpet,* and many, many, many similar books."

"Never heard of any of them," she said.

A-ha! Again I checked my dictionary, my encyclopedia—and sure enough in neither is this "Paul Horgan" so much as mentioned.

"Perhaps it's a nom de plume à clef—an anagram of the author's real name," my wife decided, and promptly worked out a few of the possibilities. Could "Paul Horgan" be—Luap Nagroh? Alphur Agon? Apul H. Groan? And then, with a laugh, she hit upon it. Of course, of course; it was that sly Nabokovian wag from Winkelman, Arizona, the well-known local barfly, humorist, and newspaper columnist, our old friend Nora! *Nora* . . . of course. Nora P. Laugh! Who else would have dared so witty, so insolent, so elaborate a bagatelle?

18

My Friend Debris

We met one evening in the streets of Santa Fe (Holy Faith!), New Mexico, in the springtime of 1959. A good year that one, excelled—at least in my experience—only by 1960 and each succeeding year. My friend Debris was staggering down Palace Avenue, supported on the arms of an artistic woman named Rini Templeton, whom I had met a short time previously in the editorial offices of a Taos newspaper called *El Crepúsculo de la Libertad.* I had not yet learned how that name was translated into American but I did know that I was supposed to be the paper's editor-in-chief. As proof of my newfound dignity I carried in an inside pocket of my 1952 Sears Roebuck wino jacket (burgundy corduroy—threads of the king) a bona fide paycheck for *one hundred dollars.* A powerful sum of money in those subbohemian, underground-beatnik days. And all for only one week's work.

How this came about is a complicated story of confusion, misunderstanding, mistaken identity, extravagant hopes, exaggerated credentials, and general good will. One day I was a student of classical philosophy subsisting on Cheez-Its in a basement pad in the undergrad ghettos of Albuquerque; a week later I was dining on rack of lamb *bouquetierre* and rice pilaf and Châteauneuf-du-Pape or something at a five-star restaurant in Taos—I forget the name of the joint—where I paid the tab by scribbling my signature on a chit and walking out with a fat flaming cigar. It's quite true, what I'd always heard: when you're rich and important you don't need money. You never touch it.

One hundred dollars a week!

I sang, as I walked along, to the tune of "Red Flag" and "O Tannenbaum," an old song of the revolution, *viz.,*

> The working class
> Can kiss my ass,
> I've got the fore-
> man's job at last!

As for Taos, New Mexico, there is little that need be added to the volumes already available on the subject. Nabokov described the town adequately in a letter to Edmund Wilson: ". . . a dismal place inhabited by faded pansies and second-rate artists." Nabokov was thinking of painters, not writers, but Taos and New Mexico as a whole suffered then and suffer still, despite pretensions, from a conspicuous lack of first-rate literary artists. D. H. Lawrence had died and been cremated nearly three decades earlier, and not in New Mexico; the gaseous essence of his mortal envelope had now become mere traces in the smog nuisance over southern France. John Nichols was a boy in New York City. William Eastlake, hidden from the world on his rancho near the village of Cuba, was more a part of Indian Country than of the "Land of Enchantment." And he would not stay. Robert Creeley was another transient. Judson Crews would soon depart for Africa. Willa Cather was in Heaven, where she had always wanted to be. And, so—who was left? Frank Waters, the Hopi transcendentalist?

Four names remain to be mentioned. Three of these, Apul H. Groan, Luap Nagroh, and the popular Nora P. Laugh, were even then collaborating on their Pulitzer Prize–winning book about New Mexico and the Rio Grande—*Great Reefer: The Story of a Land and Its People.* The fourth, the fiery and promethean poet Alphur Agon, had ceased to write, alas, and was now retired to deep seclusion on his estate in Española with his acolytes—the three furies, Frieda, Mabel, and Brett. There is nothing more to be said of the New Mexican literary scene.

Anyway, this is the story of my friend Debris. He was staggering, as I've said, marching to a drummer all his own, down the avenue and into the Plaza, propped up none too steadily by our mutual friend Rini Templeton. He seemed to be singing, a song of which I caught only the refrain, repeated with dogmatic insistence:

"Nous allons, nous allons,
Nous allons sur la motif . . ."

If I heard aright. Rini introduced us. "This is John De Puy," she said, pronouncing his name *duh-pwee,* in the correct French manner.

"Debris?"

"De *Puy,*" she repeated. "Of the well."

The tall thin fragile-looking fellow glared at me, his eyes enormous, intense, half demented, behind the thick lenses of his spectacles. His hair was bushy, curly, black, his mustache full and drooping in the style of Emiliano Zapata. Or of Bartolomeo Vanzetti. He could have passed for an anarchistic organ-grinder. Only the monkey was lacking, and the tin cup. Perhaps the monkey was on his back; I suspected more than alcohol at work here. But the drug, as I would eventually understand, was not chemical but alchemical: the alkaloids of genius.

"My name is Del Poggio," he said in deep and somber tones, mock-heroic, "and my people come from the mountains."

"From the cistern," said Rini, hugging him tightly around his lean waist. "They crawled out of a cistern."

I held out my hand. He considered for a moment, then allowed me to shake his hand. "I've heard of you," I said. "You're the artist, right?"

"The man, the artist, the failure," he corrected.

"He calls himself an artist," Rini said, "but right now he couldn't draw a sober breath."

"It is true that I am drunk," De Puy said, "but it is not true that I am always drunk. We will meet again, Abbey. Beware."

I watched them wobble past the Palace of the Governors, arm in arm, mutually supportive, bound for another bar en route to an Odetta concert. That Rini Templeton was a fine figure of a woman—still is—but De Puy looked too thin, almost emaciated; inside his stiff new Levi Strauss blue jeans there appeared to be no hams at all. No buttocks. The man would never be popular in Santa Fe. Nor get far in the art world. I assumed that I would never see him again.

But I encountered them both once more, that very evening, at the concert. I too was in love with Odetta—beautiful and magnificent black goddess, planted solid as a tree on stage, belting out her freedom songs with a power that made the house rock. I found De Puy backstage afterward, on hands and knees among the crowd that pressed upon the singer. Like me he desired only to kiss the hem of Odetta's garment, maybe lift it a little.

In the twenty-two years that have since lapsed, relapsed, prolapsed, and collapsed between us, Debris and I have shared many adventures and some misadventures, helping each other through the anxieties of fatherhood, the joys of marriage, the despair of separation and divorce, the deep purple funk of creative inertia. And survived. And thrived. We have both been very lucky. But we deserved it.

We have hiked through the Maze together. The little maze and the big maze. We have circumambulated Navajo Mountain—navel of the universe—and camped together under its slickrock buttresses. We have climbed to the shoulders of Wilson Peak, leaving the summit untouched, out of natural piety. We have blundered through the cactus forests of Arizona and penetrated to the secret heart of the canyonlands. We have dropped off

North Rim down to Thunder River, lain in the shade of limestone ledges while the sun roared like a lion three feet away, and discussed the mystery of the death of a father, of a wife—that inexplicable *disappearance.*

We have staggered together, like him and Rini, down the icy winter streets of Santa Fe, of Telluride, of Hoboken, and Manhattan—yes, Manhattan, where Debris hammered on the locked doors of Saint Patrick's Cathedral at two in the morning, demanding admittance. God would not let us in. Can't blame Him. Two kindly policemen led us away, commandeered a taxi, sent us home. Home to Moab, Utah. To Oracle, Arizona. To Ojo Caliente (Hot Eye), and Jemez Springs, New Mexico.

I saw my friend Debris, enraged, overturn a punchbowl in the Seligman Galleries, New York, and smash it against the wall, and once I saw him dip a survey pole in gasoline and hurl it like a spear, flaming, from the verge of Dead Horse Point above the Colorado River, down into darkness a thousand feet below. As a matter of course, like good sagebrush patriots, we have burned or leveled innumerable billboards together, and sanded and sugared a goodly number of earthmovers, ore trucks, front-end loaders and Caterpillar bulldozers. Naturally.

And we have quarreled, and lied, and thieved from each other when necessary: he sold my best deer rifle for an airline ticket to Zurich, whence his wife had fled; in retaliation, when I discovered the loss, I sold his household furniture to a dealer in Distressed Freight, turning a fair profit. Those were dark days in Santa Fe, and long ago, never to return.

I have touched upon certain high points, making our long friendship seem, perhaps, more bright and merry than it actually was. In truth when we are together now we spend half our time semisodden with cheap American beer, reviewing the past and previewing the future in ever more flattering light, and the other half engaged in our plodding, furtive, solitary labors, Debris at his sketchbook or easel, me at my last where I am cobbling a shoe of wood (*le sabotage*) that will kick down all doors from all jambs forever.

My friend Debris looks today more like a sheepherder than an organ-grinder, more like Einstein than Zapata. He is and appears part Basque, part Cretan, part stargazer, wholly a mystic. The rich curly dark hair has turned gray (like my beard) and his face is the lined, browned, wind-burned face of a man who has spent at least half of his fifty-odd years in the out-of-doors. Where we are happiest. Blessed with a hyperactive metabolism, Debris has never put on weight, despite the fact that he drinks beer from morning to night, every day, a continuous "transfusion" as he calls it, and eats with the gusto of a hungry wolf, moaning and groaning over his feed like a man in the throes of love. He remains as skinny and scrawny, as wiry and fibrous and hard as he was in the days of our youth.

He loves to eat. He loves to drink. He loves to cook. An insomniac, he rises always before the dawn, lights his Coleman lantern, starts the fire, brews a powerful and deadly Earl Grey tea loaded with honey and milk. He stumbles about camp in the dark, mumbling and chanting, comes presently to me and my lady with a hot steaming mug in each fist, a grin full of teeth below the Zapatista mustache. Salmon-colored clouds float on the east. Stars all over the west. We sit up naked in our ziplock sleeping-together bag.

"Drink," says the grin; "hot tea."

"It's early, Debris."

"Drink!" He thrusts the mugs into our hands, then weaves back to the campfire, there to prepare the breakfast omelets—huge mucoid globs of chicken embryo quivering with potency denied, browned and folded over the slime of melted cheese, the hot viscous kelplike green chiles, the sliced and sautéed onions, the reek of garlic and garlic salt. . . .

"My God, Debris, too much garlic."

"There can never be too much garlic."

"I hate garlic, you goddamned Frog."

"Don't whine and snivel at me, you puking Presbyterian. Eat!"

De Puy's cooking, like his art, reminds me of Poe at his most

Byronic: "Of the glory that was Greece/ And the garlic that was Rome."

His wife Tina Johnson emerges from the back of their pickup camper, approaches us through *el crepúsculo,* the twilight, of our mountain morning. She is a plump and pretty woman, brown and fair and Scandinavian, feisty but sweet, a total female, and about twenty years younger than Debris. She is his fifth wife. His fifth and *final* wife, says Tina, and hopefully John agrees.

She had come to him several years before as a student and apprentice from Evergreen College in Washington, and stayed, graduating into matrimony with honors and distinction. She is a crafty artisan, a maker of jewelry that she sells from New York to Scottsdale. She is dressed this morning like a gypsy in full skirt, flowered blouse, a scarlet kerchief on her head and golden hoops dangling from her pierced ears. She wears sandals. She plays the guitar. She smokes a pipe, farts when she feels like it, and swears like a man. A good honest woman.

I like her, and I usually don't approve of my friend's wives. His others had been too political, constantly getting poor John into trouble with their Red Brigades, Fidelismo, Maoist Mau Mau, Socialist Workers and Socialist Labor and Weathermen Underground. Distracting him from his duty, which is to paint pictures. Tina is not like that. She is a natural anarchist, like us, like all genteel, sensible, petit-bourgeois people in these days of total institutions and global power. (Our highest criminal ambition is to rob the World Bank. Give the money to the deserving poor, to you and me and Muzzie Schwartz down there on the street peddling his roasted chestnuts. Let's hear no more of this.)

Not only does Debris's wife look gypsylike, so does his summer home. He owns twenty acres on a wooded mesa in southeast Utah. From the center of his place you can see mountains and marvels in all directions: the Blue Mountains close by on the northwest, the San Juans to the east in Colorado, Sleeping Ute Mountain, Shiprock and the Chuskas and Monument Valley in the Navajo Nation, Comb Ridge and Cedar Mesa and the Bear's Ears Buttes to the west and southwest. On a clear day you can see all the way to Navajo Mountain, a hundred miles by line of sight.

For five years De Puy has been planning to build a cabin here, an A-frame on stilts, but so far he has built nothing substantial. The kitchen is a large juniper tree with ramadalike shelter attached, from the struts and spars and limbs of which hang skillets, pots, towels, rags, mirror, waterbags, canteens, shovel, ax, bucksaw, and other tools, implements, and utens. We eat breakfast on a government-surplus picnic table. John and Tina sleep in their camper-truck, a veteran GMC. The guesthouse is a tent. When in residence here they do their work in a battered housetrailer that Debris had hauled in a couple of years previously.

This housetrailer—an immobile home—is old and drafty, infested with mice, hooked up to nothing; there is no plumbing or electricity. Not needed. The trailer is jacked up on cinderblocks but not properly leveled. It sags to the east. To walk inside is like entering on the deck of a listing boat. It has always been this way. Debris and Tina like it this way.

Here in this listing trailerhouse, during the summer months, Tina manufactures her jewelry and my friend De Puy paints his paintings. His studio is small but well lighted, well ventilated. He has room for a stack of stretched canvases, a shelf of books, a worktable, the easel and the work-in-progress. There are posters, drawings, and photographs tacked to the wall—photos of friends, of natural scenes, and one of the artist himself posed dramatically, with pipe and walking stick and slouch hat, before a sunset sky. The only concession to vanity.

And what do we see on the easel? A window. An opening through a wall. In a moment I will explain.

Most of the year, eight or nine months, Debris and his wife spend in their modest home near Jemez Springs, in the high country of northern New Mexico. Harsh country—too hot in summer, cold in winter. Debris hauls and cuts a lot of firewood. And every morning, all year around, he brews his black, bitter tea. He smokes a pipe continuously, makes his own jerky, and cooks about half the time over an open fire. He drinks too much—not only beer but whatever's available with an appreciable alcoholic content. Blackberry brandy for chilly nights.

The effect of these incontinent habits has been, through the decades and so far, to keep my friend well preserved, in alcohol, tobacco, woodsmoke, tea, vitamin C, and old underwear, inside and out. He walks with a long and loping stride, uphill and downhill, through brush and over rocks, like a man accustomed to exploring, prospecting, searching. He expects to live for about 140 years—"indefinitely."

What he is seeking and what he has found appears in the strange, powerful, brooding and mystical art that has been his lifework. His graphics and oil paintings represent, clearly, recognizably, the landscape of the American Southwest—mountains, mesas, volcanoes, abysmal gorges and gleaming rivers, the stillness of the desert under vast moons and domineering suns. But De Puy's landscape is not the landscape we see with routine eyes or can record by camera. He paints a hallucinated, magical, sometimes fearsome world—not the world that we think we see but the one, he declares, that is really there. A world of terror as well as beauty—the beauty that lies beyond the ordinary limits of human experience, that forms the basis of experience, the ground of being.

Vague, pompous, pretentious words. I'm not sure what they mean. One would prefer to be precise and clear. But there is something in the art of John De Puy, as there is in a mountain or butte or canyon itself, that defies the precision and clarity of simple descriptive language. Whatever we can find to say about a desert mountain or a De Puy painting, there is always something more, obscure but ominously *present,* which cannot be said.

It will not suffice to dismiss this essential mystery as mere romanticism. The Romantics, after all, in art, music, poetry, philosophy, in action and in life, were onto something. Something real. Something as real as rock and sun and the human mind. Thus they were, and they remain—necessary. There is no "mere" about it.

Bloated rhetoric, I agree. A breezy effort at explanation. "Let Being be," said Martin Heidegger, *das Denker Kraut,* in a mere seventeen volumes. Exactly. "Whereof one cannot speak, thereof one must be silent," said Ludwig Wittgenstein in one sentence. Precisely. When Beethoven was asked to explain the meaning of one of his sonatas, he simply sat down at the piano and played it through again.

The facts in the case of J. Debris, as Poe would put it, are as follows:

Born in New Jersey during the Coolidge-Hoover era, he studied anthropology with Ruth Benedict as instructor at Columbia University; these studies brought him to the Southwest and into contact with the landforms and ancient cultures of our region. The Korean War interrupted this phase of his development. De Puy is a Navy veteran of World War II and had been enlisted (by mistake, he says) in the naval reserve. When he was called up for service in Korea he went over the hill—Absent Without Leave. At the time he believed he was Thoreau, and lived on the Navajo reservation, working at a trading post. When he was caught and tried, his military lawyer pleaded temporary insanity. The Navy locked him up in a psychiatric prison.

Debris spent six months rattling bars and chanting "More guns. Less butter. Man is made for war, woman for procreation."

The Navy gave him a medical discharge and turned him loose; the government was glad to get off so easy. Debris took advantage of his new freedom to study art and philosophy for a year at Oxford, then returned to New York for a year of Action Painting with Hans Hofmann and the push and pull school. When he'd had enough of that he came home to the West for good.

Except for journeys to France, Switzerland, Greece, and Crete, he has lived and worked ever since in the highlands of New Mexico and Utah. God's country—and the artist's. Thirty years of hectic marriages, four children, two deaths in the family, troubles and accidents, have not diminished his appetite for love, nature, life. Nor has the relative obscurity of his professional career—he makes little effort to show or promote his work—dimmed his enthusiasm for the craft and the passion of his art. He continues to paint as steadily, earnestly, furiously as before, with an ever-growing boldness and simplicity. Not so much for the glory of it—glory is fleeting—as for the joy in the act itself and for the satisfaction in the object created.

How would I place De Puy in the contemporary art scene? He belongs, I suppose, to the school called Expressionism, or to what I would call romantic naturalism, in the tradition of El Greco, Goya, Van Gogh, Nolde, Dove, Clyfford Still, Georgia O'Keeffe. And no doubt others. But in my opinion John De Puy belongs to no school but his own. In my opinion he is the best landscape painter now at work in these United States. I never tire of looking at his pictures. They have a liberating quality. They make a window in the wall of our modern techno-industrial workhouse, a window that leads the eye and the heart and the mind through the wall and far out into the freedom of the old and original world. They take us back to where we came from, long ago. Back to where we took the wrong fork in the road.

My friend is not only a great painter of romantic landscapes but also a maker of superior jerky. In return for my recipes for Voluntary Poverty Pinto Bean Sludge and R. K. Stew, he gives me his for *Jerky Supreme à la Debris*®:

Take five pounds frozen round steak or brisket, slice into thin (⅛-inch) strips. Marinate for 12 hours in a mixture of wine vinegar, Worcestershire sauce, olive oil, red chili powder, salt, garlic salt (*mais oui!*), and beer. (Heineken's will do.) (Or Black Swan.) Pin to a line in hot sun, if in an arid climate, for about twenty-four hours or until done, or dry in an oven for eight to twelve hours 200° F.; leave the oven door open about one inch to allow circulation of air. Remove. Cool. Place in pack. Place pack on back. March twenty miles into wilderness. Open pack. *Mangez!*

For the discriminating gourmet, Debris offers his jerky stew:

In pot or Dutch oven, dump onions, green peppers, potatoes (I prefer turnips myelf—I like that iron and earthy flavor), carrots, chopped celery, chili, garlic, a pound or two or three of Jerky Supreme à la Debris,® a bottle or two of red wine, and basil, oregano, more garlic, more chili, more wine, and more what have you, what the hell, I've forgotten the exact amounts or what ingredients, it all comes out fine in the end, cook until ready, eat. Will feed five hungry storm troopers or two starving artists.

Debris is willing to grant the authenticity of my concern with eating, but has somehow gotten the impression that I am not seriously interested in the art of cookery. He listens, therefore, with feigned attention at best, with impatience, with visible disinterest, as I sketch out my culinary inventions. To wit:

Voluntary Poverty Hardcase Survival Pinto Bean Sludge®

1. Take one fifty-lb sack Dipstick County pinto beans. Remove stones, cockleburs, horseshit, ants, lizards, etc. Wash in cold clear crick water. Soak twenty-four hours in cast-iron kettle or earthenware pot. (DO NOT USE TEFLON, ALUMINUM, OR PYREX. THIS WARNING CANNOT BE OVERSTRESSED.)

2. Place kettle or pot with beans on low fire, simmer for twenty-four hours. (DO NOT POUR OFF WATER IN WHICH BEANS HAVE SOAKED. VERY IMPORTANT.) Fire must be of juniper, piñon pine, scrub oak, mesquite, or ironwood. Other fuels may tend to modify or denigrate the subtle flavor and delicate bouquet of Pinto Bean Sludge.

3. DO NOT BOIL. Add water when necessary.

4. Stir gently from time to time with wooden spoon. (DO NOT DISREGARD THESE DETAILS.)

5. After simmering, add one gallon green chiles. Stir gently. Avoid bruising beans. Add one-half quart pure natural sea salt. During following twelve hours stir frequently and add additional flavoring as desired, such as, for example, ham hocks. Or bacon rinds. Or saltpork, corncobs, kidney stones, jungle boots, tennis shoes, jockstraps, cinch straps, whatnot, old saddle blanket, use your own judgment. Simmer additional twenty-four hours.

6. Ladle as many servings as desired from pot but do not remove pot from fire. Allow to simmer continuously through following days and weeks, or until contents totally consumed. Stir from time to time, gently, when in vicinity. (DO NOT ABUSE BEANS.)

7. Serve Voluntary Poverty Hardcase Survival Pinto Bean Sludge® on small flat rocks that have been warmed in sun. If flat rocks not available, any convenient fairly level surface will do. Plates may be used, if obtainable. (WEDGWOOD ONLY, PLEASE!) After serving, slather beans generously with *salsa,* ketchup, or barbecue sauce. Garnish with sprigs of fresh sagebrush. (Your guests will be amused and pleased.)

8. One cauldron of Pinto Bean Sludge, as specified above, will feed one starving artist for approximately two weeks. A grain supplement, such as rice, wheat, or maize, is needed for full protein complement.

9. The philosopher Pythagoras declared flatulence incompatible with thought and meditation. For this reason he forbade the eating of beans in his ashram. We have found, however, that thorough cooking ameliorates the condition, and custom (or solitude) alleviates the social embarrassment.

Second recipe:

Arizona Highways R.[1] K.[2] Stew®

½ cup rattlesnake grease à la blacktop
2 lbs sun-dried skunk (from the middle of the road)
¼ cup jackrabbit blood (dehydrated)
2 lbs squashed cottontail bunny
2 lbs flattened chipmunk (with tread marks)
1½ lbs macerated ground squirrel
1½ lbs laminated kangaroo rat
2 lbs elongated bull snake
2 lbs mashed house cat
2 lbs smashed dog à la asphalt
etc., etc., etc.

We are visiting a bar in the town of Garlic (a.k.a. Ajo), Arizona. The bar is full of locals, mostly citizens of the Mexican and Papago Indian preference. My friend is dancing. John has approached several of the Papago ladies—short stout barrel-shaped women with cheerful brown faces and long rich lovely hair so black it looks blue—but they have all turned him down, laughing. Even the fattest of them, who looks like the Venus of Willendorf, has declined his courteous invitation. Therefore my friend Debris, untroubled, dances alone.

He dances like Zorba the Greek, like Anthony Quinn, in the middle of the empty floor, hands clasped behind his back, old pipe smoking in his mouth, the decayed and rotten slouch hat on his head. The jukebox is playing *Mi Corazón es su Corazón* by Gabriel Cruz y sus Conjuntos. Ranchero music—guitars and violins and trumpets. A barbarous racket. Debris dances solemnly forward, then back, twirls, spreads his arms like wings and turns his face to the ceiling. Eyes closed, dancing, he flies, he soars, he sails like an eagle across the empyrean of his soul. Alone in the universe, he

[1]road [2]kill

makes it all his own. No one but me pays him any heed. Just another gringo drunk. But what a beautiful, happy, ontological gringo drunk. Only one pitcher of beer—and God entered his soul.

We drive into the desert beyond Garlic, beyond Why, beyond the ghost town of Pourquoi Non, beyond the far western borders of Hedgehog Cactus National Park where I had once been employed, for three elegant winters, as a patrol ranger. Under the moon we pass Kino Peak, the Bates Range, the Growler Range, past warning signs lettered in red on white, riddled with bullet holes where we enter the Air Force Gunnery Range. This is the bleakest wasteland east or west of the Empty Quarter. A gaunt and spectral landscape littered with .50-caliber machine-gun shells, 88-mm cannon shells, unexploded rockets, and aerial tow targets stuck nose-down in the sand like twelve-foot arrowheads. Nobody lives here but the diamondback, the fatal coral snake, the Gila monster, the tarantula and the scorpion, and us, from time to time. Debris and I love the place. God loves it. The Air Force loves it. And nobody else I know of but a Green Beret named Douglas Heiduk, who discovered it years ago.

The dirt road becomes impassable, a torture track of sand traps and volcanic rocks with flint-sharp edges, petering out in prehistoric Indian paths. A tribe called the Sand Papagos haunted the region until a century ago, lurking about the few known waterholes, ambushing bighorn sheep, Spanish missionaries, gold seekers, and other pioneers, and eating them. The one road through this desert, long since abandoned, was called El Camino del Diablo—the Devil's Highway.

And what became of the Sand Papagos? Historians say they were wiped out by the Mexican military, or by disease, or by a change in the climate. But John De Puy and I know better.

We stop the truck, shut off the motor, get out, and vomit. Feeling better we open another jug. My friend Debris hurls an empty bottle at the stars and bellows through the silence, *Chinga los cosmos!*

Nobody answers. Far to the north we can see flares, bright as molten magnesium, floating down across the sky. We hear the mutter of gunnery, like distant thunder. It's only the Air Force, hunting the last of the Sand Papagos. Something to do on a Monday night. Watching those eerie lights, Debris crossed himself and recites an introit, his version of the prayer: *"Dominus vobiscum et tu spiritu, sancto oremus, pace . . . pace . . . pace. . . ."*

Once an R.C. always an R.C. His mother was Irish, her family name Early. He'd been an altar boy, of course, long ago and far away, in another country. (New Jersey.) Although he worships at an older and grander altar now, De Puy expects to end up, as they all do, back in the arms of the Mother Church. Not by choice but because he feels he will have no choice. Frankly, he wants to live—to exist—to *be*—forever.

Why?

Out of spite.

You owe the earth a body.

But not my soul.

I seem to hear Gregorian chants in the distance, coming from far beyond and above the desert mountains. Sound of the *Dies Irae.* I shiver in the chill night, the fantasy passes. We build our ritual little fire of mesquite twigs, spread out bedrolls on the ground, contemplate the flames. The Air Force goes to bed. The silence becomes complete.

But forever? I say. That's a long time.

Only an instant, says De Puy.

I fall asleep, by slow degrees, while my friend puffs on his pipe and explains to me the peculiarities of his quaint Roman religion. He talks; I dream.

I dream of a country church in Appalachia, painted white, shaded by giant white oaks. There is a graveyard on the hillside nearby, most of the headstones at least a century old. Some of the graves are marked with rusted iron stars and standards that carry the shafts of tiny, faded American flags. The stars bear the initials G.A.R. Grand Army of the Republic. Roots and branches of the family tree. My three brothers and I are marching through the woods, rifles on our shoulders. It seems to be autumn; the dead leaves rattle beneath our feet. We march swiftly, easily, without effort, without fear, toward a joyously desired but unimaginable fulfillment. There are other men with us, ahead, behind, on both sides. We all march easily, swiftly, without effort, without speaking, toward the lights that glimmer off and on, like summer lightning, beyond the trees, beyond the dark ridge ahead. No one speaks. We move swiftly, easily . . .

De Puy is bustling about in the gloom, mumbling and grumbling, making the tea. Stars crowded over the west, opaline clouds on the east. One bird cheeps in the bush. The hackberry bush that grows by the dry wash, by the arroyo that snakes across the desert. I sit up in my sleeping bag, reach for my shirt and leather vest— the air is cold. Debris comes with the steaming mug, the maniacal grin, his mad eyes gleaming behind the glasses.

"Allons-nous," he snarls.

"No!"

"But yes!"

"But for chrissake, Debris, it's still dark."

He shoves the mug of hot tea into my hand and points over my shoulder toward the east. "Rosy fingers." He indicates the jagged pinnacles of the mountains, charcoal black and cobalt blue against the cadmium red of dawn. *"La motif,* it will not wait." Scarlet vermilion in his eyes.

I put on my hat and boots. We eat the Debris breakfast, the eggs and the cheese and the thick home-baked bread, washed down with about a quart each of the violent tea. Then the beer. Why always this nonsense of rocks, peaks, crags, sunrise skies, I ask him. Why can't you stay home, like other artists do, in a warm snug comfortable studio, and paint, well, say, what I would paint (if I didn't have better things to do), namely, a damn good-looking woman sprawled recklessly upon a divan, her peignoir a pool of black satin oozing across the floor, and in her green-gold eyes the sullen glow of an insane insatiable lust! Eh? why not?

"You're spilling your tea," De Puy says.

"But why don't you?"

He smiles, puffing on the pipe, and quotes freely from the

journal of Ferdinand Victor Eugène Delacroix: " 'The energy
which should have gone this morning into my painting I expended
instead upon the recumbent form of the model.' I had," he adds,
"about a year of that in England." He fidgets, glances at the sky,
stands up. "Time to work."

I see that he is ready; the daypack on his shoulders holding the
sketchbooks, jerky, canteen of water; his shirt pockets braced with
a battery of Marvy Markers and Pentel felt-tips of various calibers.

"Or *schmierkunst,*" I say, "why not paint *schmierkunst?* Some ab-
stract frenzy of the inner eye, like Pollock or Rothko or Gottlieb or
What's-his-name? Why not a study of your neighborhood laun-
dromat in photographic neorealism? Why not a bowl of fruit on a
green felt table? Pears? Turnips? Apples? Poker chips? Okra?"

"I've done it all," he says, slashing at the air with his walking
stick. "Now I must paint the real world. *Allons-nous!*"

Time to march.

Very well. We go.

Our job is to record, each in his own way, this world of light
and shadow and time that will never come again exactly as it is
today. And as we walk toward the sunrise, my friend Debris sings
once again the little theme which *his* friends Gauguin and Van
Gogh had also sung when they sauntered out each morning, a century before, into the rosy hills of Provence.

Allons! Allons!

Nous allons sur la motif!

19

~~~~~~

Floating

Each precious moment entails every other. Each sacred place suggests the immanent presence of all places. Each man, each woman, exemplifies all humans. The bright faces of my companions, here, now, on this Rio Dolores, this River of Sorrows, somewhere in the melodramatic landscape of southwest Colorado, break my heart—for in their faces, eyes, vivid bodies in action, I see the hope and joy and tragedy of humanity everywhere. Just as the hermit thrush, singing its threnody back in the piney gloom of the forest, speaks for the lost and voiceless everywhere.

What am I trying to say? The same as before—everything. Nothing more than that. Everything implied by water, motion, rivers, boats. By the flowing . . .

What the hell. Here we go again, down one more condemned river. Our foolish rubber rafts nose into the channel and bob on

~~~~~~

the current. Brown waves glitter in the sunlight. The long oars of the boatpeople—young women, young men—bite into the heavy water. Snow melt from the San Juan Mountains creates a river in flood, and the cold waters slide past the willows, hiss upon the gravel bars, thunder and roar among the rocks in a foaming chaos of exaltation.

Call me Jonah. I should have been a condor, sailing high above the gray deserts of the Atacama. I should have stayed in Hoboken when I had the chance. Every river I touch turns to heartbreak. Floating down a portion of Rio Colorado in Utah on a rare month in spring, twenty-two years ago, a friend and I found ourselves passing through a world so beautiful it seemed and had to be—eternal. Such perfection of being, we thought—these glens of sandstone, these winding corridors of mystery, leading each to its solitary revelation—could not possibly be changed. The philosophers and the theologians have agreed, for three thousand years, that the perfect is immutable—that which cannot alter and cannot ever be altered. They were wrong. We were wrong. Glen Canyon was destroyed. Everything changes, and nothing is more vulnerable than the beautiful.

Why yes, the Dolores, too, is scheduled for damnation. Only a little dam, say the politicians, one little earth-fill dam to irrigate the sorghum and alfalfa plantations, and then, most likely, to supply the industrial parks and syn-fuel factories of Cortez, Shithead Capital of Dipstick County, Colorado. True, only a little dam. But dammit, it's only a little river.

Forget it. Write it off. Fix your mind on the feel of the oars in your hands, observe with care the gay ripples that lead to the next riffle, watch out for that waterlogged fir tree there, clinging to the left bank, its trunk beneath the surface, one sharp snag like a claw carving the flow, ready to rip your tender raft from stem to stern. Follow that young lady boatman ahead, she knows what she's doing, she's been down this one before, several times. Admire her bare arms, glistening with wetness, and the deep-breathing surge of her splendid breasts—better fasten that life jacket, honey!—as she takes a deep stroke with the oars and tugs her boat, ferrywise, across the current and past the danger. Her passengers groan with delight.

Women and rivers. Rivers and men. Boys and girls against United Power & Gas. Concentrating too hard, I miss the snag but pivot off the submerged rock beyond, turning my boat backward into the rapids. My two passengers look anxious—

"For godsake, Ed, didn't you see that rock?"

"What rock?"

—but I have no fear. Hardly know the meaning of the word. God will carry us through. God loves fools, finds a need for us, how otherwise could we survive? Through all the perilous millennia? Fools, little children, drunks, and concupiscent scriveners play a useful function, its precise nature not yet determined, in the intricate operations of evolution. Furthermore, I reflect—

"Watch out!"

"What?"

"Rock!"

"Where?"

—as we do another graceful pivot turn off a second rock, straightening my boat to face downstream again, furthermore, it seems clear at last that our love for the natural world—Nature—is the only means by which we can requite God's obvious love for it. Else why create Nature? Is God immune to the pangs of unreciprocated love? I doubt it. Does God love *us?* Well, that's another question. Does God exist? If perfect, He must. But nobody's perfect. I ponder the ontological dilemma.

"Watch it!"

"Who?"

"The wall!"

The strong current bears us toward the overhanging wall on the outside bend of the river. A sure deathtrap. Wrapped on stone by a liquid hand with the force of a mountain in its pressure, we would drown like rats in a rainbarrel pushed under by wanton boys with brooms. ("We are as boys to wanton sports . . .") Panic, terror, suffocation—not even our life jackets could save us there. Something to think about, I think, as I contemplate the imminent danger, and meditate upon possible alternatives to a sudden, sodden, personal extinction. Walt Blackadar, I remember, world's greatest kayaker, died in similar fashion beneath a jammed half-sunken tree on the Payette River in Idaho.

"Jesus!"

"What?"

"Good Christ!"

God's love. God's elbow. We graze the wall and spin out into the sun. Not much damage: a slightly bent oarlock, a smear of powdery sandstone on the left gunwale, and my old straw hat left behind forever, snared on the branch of a shrub of some kind protruding from the rock. A last-minute pull with my oars—good reflexes here—has saved us from the deepest part of the overhang and propelled us into safety. I've said it before: Faith alone is not enough. Thou must know what thou art doing. *His Brother* sayeth it: "Good works is the key to Heaven . . . be ye doers of the Word, and not hearers only . . ." (James 1:22)

Yes, sir.

Flat water lies ahead. Our River of Sorrows, bound for a sea it will never reach, rolls for a while into a stretch of relative peace.

A good boatman must know when to act, when to react, and when to rest. I lean on the oars, lifting them like bony wings from the water, and ignore the whining and mewling from the two passengers seated behind me. Will probably be free of them after lunch; they'll find another boat. Nothing more tiresome to a thoughtful oarsman than critics.

I think of lunch: tuna from a tin, beslobbered with mayonnaise. Fig Newtons and Oreo cookies. A thick-skin Sunkist orange peeled in a crafty way to reveal a manikin in a state of urgent priapism. Salami and cheese and purple-peeled onions. Our world is so full of beautiful things: fruit and ideas and women and good men and banjo music and onions with purple skins. A virtual Paradise. But even Paradise can be damned, flooded, overrun, generally mucked up by fools in pursuit of paper profits and plastic happiness.

My thoughts wander to Mark Dubois. Talk about the *right stuff.* That young man chained himself to a rock, in a hidden place known only to a single friend, in order to save—if only for the time being—a river he had learned to know and love too much: the Stanislaus in northern California. Mark Dubois put his life on the rock, below high-water line, and drove half the officialdom of California and the Army Corps of Engineers into exasperated response, forcing them to halt the filling of what they call the New Melones Dam. For a time.

In comparing the government functionaries of the United States to those of such states as the Soviet Union, or China, or Brazil or Argentina, we are obliged to give our own a certain degree of credit: they are still reluctant to sacrifice human lives to industrial purposes in the full glare of publicity. (Why we need a free press.) But I prefer to give my thanks direct to people like Mark Dubois, whose courage, in serving a cause worthy of service, seems to me of much more value than that of our astronauts and cosmonauts and other assorted technetronic whatnots: dropouts, all of them, from the real world of earth, rivers, life.

One river gained a reprieve; another goes under. Somebody recently sent me a newspaper clipping from Nashville, in which I read this story:

> Loudon, Tenn. (AP)—Forty years of dreams and sweat have died beneath a bulldozer's blade as the Tennessee Valley Authority crushed the last two homes standing in the way of its Tellico Dam.
>
> The bulldozers arrived Tuesday hours after federal marshals evicted the last two of 341 farmers whose land was taken for the 38,000-acre, $130-million federal project.
>
> By nightfall the barn and white frame house that the late Asa McCall had built for his wife in 1939 and the home where postman Beryl Moser was born 46 years ago had been demolished. . . .
>
> "It looks like this is about the end of it," Moser said, as three carloads of marshals escorted him from his home. "I still feel the same way about it I did ten years ago: to hell with the TVA. . . ."
>
> The W. B. Ritcheys, the other holdouts, packed their furniture Monday. . . . All three families had refused government checks totaling $216,000 mailed to them when their land was condemned. . . .

Supreme Court Justice William Brennan on Tuesday rejected a plea by Cherokee Indians for an injunction to prevent TVA from closing the dam gates. Justice Potter Stewart and the 6th U.S. Circuit Court of Appeals in Cincinnati rejected the same request last Friday.

The Cherokee contend that a lake over their ancient capital and burial grounds violates their First Amendment rights of religious freedom. . . .

Sandstone walls tower on the left, five hundred feet above this Dolores River. The walls are the color of sliced ham, with slick, concave surfaces. Streaks of organic matter trail like draperies across the face of the cliff. Desert varnish, a patina of blue-black oxidized iron and manganese, gleams on the rock. A forest of yellow pine glides by on our right, so that we appear to be still in high mountain country while descending into the canyonlands. Bald eagles and great blue herons follow this river. A redtail hawk screams in the sky, its voice as wild and yet familiar as the croak and clack of ravens. The windhover bird, riding the airstream. Staring up at the great hawk, I hear human voices fretting and fussing behind my back, urging caution. A glance at the river. I miss the next rock. Can't hit them all. And bounce safely off the one beyond.

"Don't tell Preston," I suggest to my passengers. Preston— Preston Ellsworth—leader of this expedition, veteran river guide, owner and operator of Colorado River Tours, Inc., is one of the best in a difficult business. At the moment he is somewhere ahead, out of sight around the next bend. Though a sturdy and generous fellow, he might be disturbed by my indolent style of boatmanship. This sixteen-foot neoprene raft I am piloting from rock to rock belongs to him, and a new one would cost $2,300. And the rapid called Snaggletooth lies ahead, day after next.

Be of good cheer. All may yet be well. There's many a fork, I think, in the road from here to destruction. Despite the jet-set androids who visit our mountain West on their cyclic tours from St. Tropez to Key West to Vail to Acapulco to Santa Fe, where they buy their hobby ranches, ski-town condos, adobe villas, and settle in, telling us how much they love the West. But will not lift a finger to help defend it. Will not lend a hand or grab ahold. Dante had a special place for these ESTers, esthetes, temporizers, and castrate fence-straddlers; he locked them in the vestibule of Hell. They're worse than the simple industrial developer, whose only objective, while pretending to "create jobs," is to create for himself a fortune in paper money. The developer is what he is; no further punishment is necessary.

As for politicians, those lambs and rabbits—

"Watch it!"

Missed that one by a cat hair. As for the politicians—forget them. We scrape by the next on the portside, a fang of limestone under a furl of glossy water. Fatal loveliness, murmuring at my ear. I glide into a trough between two petrified crocodiles and slide down the rapid's glassy tongue into a moderate maelstrom. I center my attention on the huge waves walloping toward us. We ride them out in good form, bow foremost, with only a stroke now on one oar, now on the other, to keep the raft straight.

We leave the forest, descending mile after mile through a winding slickrock canyon toward tableland country. It is like Glen Canyon once again, in miniature, submerged but not forgotten Glen Canyon. The old grief will not go away. Like the loss of a wife, brother, sister, the ache in the heart dulls with time but never dissolves entirely.

We camp one night at a place called Coyote Wash, a broad opening—almost a valley—in the canyon world. After dark one member of the crew, a deadly pyromantic, climbs a thousand-foot bluff above camp and builds a bonfire of old juniper and piñon pine. He is joined by a second dark figure, dancing around the flames. As the flames die the two shove the mound of glowing coals over the edge. A cascade of fire streams down the face of the cliff. Clouds of sparks float on the darkness, flickering out as they sink into oblivion. A few spot fires burn among the boulders at the base of the cliff, then fade. The end of something. A gesture—but symbolizing what?

Maybe we should all stay home for a season, give our little Western wilderness some relief from Vibram soles, rubber boats, hang gliders, deer rifles, and fly rods. But where is home? Surely not the walled-in prison of the cities, under that low ceiling of carbon monoxide and nitrogen oxides and acid rain—the leaky malaise of an overdeveloped, overcrowded, self-destroying civilization—where most people are compelled to serve their time and please the wardens if they can. For many, for more and more of us, the out-of-doors is our true ancestral estate. For a mere five thousand years we have grubbed in the soil and laid brick upon brick to build the cities; but for a million years before that we lived the leisurely, free, and adventurous life of hunters and gatherers, warriors and tamers of horses. How can we pluck *that* deep root of feeling from the racial consciousness? Impossible. When in doubt, jump out.

Ah yes, you say, but what about Mozart? Punk Rock? Astrophysics? Flush toilets? Potato chips? Silicon chips? Oral surgery? The Super Bowl and the World Series? Our coming journey to the stars? Vital projects, I agree, and I support them all. (On a voluntary basis only.) But why not a compromise? Why not—both? Why can't we have a moderate number of small cities, bright islands of electricity and kultur and industry surrounded by shoals of farmland, cow range, and timberland, set in the midst of a great unbounded sea of primitive forest, unbroken mountains, virgin desert? The human reason can conceive of such a free and spacious world; why can't we allow it to become—again—our home?

The American Indians had a word for what we call "wilderness." For them the wilderness was home.

Another day, another dolor. The dampness of the river has soaked into my brain, giving it the consistency of tapioca. My crackpot dreams fade with the dawn. Too many questions, not enough answers.

We are approaching Snaggletooth Rapid at last. A steady roar fills the canyon. My passengers, a new set today, life jackets snug to their chins, cling with white knuckles to the lashings of our baggage as I steer my ponderous craft down the tongue of the rapid, into the maw of the mad waters. I try to remember Preston's instructions: ferry to the right, avoiding that boat-eating Hole beyond the giant waves; then a quick pull to the left to avoid wrapping the boat upon Snaggletooth itself, an ugly talon of rock that splits and divides the main force of the river.

I grip the oars and shut my eyes. For a moment. The shock of cold water in the face recalls me to duty. A huge wave is rising over the port bow, about to topple. Pull to the right. The wave crashes, half-filling the boat. We ride down past the side of the Hole, carried through by momentum. The Tooth looms beyond my starboard bow, an ugly shark's fin of immovable stone. Pull to the left. We slip by it, barely *touching*—dumb luck combined with blind atavistic natural talent. The boat wallows over the vigorous vee-waves beyond. Wake up. I'm drifting beyond the beaching point. I strain at the oars—oh, it's hard, it's hard—and tug this lumpen-bourgeois river rig through the water and into the safety of an eddy. My swamper jumps ashore, bowline in hand. We drag the raft onto the sand and tie up to a willow tree.

Safely on the beach I watch (with secret satisfaction) the mishaps of the other oarsmen. And oarswomen. Nobody loses or overturns a boat, but several hit the Tooth, hang there for awesome seconds, minutes, while tons of water beat upon their backs. They struggle. Hesitation: then the boats slide off, some into the current on the wrong side of the rock to go ashore on the wrong side of the canyon. No matter; nobody is hurt, or even dumped in the river, and no baggage is lost.

Recovered, reassembled, we eat lunch. We stare at the mighty rapids. We talk, meditate, reload the boats and push out, once again, onto the river.

Quietly exultant, we drift on together, not a team but a family, a human family bound by human love, through the golden canyons of the River of Sorrows. So named, it appears, by a Spanish priest three centuries ago, a man of God who saw in our physical world (is there another?) only a theater of suffering. He was right! He was wrong! Love can defeat that nameless terror. Loving one another, we take the sting from death. Loving our mysterious blue planet, we resolve riddles and dissolve all enigmas in contingent bliss.

On and on and on we float, down the river, day after day, down to the trip's end, to our takeout point, a lonely place in far western Colorado called Bedrock. Next door to Paradox. There is nothing here but a few small alfalfa farms and one gaunt, weathered, bleak old country store. The store is well stocked, though, with Michelob beer, and Budweiser (next morning we'll find among us a number of sadder Budweiser men), and also a regional brew known as—Cures? Yes, Cures beer, a weak, pallid provincial liquescence brewed, they say, from pure Rocky Mountain spigot water. Take a twelve-pack home tonight. Those who drink from these poptop tins will be, in the words of B. Traven, America's greatest writer, "forever freed from pain."

Three of the boat people are going on down the Dolores to its junction with the Colorado, and from there to the Land of Moab in Darkest Utah. My heart breaks to see them go without me. But I have a promise to keep. Preston Ellsworth has business waiting in Durango; the others elsewhere. Must all voyages end in separation? Powell lost three of his men at Separation Rapids, far down there in *The* Canyon. And Christopher Columbus, after his third voyage to the Indies, got in trouble with his royal masters and was sent back to Spain in chains, leaving his men behind on Hispaniola.

Which made no difference. There will always be a 1492. There will always be a Grand Canyon. There will always be a Rio Dolores, dam or no dam. There will always be one more voyage down the river to Bedrock, Colorado, in that high lonesome valley the pioneers named Paradox. A paradox because—anomaly—the river flows across, not through, the valley, apparently violating both geo-logic and common sense. Not even a plateau could stop the river. Their dams will go down like dominoes. And another river be reborn.

There will always be one more river, not to cross but to follow. The journey goes on forever, and we are fellow voyagers on our little living ship of stone and soil and water and vapor, this delicate planet circling round the sun, which humankind call Earth.

Postscript

No more. That was my final river trip, whichever one it was. And I'm back home resting at last, preparing to go to work on my great book, working title "Fat Masterpiece," when the phone rings and somebody at Sobek, Inc., calls me up. It's Richard Bangs, the boss.

"Abbey," he says, "we're going down the Zambezi in October."

"Bon voyage."

"We need an official scribe."

"No!"

"We're starting at Victoria Falls. It's never been run before."

"I never heard of it."

"It's in Africa."

"No."

"Yes."

"If I see it they'll dam it."

"They're going to dam it anyway. You better come."

"Oh Christ . . ."

"That's right. You'll need shots."

"I know."

"A passport, visas—"

"Yes."

"And so on."

"I know."

Shall we gather at the river? The beautiful, the beautiful river? Gather with the saints at the river, that flows by the throne of the Lord?

Well . . . I guess so. One more time.

ALSO BY EDWARD ABBEY

Abbey's Road
The "Thoreau of the West" writes about places all over the world, from Australia to Mexico to the American West. Illustrated by the author.
$6.75 paperback   ISBN: 0-525-03001-8

Good News: A Novel
An hilarious parable of Abbey's beloved American desert after the Fall.
$6.95 paperback   ISBN: 0-525-03467-6

The Journey Home
Some words in defense of the American West. Illustrated by Jim Stiles.
$6.75 paperback   ISBN: 0-525-03700-4

Available at bookstores or from E. P. Dutton. To order from Dutton, list titles and ISBN numbers. Send a check or money order for the retail price plus appropriate sales tax and 10% for postage and handling to Dept. CW, E. P. Dutton, Inc., 2 Park Avenue, NY 10016. New York residents must add sales tax. Allow up to six weeks for delivery.

21 DAY BOOK

3 200 00013 634

Abbey, Edward
    Down the river

10/82

NEW HANOVER COUNTY
PUBLIC LIBRARY
201 CHESTNUT STREET
WILMINGTON, N. C. 28401